Best Bike Rides
Detroit and Ann Arbor

Help Us Keep This Guide Up to Date

Every effort has been made by the author and editors to make this guide as accurate and useful as possible. However, many things can change after a guide is published—roads are detoured, phone numbers change, facilities come under new management, etc.

We would love to hear from you concerning your experiences with this guide and how you feel it could be improved and kept up to date. While we may not be able to respond to all comments and suggestions, we'll take them to heart and we'll also make certain to share them with the author. Please send your comments and suggestions to the following address:

Globe Pequot Press
Reader Response/Editorial Department
P.O. Box 480
Guilford, CT 06437

Or you may e-mail us at:
editorial@GlobePequot.com

Thanks for your input, and happy riding!

BEST BIKE RIDES® SERIES

Best Bike Rides
Detroit and Ann Arbor

Great Recreational Rides in Southeast Michigan

ROB PULCIPHER

FALCONGUIDES

GUILFORD, CONNECTICUT
HELENA, MONTANA

AN IMPRINT OF ROWMAN & LITTLEFIELD

Contents

Paved Roads

Dirt Roads and Bike Paths

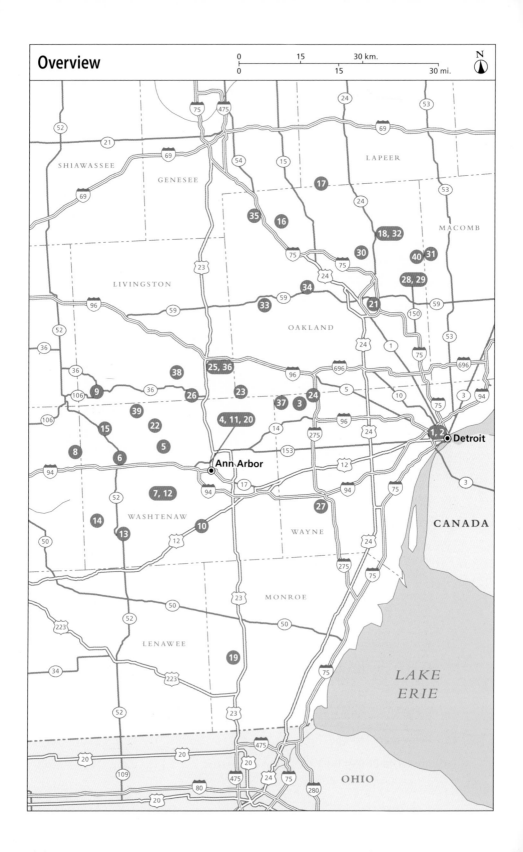

Mountain Bike Trails 🖼

Acknowledgments

First, I want to thank my wife, Connie, for her companionship and input on some of these rides and for giving me the space and encouragement to put all of this together. I also want to thank those who've shown me new places, helped me rediscover old places, and opened my eyes to the opportunities out there: Ben Caldwell, Wendy Caldwell, Norm Cox, Norm Roller, Amy Kuras, Rich Stark, Brian Rosewarne, Tom Pilutti, Jay Ellis, Joe Lekovish, Andy Staub, Bob Spleet, Mike Casey, Kevin LaRoe, Dennis Pontius, Leslie Isaacs, Ed Brewer, Nate Kearns, Jen Conine, Mike Solomon, Keith Riege, Jason Jones, Yao-Fen You, Tony Klein, Rob Walker, Linda Briggs, Duane Menter, Cullen Watkins, Todd Scott, Scott Goocher, Noah Hall, and Bob Tetons. I also want to thank Charles Reynolds, who's unfortunately no longer with us, but who rode with me through thick and thin over many sections of the terrain covered in this book. I also want to thank those whom I left off this list and will let me know later. You can scold me now.

There are also groups and organizations that were invaluable in helping to compile the massive amounts of resources and information that served as a guide to my adventures: m-bike.org, detroit1701.org, the Michigan Department of Natural Resources, the Michigan Mountain Bike Association, the Rails-to-Trails Conservancy, the Michigan Trails & Greenways Alliance, Huron-Clinton Metroparks, the League of Michigan Bicyclists, the staff at the Hub of Detroit bike shop, the staff at the Wheelhouse bike shop, the Greenway Collaborative, and the Ann Arbor Bicycle Touring Society.

Other resources that were extremely helpful were *Detroit City Is the Place to Be*, by Mark Binelli, and *Metroparks for the People*, by Cynthia Furlong Reynolds.

I also want to thank all those who volunteer to expand, maintain, and improve bike paths and mountain bike trails in the region. And to those who work to improve the conditions for cyclists on our roadways: You're the unsung heroes out there who keep things going.

There are also the people I met along the way, and whose names I didn't get, who filled me in on all kinds of things that I would have missed, or who were just friendly and made each ride that much better for their kindness. You remind me why this is such a special way to spend time.

Introduction

Imagine a segment of land that radiates from a hub stretching out 50 miles or more. Imagine you on a bike within that wheel of land cycling over hundreds of miles of dirt, cinder, and paved trail systems, along thousands of miles of paved and dirt roads, through the heart of busy major cities and towns that have helped shape our country's history, or on the quietest country byways that encompass forests rich with maples, oaks, and hickories. Imagine marshlands, teeming with wildlife. Imagine a glacially shaped land with winding, ever-rolling hills where a new view unfolds minute by minute, or where the land is arrestingly flat and the panorama is farm fields dotted with structures built in the early years of settlement, many still in use.

Imagine riding along a field edge watching a flock of prehistoric-looking sandhill cranes fanned across the sky above cackling their eerie staccato call, then cruising down a historic town's brick-building-lined main street ten minutes later. Imagine riding along a path that leads from a congested urban area, across major highways, then transforms to farm fields, then quiet forests with mature tunnels of old trees arching over you cathedral-like in their protection, experiencing all of it in an hour or two.

Imagine a route in that same stretch of land where it's possible to ride year-round and see a whole different place from season to season. Imagine within that stretch many people dedicated to expanding the network of trails and pathways so you can explore even farther, even deeper.

How can countryside and city, wild nature and human habitation, coexist in a landmass jammed with people, the most populous area in the state as a matter of fact…and growing?

I can tell you that it does exist. I've ridden there. All over it. I still do. I live in it. It's in an imaginary land that's real, called Southeast Michigan. I can't tell you how it came together, though I know it took a lot of people's efforts. In fact, it stretches far beyond that small radius. There's more to explore.

Within these pages are forty of my version of the "best" bike rides in the region. You may disagree with my selection, and for good reason—forty doesn't even begin to do it justice. There are hundreds of great bike rides within these boundaries, maybe thousands. I've ridden a lot of those, too. I wanted to put them in, but I had to stop somewhere. You, I'm sure, have your own "best." There are plenty of "bests" to share.

What's more, there are all kinds of places to ride a bike. They often require a bike made for that specific use, though some bikes will do many of these things at once. In this case it came down to an awareness of what's out there and selecting the rides that I thought were excellent examples of what the region has to offer. It meant looking at all the opportunities and selecting from a good palette of options.

I came to realize that this region has a great balance of the four major biking food groups—paved roads, dirt roads, bike paths, and mountain bike trails—so I wandered all over the land and found that the "best" were pretty evenly split among these groups. If anything, the humble bike path may edge out all other uses in terms of popularity and extensiveness of its existing and ever-expanding network, but it was only winning by a small margin. Still, it's hard to beat a nice ride on a bike path that often cuts through dense population areas yet feels as removed as a quiet northern Michigan rural lane. If you're a mountain biker, the mountain bike trail system in Southeast Michigan is varied and wide-ranging, from tight and technical to fast and flowing, from small lunchtime escapes to full-day adventures. There are dirt roads as well, something not every part of the country has. The dirt roads are rapidly growing in popularity in the area due to the improvements of bicycles designed to ride such terrain, the widespread network of options in some parts of the region, and the lack of heavy traffic. The paved roads, though sometimes limited by the dominance of the automobile and the paucity of bike lanes in many areas, are still found in some of the most beautiful parts of the region and, surprisingly to many, in the heart of Detroit, where biking is very popular, and they allow closer appreciation of all that great, conflicted city has to offer.

Whatever kind of biking you do, Southeast Michigan has many options to choose from, many varieties of terrain to wander through. It's only limited by your imagination. Check them out. I think you'll be impressed. If you live here, it will make you proud to reside in such a beautiful area, and proud of those who care enough to help shape its beauty and its healthy recreational opportunities. If you don't live here, you'll find a range of sometimes dramatic, sometimes simply pleasant, options to explore atop a bicycle. Pleasant options. That's not a bad way to spend a few hours. They're here. Go find them.

PREPARATION

There are all kinds of debates out there about whether helmets are necessary. It's a very personal decision, but through my own tumbling experiences, and those of people who didn't wear one and now have closed head injuries, I'm a strong believer in helmet use.

There are also a few things that will put you at ease during a ride. One is to have some knowledge of your bike and how to perform basic maintenance and repair on it. Small things like checking and topping up air pressure in the tires and lubricating the chain and other moving parts will help keep the bike moving forward rather than stopped at the side of the road. And when issues do arise far from home, you'll know how to fix them and you'll have the tools you need to do so.

Some basic items to pack along are a multitool with chain breaker, a spare tube, a tube patch kit, a portable tire pump, a cell phone, and a few extra dollars for those unexpected needs along the way. Sometimes you're out longer than you expect and you end up riding the last few miles in darkness. This is often daunting even with lights, but downright scary (to drivers, pedestrians, and you) without them. If you're going out at a dim or dark hour, have a headlight and taillight handy.

Water is a necessity on most rides, and a small snack is nice to keep your energy up.

How to Use This Book

THE RIDES

Since this book is divided into three major categories, there are many ride options and even the opportunity to mix them around. You can choose by distance, but be aware that a 10-mile ride on smooth pavement takes less effort than that same distance on a mountain bike trail. Adjust accordingly when trying to find a ride that matches your intent.

Some of the routes are rather long, but it doesn't mean that you're required to do exactly what I've laid out. If time is limited, do a part of it. If you have plenty of time, do it twice, or connect a couple together. Most important, do the ride that will leave you yearning for more. This is about recreation and enjoyment. I'm a big believer in taking the recreation word to heart. If you come back feeling rejuvenated—and everyone has their own definition of that feeling—then you'll keep riding week after week, year after year. Mix things up. Ride one day with a friend, another with a group, and another on your own. Do it fast or do it slow or do both. Make it fun. These routes are suggestions, not prescriptions. If you want to do them backward, sideways, or upside down, then by all means make them yours. Find some maps and wander off track. Explore. It's your ride in the end.

The only places I've indicated riding level in the Ride Finder is on the mountain bike trails and the paved pathways. Mountain bike trails are the one place where ability is crucial so riders don't get miles back on a trail (often one-way) and find themselves way over their skill level and dangerously fatigued. Conversely, the paved pathways are, on the whole, very beginner friendly as long as distance is taken into consideration.

TRAFFIC

The nature of cycling puts us out in the world. For the most part, road rides are usually more immersed in traffic than other types of rides. Road conditions vary for many reasons: time of day, or some roads feel dicey due to the speed of the traffic and the narrow width of the shoulder. Most of the road routes in this book are in low to moderate traffic areas, but there are occasions when the route requires a section to connect along a busy roadway, or the roadway is great to ride along, but the shoulder is narrower than preferred. There may be a time when road commissions truly take cyclists into consideration, and in some cases they do. But many times it's a choice between riding with what's there or not going at all. I've tried to make clear in the descriptions what the conditions are.

Cycling pathways are not immune from traffic issues either. Usually these are roadway crossing–related rather than problems associated with riding alongside vehicles. Some pathway crossings are downright dangerous with fast-moving traffic, no signal lights, or they're at odd angles to the road. Take extra care at these and be patient until you feel comfortable crossing. You're out to have fun on your bike, not play car tag. Cars tend to win those games.

Dirt roads are, for the most part, pretty quiet, but in Michigan, unless posted otherwise, the speed limit on these is 55 mph. That's fast even on a paved road, much less a narrow country dirt road. There are moments—rare but they do happen—when drivers decide to drive the legal maximum speed limit in unsafe conditions. Watch out for these yahoos and give them a wide berth. Also, many dirt roads have blind curves and blind hills. In most conditions, stay to the right and be cautious. An oncoming car can appear out of nowhere. Don't let the bucolic setting lull you into a false sense of complacency. Always ride defensively.

Mountain bike trails sometimes cross vehicular roadways, or even pedestrian pathways. Be aware of your surroundings so you come back as healthy as when you left. Be courteous to hikers, horseback riders, and other cyclists, and you'll help maintain goodwill with those groups. You're all there to enjoy the outdoors together.

As with all cycling endeavors, one cyclist carries the burden of many. Your actions and reactions will be interpreted as that of the whole cycling community. The more we can build goodwill in the larger community as a whole, the more we'll be welcome and not hindered when working to expand our recreational role and our opportunities.

GPS COORDINATES

GPS is not an exact science. It's often an approximation with a margin of error. My readings may be slightly different than yours due to atmospheric conditions, overhead cover, ride speed, and satellite connections. I've found that even riding the same exact route on different days and taking a reading with the same device can give me slight variations in readings.

So, as a disclaimer, you may find that the readings you get differ from mine. Take these variables into account when following a route's course. Look for other markers as well in order to keep on track. I've noticed that this is especially important on trails that are under dense tree cover.

Ride Finder

BEST RIDES FOR FAMILIES

21. Clinton River Trail
22. Hudson Mills Metropark
23. Huron Valley Rail Trail and Lyon Oaks County Park Connector
25. Island Lake–Kensington–Milford
27. Lower Huron–Willow–Oakwoods Metroparks
28. Macomb-Orchard Trail
29. Paint Creek Trail
30. Polly Ann Trail
31. Stony Creek Pathway
37. Maybury State Park
40. Stony Creek Mountain Bike Trail

BEST RURAL RIDES

5. Dexter–Chelsea–Patterson Lake
6. Chelsea–Waterloo
7. Parker–Fletcher Route
8. Clear Lake–Huttenlocker
9. Gregory–Munith
10. Saline–Clinton
11. Ann Arbor–Walsh
12. Ellsworth–Waters
13. Manchester–Bethel Church
14. Sharon Area
15. North Lyndon–Embury
16. Holly Recreation Area and Environs
17. Ortonville Recreation Area and Environs
18. Lake Orion–Metamora
19. Petersburg–Monroe
26. Lakelands Trail
28. Macomb-Orchard Trail
30. Polly Ann Trail

BEST URBAN RIDES

1. Downtown Detroit
2. Detroit: Belle Isle–Indian Village–Heidelberg Project

3. Hines Drive
20. Border-to-Border Trail: Ann Arbor to Ypsilanti
24. I-275 Metro Trail

BEST FLAT RIDES

1. Downtown Detroit
2. Detroit: Belle Isle–Indian Village–Heidelberg Project
19. Petersburg–Monroe
21. Clinton River Trail
23. Huron Valley Rail Trail and Lyon Oaks County Park Connector
26. Lakelands Trail
28. Macomb-Orchard Trail
29. Paint Creek Trail
30. Polly Ann Trail
31. Stony Creek Pathway
35. Holdridge (North)

BEST HILLY RIDES

3. Hines Drive
4. Huron River Drive: Ann Arbor to Dexter
5. Dexter–Chelsea–Patterson Lake
6. Chelsea–Waterloo
7. Parker–Fletcher Route
8. Clear Lake–Huttenlocker
9. Gregory–Munith
10. Saline–Clinton
11. Ann Arbor–Walsh
12. Ellsworth–Waters
13. Manchester–Bethel Church
14. Sharon Area
15. North Lyndon–Embury
16. Holly Recreation Area and Environs
17. Ortonville Recreation Area and Environs
18. Lake Orion–Metamora
20. Border-to-Border Trail: Ann Arbor to Ypsilanti
23. Huron Valley Rail Trail and Lyon Oaks County Park Connector
24. I-275 Metro Trail
25. Island Lake–Kensington–Milford
32. Bald Mountain North

33. Highland Recreation Area

35. Holdridge (West and East)

34. Pontiac Lake

36. Island Lake Mountain Bike Trail

37. Maybury State Park

38. Murray Lake–Torn Shirt

39. Potawatomi Trail

40. Stony Creek Mountain Bike Trail

BEST RIDES FOR BEGINNERS

20. Border-to-Border Trail: Ann Arbor to Ypsilanti

21. Clinton River Trail

22. Hudson Mills Metropark

23. Huron Valley Rail Trail and Lyon Oaks County Park Connector

24. I-275 Metro Trail

25. Island Lake–Kensington–Milford

26. Lakelands Trail

27. Lower Huron–Willow–Oakwoods Metroparks

28. Macomb-Orchard Trail

29. Paint Creek Trail

30. Polly Ann Trail

31. Stony Creek Pathway

35. Holdridge (North)

36. Island Lake Mountain Bike Trail

37. Maybury State Park

40. Stony Creek Mountain Bike Trail

BEST RIDES FOR INTERMEDIATES

26. Lakelands Trail (Hamburg to Stockbridge)

32. Bald Mountain North

33. Highland Recreation Area

34. Pontiac Lake

35. Holdridge (West)

36. Island Lake Mountain Bike Trail

37. Maybury State Park

38. Murray Lake–Torn Shirt (Murray Lake)

39. Potawatomi Trail

40. Stony Creek Mountain Bike Trail

Map Legend

75	Interstate Highway	✈	Airport
23	US Highway	⏝	Bridge
14	State Highway	■	Building/Point of Interest
52	Featured State/Local Road	▲	Campground
	Local Road	†	Church
	Featured Bike Route	🎓	College/University
	Bike Route	🍴	Dining
	Railroad	◉	Large City
	Trail	17.1 ◆—	Mileage Marker
	State Line	🏛	Museum
	County Line	🅿	Parking
	Small River or Creek	⯭	Picnic Area
	Marsh/Swamp	o	Small City/Town
	Body of Water	🔺	Small Park
		①	Trailhead
	State Park/Forest/Wilderness/ Preserve/Recreational Area	①	Trail Markers
	Nontarget State/Country Fill	❓	Visitor/Information Center

BEST RIDES FOR ADVANCED CYCLISTS

26. Lakelands Trail (Hamburg to Stockbridge)
33. Highland Recreation Area
34. Pontiac Lake
35. Holdridge (East)
38. Murray Lake (Torn Shirt)
39. Potawatomi Trail
40. Stony Creek Mountain Bike Trail

PAVED ROADS

The paved bike rides in this book are skewed toward the western side of Southeast Michigan, with a few notable exceptions. This is due mainly to the expansion of roadways in Metro Detroit in favor of the automobile with secondary regard to the bicycle. As the region is the home of automobile manufacturing, that might be expected, though there are inroads (so to speak) in the introduction of bike lanes in some areas. Let's hope these continue and even thrive in the coming years.

There are a lot of roads not mentioned in this book that are worth riding for those who are comfortable in high-traffic areas or in areas with minimal road shoulders. Both upriver and downriver from Detroit proper there are all kinds of places to discover. *Adventure Cycling* even created a recent route through the region that follows the path of the Underground Railroad. There are also places like Grosse Ile in the downriver area that offer beautiful views of the Detroit River and across into Canada, but as of this writing there are few public places to park on the island, and though there's an inner island pathway, the most fascinating stretch to ride is along the river, which is on a very narrow road with no shoulder and no parkland to dawdle in. Similarly, the Grosse Pointe area to the north has magnificent views over Lake St. Clair but no dedicated bike lane on a road with fast-moving traffic. Still, if those environments are comfortable to you, they're worth pedaling through. In many areas, both up and downriver, there are efforts to make more bike-friendly connections, but they haven't come to fruition yet. Some of the pieces are in place, but they have yet to connect into a coherent whole. Stay tuned.

In the meantime, there are still excellent places that a dedicated road bike enthusiast can explore in relative comfort. Downtown Detroit is a wonderful place to ride. Two routes are specified, but there could be more, such as one stretching into Hamtramck, and others that take into account some of the early auto industry around Highland Park that would also include the fascinating homes in the Boston Edison area. The routes presented, though, will give you great insight into why so many people care about Detroit and about its future. One takes you from the edge of downtown to Belle Isle, through the historic neighborhood of Indian Village, and over to the inspiring Heidelberg Project. The other goes through the Eastern Market, into the heart of the downtown skyscrapers, out to New Center where GM and the

Cyclist in Detroit's historic Brush Park neighborhood

Fisher Brothers tried to create a New Town Center (hence the name) in the early years of last century, past Motown, back through a rejuvenating Midtown and Wayne State campus area, and over to Corktown and Mexicantown. It's nonstop history all along the way, with some pleasant surprises thanks to the attention and care now paid to some of these areas.

Hines Drive cuts a diagonal swath along the River Rouge through many municipalities, with dozens of connected parks that create one highly popular recreational greenway. It's popular all day, year-round. It gets Metro Detroiters outside, keeps them fit, and lets them play, and they definitely take advantage of it. For some, it is *the* place to ride a bike.

The other great place to ride a road bike is on the rural roads of Washtenaw County. Leave Ann Arbor or Ypsilanti and it doesn't take long to find a nice rural road to venture out on. Some of the roads don't have wide shoulders, but the traffic volumes are reasonably low and the sheer number of riders and bike groups along these roads has made them a share-the-road experience for those who like their tires on pavement. In addition, the small towns—Saline, Chelsea, Dexter, Manchester—are accustomed to cyclists in their midst, and they offer bike-friendly amenities such as welcoming cafes and nearby bike shops. And when you get into the countryside, it's one great rolling, forested, marshy, farmstead-laden landscape with plenty of wildlife to ogle. So, yes, there's plenty to explore if you like your bike to stay on the tarmac.

Downtown Detroit

We've all heard the stereotype of Detroit as a place in decline, a place beyond repair. This ride will open your eyes to another Detroit, a city that feels alive and filled with possibilities even with the awareness that there are many areas of decay and blight as well. Much of this ride goes through the heart of Detroit, weaves through thriving neighborhoods, rolls into viable commercial areas, passes well-maintained historic buildings and sites, and lets you experience a city that truly has soul.

This is the core Detroit ride, and even though there's much more to experience about Detroit than this, this is chock-full of so much of what Detroit is, has been, and will be that you'll be able to get a good feel for the place after riding almost 24 miles. This ride is a dynamically varied urban experience evoking emotions of both the sadness of loss and the joy of seeing vibrant areas in the midst of rejuvenation. The combination of quiet vs. congested, compact vs. open, loss vs. restoration, hope vs. despair, art alongside commerce, all coexisting within a few square miles is an urban immersion in dramatic contrasts.

Start: William G. Milliken State Park at Rivard Plaza

Length: 23.7 miles

Approximate riding time: 2–4 hours

Best bike: Road or hybrid

Terrain and trail surface: Paved road, sometimes rough, mostly flat

Traffic and hazards: Urban riding. Not all drivers are thinking about you. Be careful of doors opening from parked cars. Most streets are quiet even though they can be quite wide. Downtown, especially in the necklace, can get congested with many lanes of anxious traffic one minute, no cars around the next.

Things to see: A major urban city with tall buildings and cavernous streets, wide-open spaces, university area energy, Motown, New Center

Area, Midtown, well-cared-for neighborhoods such as Woodbridge, Mexicantown, and Corktown, beautifully restored blocks like that on Canfield and Ferry Avenue, abandoned buildings, gloriously restored cathedrals, and many other experiences all within a 24-mile ride

Maps: Universal Map: Detroit Greater Area; *DeLorme: Michigan Atlas & Gazetteer*, page 32

Getting there by car: From Jefferson and Woodward Avenue (at the hub of all roads leading out of downtown Detroit), drive east on Jefferson to Rivard Street. Turn right onto Rivard. Turn left onto Atwater Street, then the first right into the William G. Milliken State Park parking area. The Riverwalk leads from Rivard Plaza adjacent to the parking area. GPS: N42 19.853 W83 01.879

THE RIDE

Many speak of the ease of riding in Detroit. On many days, even on the major streets, that's true. The roads are often wide and the traffic volumes low. It is still a city, though. In the very core, and in other select areas of Detroit, traffic can be urban (impatient) and active (squirrely). That said, most of the ride is reasonably comfortable.

Leave the William G. Milliken State Park parking lot and take a right (heading east) onto Atwater Street. Take this past Orleans Street to the bike path (mile 0.3) and take a left. Cross two streets at grade level, and after Woodbridge Street you'll enter the Dequindre Cut. For the next mile the pathway passes below street level until it rises up to Gratiot Avenue at the north end. Eventually it will go to Mack Avenue, past the Eastern Market. The Cut is actually an old Grand Trunk Railroad line that's now a greenspace with a 20-foot-wide paved pathway. It's all well-maintained and well-patrolled. There's also some fascinating graffiti to ogle on the walls along the way.

At the other end, rise up to Gratiot Avenue and stay on the sidewalk as you take a left, crossing over the Cut. Follow this to Riopelle Street (mile 1.6) and take a left onto this side street that then swings right on the next block onto brick-paved Service Street. This old street is behind a block of brick buildings that serve as a minor renaissance community. The block is part of what makes pride of place a theme throughout the city in various pockets.

Turn right onto Russell Street, cross Gratiot and then the Fisher Freeway bridge, and you're now entering the Eastern Market area. Eastern Market dates back to the 1850s, and it's now more vibrant than ever. There are excel-

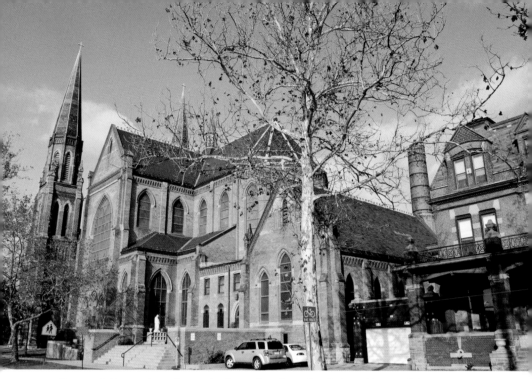

The second oldest continuously operating Roman Catholic parish in the United States and the site of the first building constructed in Fort Pontchartrain du Detroit

lent restaurants and daily markets and shops in the area, but it really comes to life on Saturday when the open-air farmers' market fills the covered sheds. For a quick spin through the market area, take a right onto Winder Street and arc around the block with a left onto Market Street and another left onto Adelaide.

Return to Russell Street and proceed north (right) to Wilkins Street. Turn left and cross over the Chrysler Expressway (I-75) and proceed to Brush Street. Take a left. This area is the historic Brush Park neighborhood, once filled with Victorian residences owned by the city's elite. Though the area is now more sparse, there are still plenty of the houses in various states of complete renovation, disrepair, or somewhere in between. A short detour down Edmund Place (mile 2.8), with its restored houses, reveals the amazing architecture that once covered the area.

Continue south on Brush Street and cross back over the Fisher Freeway, beyond which you'll enter the land of professional sports, passing between Comerica Park (home of the Detroit Tigers) and Ford Field (the Detroit Lions' gridiron). The scale and aura of both of these are imposing as you pedal past on your small bicycle.

Proceed to Madison Street and take a right. You're now at the outer periphery of what is known as the Necklace or inner core of downtown, but instead of immersing just yet, you'll ride back around to the front of the Tigers' Comerica Park, worth the visual enjoyment, past the Detroit Athletic Club and Grand Circus Park on the way. Facing the ball park, across Woodward Avenue, is the Fox Theater. The sign is large-scale and dramatic. Built in 1928, the theater was restored in 1988. Its history is long and varied, including films from the silent era and performances by Elvis Presley and Motown artists among many others.

Swing over to Woodward and head north. Woodward is the central street heading out from the "hub" of the city's core, with a vaunted history of its own and much to see along its length. Among the sights are the Bonstelle Theatre (mile 4.5), originally a synagogue built in 1902 and designed by the ubiquitous Albert Kahn (who lived nearby in Brush Park); it is now a playhouse owned by Wayne State University.

Farther along is the Max Fisher Music Center (mile 4.7), home of the Detroit Symphony Orchestra. Farther yet is the rich red limestone First Congregational Church at East Forest Avenue built in 1891. Another magnificent church, the Cathedral Church of St. Paul, is at mile 5.2 just before Warren Avenue. This was where Henry Ford's funeral service was held in 1947.

Another block up is the Detroit Institute of Arts (DIA), indicating that you're now in the Cultural Center Historic District. The main exterior material of the DIA is white marble, built in 1927. Its 100 galleries house major artworks from around the world. The renowned Diego Rivera fresco "Detroit Industry" is there as well, a dramatic visual representation of Detroit's past, controversial when it was first unveiled.

Pedal to the next block and take a right onto Ferry Avenue. You'll be immediately struck by the dramatic homes on this street. In particular, note the extravagant Chateaux-style house on the corner of Woodward and Ferry, known as the Colonel Frank J. Hecker House, dating to 1888. Farther down the street on the east side is the Inn on Ferry Street, which is actually four restored Victorian houses, now popular accommodations for visitors to Detroit. More restored Victorian houses line the street.

Take a left onto Saint Antoine Street and follow the route back to Woodward Avenue. Head north once more. Pass below the railroad underpass and make your way to West Grand Boulevard. The left turn onto West Grand is not the easiest due to traffic and layout, but carefully arc your way across the street and head west. This area, known as the New Center, holds a unique history in the annals of Detroit and is worth exploring. Grand Boulevard itself plays an interesting role in the city's development. Begun in 1891, it was built as a ring road to wrap around the city. It was thought to be the ultimate limits of the city's expansion at the time.

The "new" in New Center came from the visions and hopes for a new commercial center in Detroit by the Fisher brothers (Fisher Body) and William Durant (co-founder of GM), among others. Albert Kahn's handiwork designed some of the signature buildings, including the GM Building (1923; now known as Cadillac Tower Building) on the south side of the street and the Fisher Building (1927) on the north side. (GM's headquarters are now in the Renaissance Center along the Detroit River.) The Henry Ford Hospital, begun by Henry Ford in 1915, is farther west on the right just past the Lodge Freeway.

Now, get ready to do some dancing in the street. Just a couple of blocks past the hospital is the renowned Hitsville USA founded by Berry Gordy at 2648 W. Grand Blvd. (mile 8.1), home of Motown, where "Dancing in the Street" (Martha and the Vandellas) was recorded, along with hundreds of other hits by well-known Motown artists. This is not just your imagination. You are in the heart of where music history was grooved into the souls of music lovers around the world in the '60s. Guided tours are available year-round (motownmuseum.org).

Take a left onto Holden Street and follow it all the way to the end where there's a pedestrian overpass that will take you over the Lodge Freeway. Be aware, this is a rather run-down section in what was once a thriving neighborhood, offering another perspective on life in Detroit.

Follow Holden to 3rd Street, take a right, and cross over the Edsel Ford Freeway on the overpass. You're now entering the realm of Wayne State University, founded in 1868, at that time called Detroit Medical College. The route will zigzag you through this Midtown area. Soak up the student vibe as you ride through one of the most rapidly growing and desired areas of Detroit.

Pass Warren Avenue and just beyond Hancock Street there's a pedestrian cut-through in the boulevard. Do a 180-degree turn and then go east on Hancock. Two blocks up, on the corner of Cass and Hancock, is the vibrant and dramatic-looking Old Main building. It was originally built as Central High School in 1896 and served as a central focus on campus for years to come.

Take a right onto Cass Avenue and head south 2 blocks to Prentis Street and take a right. Return to 3rd Street and take a left. Take another left onto Canfield Street. Note that the granite block paving is a challenge for small bike tires, so opt for the sidewalk on either side to explore this block's elegant houses on both sides of the street. You'll want to stop and look at the fine detail on many of these restored 1870s homes and savor the restored beauty of the streetscape as well. Though only a block long, it steps into a whole different time.

Continue east to Cass Avenue again and take a right. If you're in need of a snack break at this point, the Avalon Bakery is a block up on the right on Willis Street. It's a good mid-route place to replenish, as there's still much more to explore on this ride.

Once rested and refreshed, continue south on Cass to Selden Street and take a right. Cross the Lodge Freeway on a pedestrian overpass and you'll enter into the Woodbridge neighborhood. Follow the route into the heart of an area that's experiencing a revival. Though many neighborhoods in Detroit have been partially demolished, the large Victorian homes in Woodbridge remained largely intact, and many are in the midst of renovation. It's a pleasant spin down these quiet streets. If you're a baseball fan, the home of the Detroit Tiger great Ty Cobb, or more accurately his side of a duplex, is at 4117 Commonwealth St.

After Woodbridge, head southeast on Grand River and then south on Trumbull Street to Spruce. Take a right. Go 1 block to Cochrane and take a left. In another block you'll come to a pedestrian overpass that crosses over the Fisher Freeway. Once on top, you'll get a splendid view of the old Tiger Stadium, but it will be there in your imagination only. The stadium was torn down in 2008. It was the home of the Detroit Tigers for over a century. There's a makeshift diamond in the open park that's often in use by the local community.

Take a right onto Michigan Avenue and pass a line of stores on this very wide street. This area is seeing a resurgence of activity particularly as a place to go for food and drink. There's the popular Astro Coffee shop and the renowned Slows BarBQ, among others.

Pass through the light at 14th Street and take a left into Roosevelt Park. You're now riding straight toward one of the most iconic buildings in the city. The Michigan Central Station (1913) is a stunning sight, standing so prominently in the area. Even as an unused building in decay, it has a dignity that many actively used buildings lack.

Continue to the right of the station and follow Vernor Highway under the railroad bridge that leads into Mexicantown. Turn left onto Sainte Anne Street and roll up to Bagley Avenue. Take a right and pass the restored Matrix Theater and on toward the Bagley Pedestrian Bridge. On the left at the base of the bridge is a Michigan Information Center (with public restrooms). Cross the bridge and enter the heart of Mexicantown, where you'll be surrounded by restaurants and specialty shops.

Go right onto 24th Street and out to Vernor Highway. Vernor is an active commercial strip in Mexicantown. Ride to Scotten Street (mile 15.1) and turn left. Swing past Clark Park and back through the Mexicantown residential area. This is one of the dynamic neighborhoods in Detroit and this is apparent as you pass through an area of well-tended yards and homes.

Cross over the Bagley Pedestrian Bridge once more and cruise back to Sainte Anne Street and take a right. The highlight is a few blocks down at the corner of Lafayette Boulevard with the Ste. Anne de Detroit Catholic

Church (1886). Architecturally, its orange brick Victorian Gothic style makes it a wonder to behold. The parish itself began with the original settlers in the area in 1701.

Take Lafayette east to 16th, then Bagley, then Wabash, and back out to Michigan Avenue. Take a right onto Michigan Avenue and another right onto 12th Street (Rosa Parks Boulevard). Ride a couple of blocks to Leverette Street and you're now in the heart of Corktown, settled primarily by the Irish from County Cork, Ireland, in the 1850s. The neighborhood is in the midst of revitalization, and the original Federal-style detached houses and attached row houses lend this area a unique charm. Follow the route over to Bagley, onto 6th, then over the Lodge Freeway on Michigan Avenue into downtown Detroit.

At the corner of Michigan Avenue and Shelby Street sits Lafayette Greens, a garden built on the site of where the historic Lafayette Building was torn down in 2009. Built by Compuware, it serves as both a park and a garden that grows food it donates to groups in the community.

Turn right onto Griswold Street and ride through the cavernous downtown financial district to the Guardian Building at 500 Griswold. This is a stunning example of Art Deco architecture, with intricate design elements incorporated both inside and out.

Take a left onto Larned Street and look up to your right. You're paralleling the People Mover, a monorail that loops throughout the downtown area. As you cross Woodward Avenue, glance to the right for a view of the *Spirit of Detroit* sculpture. This is the "hub" of the wheel of streets that spoke in all directions. It can get busy and congested, as it is the conflation of all those streets.

Continue on to Brush Street (mile 20.4) and take a left. Note the stately Roman Baroque style Wayne County Building on the left as you pass Congress Street. You're rolling into the Bricktown/Greektown district, known for its restaurants and in recent years a large casino. Turn right onto Monroe Street, the heart of Greektown. A couple of blocks down is the majestic Old St. Mary's Roman Catholic Church across St. Antoine Street on the right.

Take a left onto St. Antoine and ride up to Gratiot. Take a left. Follow it a few blocks down to Randolph Street and take a right into the Germantown district. It's a pleasant, tight series of blocks that give the sense of an earlier Detroit. Take a loop around historic Harmonie Park, where early immigrants once gathered to sing their lieder, then take a left onto Grand River Avenue. Work your way up to Grand Circus Park (1850) via Broadway Street and do a counterclockwise loop around that. Grand Circus Park, bisected by Woodward Avenue, is in a sense the gateway to the core downtown area. It's at the heart of the theater district, with the nearby Fox Theater and the Opera House.

Once around to the other side, turn right onto Washington Boulevard, make your way down to Grand River Avenue and turn left, then right onto Woodward. This is the spine of the Financial District that takes you past Campus Martius Park, a major gathering place. This is the point from which all the coordinates (for instance, the Mile Roads) are measured in Detroit.

Follow Woodward to Jefferson Avenue. Cross over this multilane behemoth, past the statue of Joe Louis's arm into the heart of the plaza itself. There are various large sculptures on display, including a pylon by Isamu Noguchi, but by far the most well-known piece is Noguchi's fountain farther in.

To the right of the fountain (on the southwest side) is a wide pathway ramp (bike friendly) that leads to the Detroit Riverwalk. It enters the Riverwalk in front of the *Detroit Princess* Riverboat. Turn left (east) onto the walk. A short way up is the Gateway to Freedom International Memorial dedicated to the Underground Railroad. Detroit played a prominent role as a ready connection to Canada. Proceed east past the Port Authority Building to the prominent Renaissance Center. This is now the General Motors Headquarters, among many other companies. In many ways it's a city unto itself as you'll see if you wander inside. The steps along the river are a great place to people-watch and to observe the boats passing by.

Continue to Rivard Plaza and you're back where you began. This is a pleasant spot to recover from your ride as well, with a concession stand, plenty of outdoor seating with tables, and a clean, well-tended restroom.

Bike Rentals

The Hub of Detroit/Back Alley Bikes: 3611 Cass Ave., Detroit, MI 48201; (313) 833-0813; thehubofdetroit.org
The Wheelhouse (seasonal): 1340 E. Atwater St., Rivard Plaza on the Detroit RiverWalk, Detroit, MI 48207; (313) 656-BIKE (2453); www.wheelhousedetroit.com

MILES AND DIRECTIONS

0.0 Begin at William G. Milliken State Park in the Rivard Plaza. Head east on Atwater Street.

0.3 Take a left onto the pathway leading to the Dequindre Cut.

1.4 After rising up from the Cut, take a left onto the sidewalk along the south side of Gratiot Avenue.

1.6 Turn left onto Riopelle Street, then take a right onto Service Street.

1.8 Turn right onto Russell Street and cross Gratiot Avenue.

1.9 Turn right onto Winder Street and take a quick tour around a block of the Eastern Market. Turn left onto Market Street, then left again onto Adelaide Street, then right onto Russell Street.

2.3 Turn left onto Wilkins Street and cross over the Chrysler Expressway.

2.8 Turn left onto Brush Street into the Brush Park Area. Cross over the Fisher Freeway, and pass between Ford Field and Comerica Park.

3.5 Turn right onto Madison Street.

3.7 Turn right at the edge of Grand Circus Park onto Witherell Street and pass by the front of Comerica Park.

3.9 Turn left onto Montcalm Street, then right onto Woodward Avenue and cross over Fisher Freeway once more. Follow Woodward through the Arts & Cultural Center area. Be aware that Woodward is busy at times, as it is a main artery in Detroit as well as a bus route.

5.6 Turn right onto Ferry Avenue.

6.1 Turn left onto St. Antoine Street, then left again a block up at Palmer Avenue.

6.3 Turn right onto Brush Street and cross the Edsel Ford Freeway.

6.5 Turn left onto Antoinette Avenue.

6.7 Turn right onto Woodward Avenue.

7.2 Turn left onto West Grand Boulevard. This is a sometimes busy, multilane intersection. Cross with care. Pass the GM Building, the Fisher Building, cross over the Lodge Freeway, and pass Henry Ford Hospital. Hitsville USA (Motown) is ahead on the left.

8.2 Just past Hitsville USA, turn left onto Holden Street.

8.7 Go over the Lodge Freeway on the pedestrian crossing, then take Forsythe Street to 3rd Avenue.

9.0 Turn right onto 3rd Avenue. Ride over the Edsel Ford Freeway and pass through the Wayne State University area and into Midtown.

9.7 Take the jog around the median on 3rd and return to Hancock Street.

10.0 Turn right onto Cass Avenue.

10.1 Turn right onto Prentis Street.

10.3 Turn left onto 3rd Avenue.

10.4 Turn left onto Canfield Street.

10.7 Turn right onto Cass Avenue.

11.0 Turn right onto Selden Avenue; follow it to the pedestrian overpass that crosses the Lodge Freeway.

11.6 Turn right onto Trumbull Avenue into the Woodbridge area.

11.7 Turn left onto Alexandrine Street, then go for 1 block to Commonwealth Street; turn right (Ty Cobb house is on the left); at the next block take a left onto Willis Street, then another left onto Avery Street.

12.1 Turn left onto Grand River Avenue.

12.3 Turn right onto Trumbull Avenue.

12.7 Turn right onto Spruce Street.

12.9 Turn left onto Cochrane and 0.5 block ahead, beyond Pine Street, turn left onto the spiral climb up the pedestrian overpass that crosses the Fisher Freeway. Descend from the ramp and continue south (right) on Cochrane alongside the old Tiger Stadium field.

13.3 Turn right onto Michigan Avenue.

13.6 Turn left onto the Vernor Highway in front of the old Michigan Central Train Station. Stay to the right and pass under the railroad tracks.

14.1 Turn left onto Sainte Anne Street.

14.3 Turn right onto Bagley Street.

14.4 On the left is the Michigan Welcome Center. Straight ahead is the Bagley Street Pedestrian Bridge. Cross the bridge over the Fisher Freeway and once over continue on Bagley Street.

14.6 Turn right onto 24th Street, then a block up turn left onto Vernor Highway. This is a main artery and an active commercial area. Be aware that traffic can be busy at times.

15.1 Turn left onto Scotten Street and ride alongside Clark Park.

15.4 Turn left onto Porter Street, take it 1 block to Hubbard Street and turn right.

15.7 Turn left onto Lafayette Boulevard, and 1 block up take another left onto Vinewood Street, a quiet, well-cared-for neighborhood in Mexicantown.

16.2 Turn right onto Bagley Street and return through the heart of Mexicantown once more, over the Bagley Street Pedestrian Bridge, and back onto Bagley going east.

16.8 Turn right onto Sainte Anne Street.

17.2 Take a left onto Lafayette Boulevard.

17.4 Turn left onto 16th Street.

17.7 Turn right onto Bagley Street.

17.9 Turn left onto Wabash Street and head into Corktown.

18.2 Turn right onto Michigan Avenue.

18.4 Turn right onto 12th Street.

18.5 Turn left onto Leverette Street.

18.8 Turn right onto Trumbull Street, then a block over turn left onto Bagley Street.

19.1 Turn left onto 6th Street then right onto Michigan Avenue. Cross over the Lodge Freeway.

19.8 Turn right onto Griswold Street.

20.1 Turn left onto Larned Street. This is the heart of the financial district in Detroit, and it's the "hub" of the radius of streets fanning out over the area. Traffic and buses can make maneuvering on a bicycle a challenge during certain times of day.

20.4 Turn left onto Brush Street. Pass through Bricktown and on into Greektown.

20.6 Turn right onto Monroe Street.

20.8 Turn left onto St. Antoine Street.

21.0 Turn left onto Gratiot Avenue.

21.2 Turn right onto Randolph Street and into Germantown, pass the park and swing back around it onto Grand River Avenue.

21.4 Turn right onto Broadway Street.

21.6 Turn right onto Witherell Street and circle around Grand Circus Park, first left onto Adams Street, then left onto Park Avenue.

21.9 Turn right onto Washington Boulevard.

22.0 Turn left onto Grand River Avenue.

22.2 Turn right onto Woodward Avenue. Pass Campus Martius, then cross Jefferson Avenue using the signalized crossing. Jefferson, a multi-lane street, is busy most times of day, with traffic crisscrossing all over. Cross carefully with the aid of the signalized pedestrian signal straight into Hart Plaza. Toward the back of Hart Plaza there's a ramp to the right that leads down to the Detroit Riverwalk.

22.9 Turn left onto the Riverwalk and ride east, past the Gateway to Freedom Memorial and the Renaissance Center.

23.7 Arrive back at Rivard Plaza in the William G. Milliken State Park.

RIDE INFORMATION

Local Events/Attractions
Architectural Tour via the Wheelhouse: (313) 656-BIKE (2453); www.wheel
housedetroit.com
Beat the Train Ride: A group bike ride around downtown every Saturday
morning in the warm months; www.beatthetrain.org
Campus Martius: Public events held throughout the year; www.campus
martiuspark.org
Detroit Institute of Arts (DIA): Don't miss the Rivera mural. It's a great and
wonderfully controversial visual representation of Detroit's industrial heritage; www.dia.org
Eastern Market: Saturday farmers' market; www.detroiteasternmarket.com
Hart Plaza: Great sculpture park as well as a popular festival area (see the
fountain by Isamu Noguchi); 1 Washington Blvd., Detroit, MI 48226
Motown Museum: Tours of the home where the Motown hits originated;
www.motownmuseum.org
Tour De Troit: A group bike ride around downtown Detroit in September;
www.tour-de-troit.org

Restaurants
Astro Coffee: 2124 Michigan Ave., Detroit, MI 48216; (313) 638-2989
Avalon International Breads: Excellent bakery/cafe; 422 W. Willis St., Detroit,
MI 48201; (313) 832-0008
Cafe Con Leche: 4200 W. Vernor Hwy., Detroit, MI 48209; (313) 554-1744
Motor City Brewing Works: 470 W. Canfield St., Detroit, MI 48201; (313) 832-2700
Russell Street Deli: 2465 Russell St., Detroit, MI 48207; (313) 567-2900
Slows Bar BQ: 2138 Michigan Ave., Detroit, MI 48216: (313) 962-9828
Supino Pizzaria: 2457 Russell St., Detroit, MI 48207; (313) 567-7879
Woodbridge Pub: 5169 Trumbull St., Detroit, MI 48218; (313) 833-2701

Accommodations
The Inn on Ferry Street: innonferrystreet.com

Restrooms
Start/Finish: Excellent facilities at the Rivard Plaza where the ride begins
Mile 14.4: State of Michigan Welcome Center in Mexicantown

Detroit: Belle Isle–Indian Village– Heidelberg Project

Rivard Plaza along the Detroit Riverwalk at William G. Milliken State Park serves as the starting point for this ride. The 28-mile Detroit River, short by river standards but large in its historical role, gives one a sense of Great Lakes grandeur. It connects Lake Erie and Lake St. Clair, eventually linking to three of the other Great Lakes to the north and west and to Lake Ontario and the St. Lawrence Seaway to the east. It looks across at Canada, it was a major crossing for the Underground Railroad, it played a strong role in the settling of America, and has served as one of the busiest waterways in the country where large ships from all over the world still slide by with substantial cargo.

A view north reveals Belle Isle, the first destination for this ride. From there, it's on to Indian Village, a residential area lined with majestic homes built in the early 20th century by wealthy and prominent citizens in the city. After that it's on to Tyree Guyton's Heidelberg Project, one of the most unique living art projects anywhere. Then it's a tour through Elmwood Cemetery and finally a return to the William G. Milliken State Park via the Dequindre Cut, a popular linear park that was once a railroad corridor.

Start: William G. Milliken State Park at Rivard Plaza

Length: 20.5 miles

Approximate riding time: 1.5–3 hours

Best bike: Road or hybrid

Terrain and trail surface: Pavement, mostly flat

Traffic and hazards: Pedestrians and other users on the Riverwalk. The streets are reasonably low in traffic volume with wide lanes, but this is a city and city drivers can be aggressive at times. Always ride defensively.

Things to see: Major recreational outlets and aesthetic features in Detroit: the Detroit Riverwalk, Belle Isle, Indian Village, the Heidelberg Project, Elmwood Cemetery, and the Dequindre Cut

Maps: Universal Map: Detroit Greater Area; *DeLorme: Michigan Atlas & Gazetteer,* page 34

Getting there by car: From Jefferson and Woodward Avenue (at the hub of all roads leading out of downtown Detroit), drive east on Jefferson to Rivard Street. Turn right onto Rivard. Turn left onto Atwater Street, then the first right into the William G. Milliken State Park parking area. The Riverwalk leads from Rivard Plaza adjacent to the parking area. GPS: N42 19.853 W83 01.879

THE RIDE

Roll northeast from the Rivard Plaza in the William G. Milliken State Park along the Detroit Riverwalk. The view across the river is Windsor, Ontario, and the view upriver is that of Belle Isle Park, the first major destination.

A short way up, the path swings north to Atwater Street. Take a right and follow this up to where it Ts at River Place Drive as you pass between old brick warehouses and recently restored parkland along the river. Chene Park on the right is a popular concert venue in the summer months.

At the T on Joseph Campau Street, swing a quick right, then a left back onto the Riverwalk. To the left is a cluster of restored warehouses now primarily in use as upscale residential buildings. This section of the Riverwalk also passes the imposing, relatively new UAW/GM building, then wends its way past a small marina, over to Wright Street and left onto Mt. Elliott Street. You'll ride past the Iron Street Lofts, another historic, restored warehouse building and follow Mt. Elliott Street up to Jefferson Avenue. Turn right (east) onto Jefferson and ride to East Grand Boulevard, the entrance to the bridge that takes you to Belle Isle.

Belle Isle

Turn right off Jefferson Avenue onto the MacArthur Bridge and feel the breeze pick up. It's a 6.7-mile loop beginning on Jefferson Avenue, over the bridge, one counterclockwise loop around the island, returning over the bridge to Jefferson. The island is mostly flat, but even if there aren't any hills to challenge you, usually there's a headwind, tailwind, or crosswind on various parts of this ride to keep you pedaling.

Swing right as you descend off the bridge and you'll soon have a great panoramic view downriver of downtown Detroit. For all its challenges over the years, Detroit still has a fascinating skyline. The park areas on the west side of the island are expansive, with plenty of opportunities for a picnic or just a place to sit and take a break and enjoy the view.

Ride the pathway to the western tip of the island, then swing east and back onto the roadway, and there are sweeping vistas of Ontario on the right and some nice architecture on the left as you cruise along. Belle Isle was designed in part by Frederick Law Olmsted, the man who also designed Central Park in New York City, and there are similar landscape features such as internal ponds, long vistas, an integration of vehicular and nonmotorized traffic while retaining the natural setting, and interesting architectural and sculptural features. The intended purpose of a large greensward is a welcome relief in the midst of a major urban area. The sightings of occasional passing international freighters are a bonus.

There's much to enjoy and explore, but of special visual interest is the Belle Isle Casino building (not used for gambling, but for special events, at mile 4.0 from the beginning of the ride), the Anna Scripps Whitcomb Conservatory (mile 4.6) designed by Albert Kahn, and the Detroit Yacht Club (mile 7.0).

The route includes a quick sidetrack into the center of the island on Inselruhe Avenue, but there are other byways to explore as well. Leave the island over the same bridge.

Indian Village

Once off the bridge, continue north on East Grand Boulevard to Agnes Street (mile 10.2), a pleasant, quiet residential street that connects to the next destination, Indian Village. Continue east to Seminole Street (mile 10.8) and take a right. You'll be immediately struck by the grand eloquence of the houses around you.

Indian Village is a neighborhood where affluent Detroiters in the auto industry like Edsel Ford built large homes designed by prominent architects such as Albert Kahn (his fingerprints are all over Detroit) and Louis Kamper in the early 20th century.

Roam down a block to Lafayette Street, then turn left and ride another block to Iroquois Street and take another left. You've begun the large rectangular loop that will take you by one magnificent home after another, most of them restored to their original splendor. Ride slowly to savor the details, 6 blocks north to Goethe Street (mile 12.0) and take a left. Go 1 block back to Seminole, turn left again, and follow that to where you began on Agnes.

Follow Agnes west to Seyburn Street and take a right. Go 2 blocks to Kercheval Street and take a left. Head west to Mt. Elliott (mile 14.2) and take a

Once the route of the Grand Trunk Western Railway, the Dequindre Cut is now a popular below-grade dedicated greenway.

right. Go north, past Vernor Highway to Heidelberg Street (mile 14.7). Turn left onto Heidelberg Street.

Heidelberg Project

There's something so unique about the Heidelberg Project. Outdoor sculpture is usually an object of some kind, often at a small scale to its grand environmental surroundings. The Heidelberg Project is an art installation that takes up a few city blocks. There have been moments in its history when the City has attempted to tear it down, and though parts have been demolished, much of it still stands and it's now protected.

It was begun in 1986 by Tyree Guyton and his grandfather Sam Mackey as a response to the 1967 Riots and the decay of a neighborhood where Guyton grew up. It's still a living, perpetually changing project.

There are painted, multicolored polka dots everywhere, plus signs, and abstract faces; found objects such as toys, dolls, shopping carts, and even cars; words such as "war" and "god" are scrawled all over. And, of course, the houses themselves are festooned with much of the above and more. It's a lot to take in.

According to Guyton, "the philosophy of the Heidelberg Project is to take nothing and to take that nothing and to create something very beautiful, very whimsical, to the point that it makes people think…[It's] transforming something, nothing into something, building bridges, creating hope, giving young people a chance to be creative, it's going to live on. It's bigger than me." See www.youtube.com/watch?v=wbdfY2NArOU.

Loop 1 block down to Ellery Street, take a right and go 0.5 block to Elba and take another right. This street is also a part of the art display. Go east to Mt. Elliott and take a right. Follow this back south past Vernor and then past the Mt. Elliott Cemetery to Lafayette Street (mile 16.0) and take a right. Take this to Robert Bradby Drive and take a right. Go 0.5 block (mile 16.4) and turn right into Elmwood Cemetery.

Elmwood Cemetery

Enter the cemetery past the Gothic Revival Gatehouse, built in 1876. The cemetery website says that Elmwood Cemetery is "the oldest continually operating, non-denominational cemetery in Michigan." The cemetery was established in 1846 and it holds some of Detroit's most prominent citizens (Lewis Cass, Zina Pitcher, and Coleman Young, to name a few) as well as those laborers who helped to build the city.

Its design was updated by Frederick Law Olmsted in the 1890s on a rolling piece of land that is carefully crafted and laid out to flow with the natural features. The roadways wind in and around the knolls, and though the entire property is only 82 acres, it's not hard to get disoriented due to the twisting flow of the roads. The route on the map is only a suggestion. Each road in here is worth taking. Keep in mind, you're never far from the entrance and let the beauty of the place guide you.

At some point you'll see the highly charming Gothic Revival Chapel, constructed in 1856. It truly does put you in another place and time.

Return to the entrance and turn left onto Robert Bradby Drive, then take a right onto Lafayette. Follow this to Chene Street (mile 17.8) and take a right. Chene Street eventually swings around to become Antietam Avenue. Take this to St. Aubin Street (mile 18.7) and take a right up to Gratiot Avenue. I recommend you take a left onto the sidewalk on the south side of Gratiot. It's a substantial sidewalk, and a short way up it leads you to the entrance ramp (mile 19.0) into the Dequindre Cut. Turn left onto the ramp and begin your descent.

Bike Rentals

The Hub of Detroit/Back Alley Bikes: 3611 Cass Ave., Detroit, MI 48201; (313) 833-0813; thehubofdetroit.org
The Wheelhouse (seasonal): 1340 E. Atwater St., Rivard Plaza on the Detroit Riverwalk, Detroit, MI 48207; (313) 656-BIKE (2453); www.wheelhousedetroit.com

Dequindre Cut

The Dequindre Cut is actually a section of an old railway line, the Grand Trunk Western Railroad, that's now a wide, two-way, nonmotorized pathway.

It's called a cut because it descends below street level and crosses under major streets such as Lafayette Street and Jefferson Avenue. It's bordered by high walls, much of it covered by dramatic and well-crafted graffiti. The pathway and adjoining greenspace is well-patrolled and well-maintained its entire length.

Eventually the Dequindre Cut will connect farther north to the Eastern Market, a well-known, well-loved, and historical farmers' market in Detroit. For now it goes from Gratiot Avenue on the north to Atwater Street on the south.

Return

At Atwater Street (mile 20.1), take a right and return along the Riverwalk (left at mile 20.2) to the starting point in Rivard Plaza where there's a concession stand for post-ride refreshments, with tables and chairs for you to relax in and watch the world go by.

MILES AND DIRECTIONS

0.0 Leave Rivard Plaza heading east along the Riverwalk. A short way up, the path swings north.

0.3 Turn right onto Atwater Street.

0.9 Turn right onto River Place Drive. This leads back to the Riverwalk, where you'll swing left, heading east. The path follows the river, then turns left, away from it at Harbortown.

1.7 Turn right onto Wright Street, then turn left onto Mount Elliott Street. (Note: in the future this may continue along the river to the Belle Isle Bridge, but that connection is not yet available.)

2.0 Turn right onto Jefferson Avenue. This is a busy main thoroughfare, but the lanes are wide enough to readily accommodate cyclists.

2.4 Swing to the right, onto the Belle Isle Bridge.

3.0 Once across the bridge, swing right onto Sunset Drive and begin the tour around the perimeter of Belle Isle.

3.5 While the roadway arcs left at this point, in order to get to the far western tip of Belle Isle with its wide-open views of Detroit, hop onto the pathway and follow it around until it reenters onto Casino Way a short way ahead. There are public restrooms at this location as well.

3.7 Reenter Casino Way and continue east. Follow the perimeter road all the way around the island, past the yacht club, until reaching Inselruhe Avenue on the other side.

8.0 Turn left onto Inselruhe Avenue for a quick out-and-back view of the inner workings of the island.

9.2 Return to the bridge and cross over, cross Jefferson Avenue, and continue up East Grand Boulevard.

10.2 Turn right onto Agnes Avenue.

10.8 Turn right onto Seminole Street and enter into the Indian Village neighborhood. Go 1 block down and turn left onto Lafayette Street, then left again onto Iroquois Street the next block over.

12.0 Turn left onto Goethe Street, then a block over turn left again onto Seminole Street.

Detroit: Belle Isle–Indian Village–Heidelberg

12.8 Turn right onto Agnes Street once again.

13.1 Turn right onto Seyburn Street.

13.4 Turn left onto Kercheval Street.

14.2 Turn right onto Mount Elliott Street.

14.7 Turn left onto Heidelberg Street into the heart of the Heidelberg Project. Go around the block, turning right at Ellery Street, then right at Elba Place, and right again onto Mount Elliott Street.

16.0 Turn right onto Lafayette Street.

16.4 Turn right onto Robert Bradby Drive, then right, into the entrance for the Elmwood Cemetery. Follow the route through the cemetery. To be honest, the route options through the cemetery are numerous and convoluted, but the views are long, and even accounting for a few moments of misdirection it's easy to find your way back to the gatehouse.

17.4 Having returned to Lafayette Street after exiting the cemetery and turning left onto Robert Bradby Drive, turn right onto Lafayette.

17.8 Turn right onto Chene Street. This swings around and becomes Antietam Avenue.

18.7 Turn right onto St. Aubin Street.

18.9 Turn left at Vernor Highway onto the sidewalk, which then swings onto the sidewalk on the south side of Gratiot Avenue.

19.0 Take the ramp to the left, down into the Dequindre Cut.

20.1 Turn right onto Atwater Street.

20.2 Turn left onto the Riverwalk bike path and follow it back to Rivard Plaza.

20.5 Arrive back at Rivard Plaza.

RIDE INFORMATION

Local Events/Attractions
Architectural Tour via the Wheelhouse: (313) 656-BIKE (2453); www.wheelhousedetroit.com
Beat the Train Ride: A group bike ride around downtown every Saturday morning in the warm months; www.beatthetrain.org

Campus Martius: Public events held throughout the year; www.campus martiuspark.org

Detroit Institute of Arts (DIA): Don't miss the Rivera mural. It's a great and wonderfully controversial visual representation of Detroit's industrial heritage; www.dia.org

Eastern Market: Saturday farmers' market; www.detroiteasternmarket.com

Hart Plaza: Great sculpture park as well as a popular festival area (see the fountain by Isamu Noguchi); 1 Washington Blvd., Detroit, MI 48226

Motown Museum: Tours the home where the Motown hits originated; www.motownmuseum.org

Tour De Troit: A group bike ride around downtown Detroit in September; www.tour-de-troit.org

Restaurants

Astro Coffee: 2124 Michigan Ave., Detroit, MI 48216; (313) 638-2989

Avalon International Breads: Excellent bakery/café; 422 W. Willis St., Detroit, MI 48201; (313) 832-0008

Cafe Con Leche: 4200 W. Vernor Hwy., Detroit, MI 48209; (313) 554-1744

Motor City Brewing Works: 470 W. Canfield St., Detroit, MI 48201; (313) 832-2700

Russell Street Deli: 2465 Russell St., Detroit, MI 48207; (313) 567-2900

Slows Bar BQ: 2138 Michigan Ave., Detroit, MI 48216; (313) 962-9828

Supino Pizzaria: 2457 Russell St., Detroit, MI 48207; (313) 567-7879

Woodbridge Pub: 5169 Trumbull St., Detroit, MI 48218; (313) 833-2701

Restrooms

Start/Finish: Excellent facilities at the Rivard Plaza where the ride begins

Mile 3.5: Public restrooms in the brick building near the western tip of Belle Isle

Hines Drive

Hines Drive is nearly legendary at this point. Frankie Andreu, former pro cyclist and Dearborn native, has trained here, as have many of the top racers in the state. It's ridden by just about every level of rider, from the casual coaster to the weekend wanderer to the hard-core bike racer. Groups fly by, or they slowly amble past, chatting away. There's a parallel bike path that's as popular as the road.

On weekends from early May to late September, over 6 miles of the drive are closed to vehicles for specified periods of time. The whole wide road opens to self-powered pursuits. Those 6 miles get filled with mostly cyclists, but also Rollerbladers and walkers. This indicates the popularity of its use for recreation. It's as much fun to come and people-watch as it is to ride, but it's best to do both.

Plus, it connects Northville in the northwest to Dearborn to the southeast, and ties in other municipalities along the way. That makes it a very popular commuter route. It parallels the Middle Rouge River its entire length. It occasionally floods, and that's actually part of the plan.

Start: Northville West parking area off Hines Drive just south of 7 Mile Road

Length: 34.0 miles both ways

Approximate riding time: 2–3 hours

Best bike: Road or hybrid

Terrain and trail surface: Paved road

Traffic and hazards: There is a wide bike lane and cars normally travel at reasonable speeds, but there are also a lot of bikes at times, and jostling around them requires care. There are also numerous busy intersections, particularly on the western half of the ride. There are clear signal lights, however.

Other users can make things difficult on busy days. There are all kinds of riders, fast racers and inexperienced riders, drifting families, joggers, and wide-swinging Rollerbladers. Keep an eye out for the unexpected.

Be aware that this is also a very popular route for vehicles. It's a nice drive and sometimes it's packed with cars, especially during the rush hours.

Things to see: This is a verdant river valley in a large population area. It's a respite from all the suburban development. Large mature trees, rolling green vistas, activities such as cricket, baseball, or soccer, historic buildings, ponds, and stretches of the Rouge River.

This is a beautiful, well-maintained, rolling roadway with a wide bike lane on each side most of the way.

Maps: *DeLorme: Michigan Atlas & Gazetteer,* page 33

Getting there by car: From I-275 take exit 169A headed west on 7 Mile Road. Follow this 2.4 miles to Northville Road. Turn right and go 0.1 mile to the continuation of 7 Mile Road and turn left. Go 0.3 mile to the turn onto Hines Drive to the left. Turn left in 0.3 mile into the Northville West Park parking area. GPS: N42 25.288 W83 28.669

THE RIDE

The Hines Drive greenway has been around since the 1930s when Henry Ford deeded much of his land holdings to Wayne County and Edward Hines shepherded his vision of a long linear riverine park to reality. Hines was a roadway innovator in many ways, cited as the first builder of a concrete road in the world along Woodward Avenue in 1909. He also came up with the idea of the middle road stripe to separate traffic moving in opposite directions as well as roadway snow removal; he was also an early advocate of highway beautification. To add one more bicycle-related item to his palmares, he was also one of the organizers of the League of American Wheelmen and served as its chief counsel. So Hines Drive is more than just a road. It honors an early pioneer who shaped the country's true meaning of parkway. Give Mr. Hines his due as you slowly meander or hammer your legs into shape along this long greensward.

This is an out-and-back ride. There is no loop, but the perspectives are different in each direction, and the road is wide enough that it can almost feel like two separate paths that just happen to parallel one another. Part of the reason the road is so wide is the ample bike lane on each side. Groups can ride in this lane two abreast without hindering other traffic.

The descent from the Northville West park area is long, fast, and sweeping. It's a great way to enter into the Rouge River corridor. (Forget for now

Bicycling is a highly popular activity along the route.

that this is the return climb, the biggest of the entire ride.) Enjoy it. Also, keep in mind that all around you is a green park and a short way beyond that is a bustling metro area bursting with urban energy. You are cruising through the respite from that hustling world. The contrast is quite distinct as you watch traffic clustering at intersections with lines of cars queued up as you roll happily along in the open air.

Once the rapid downhill tapers, the road levels off somewhat with long gentle ups and downs. That's Hines Drive. The terrain isn't overly sharp, but after a long ride over those rollers you realize that the legs got a workout.

Also, be aware that there's a bike path that parallels Hines Drive. It sometimes follows along the edge and sometimes dips back behind a park, returning on the other side. If paths are your preference, or if for some reason a break from the road is in order, try the path. It's in good shape most of the way, with only a few spots where the paving could use some maintenance. It's a whole different way to enjoy this unique park and well worth the change of pace.

Many roads do crisscross through and over Hines Drive, and it is possible to get misdirected, though for the most part the road is clearly marked. Confusion may occur at the T into Northville Road at mile 1.8. This is even more challenging on the return trip. You'll need to watch for this turn, as there's no T as a reminder from the other direction. Turn right, pass 5 Mile Road, and go beneath the railroad viaduct. Continue to mile 2.2, where Northville Road and Hines Drive once again diverge at a Y. Stay to the right, remaining on Hines Drive.

The rest of the ride is pretty straightforward. You can now concentrate on the many parks and activities going on all around you. I've even passed a cricket match in progress—not your normal American pastime, but with the many cultures that live in the Detroit metro area, a pleasant reminder of the diversity such an area offers.

In fact, one of the most interesting things to realize is that Hines Drive isn't just one long park, but many parks and recreational options linked together, with diverse activities taking place in each one. Not to mention those who use it as a place to eat lunch, as a background for photography sessions, to sunbathe, or to get a little work done in the open air. It's not unusual to see someone in a suit with a laptop propped open on a picnic table. Hines is all things to all people, and you, on your bike, are just another participant in the show.

There are also a series of mill names along the ride: Gunsolly Mills, Newburg Mill, and the most prominent of all, Nankin Mills at mile 9.4. Mills were some of the first businesses in the region during its early settlement by Europeans. Nankin Mills is now the headquarters of the Wayne County Park System and an historical interpretive center open to the public. This stately piece of architecture was built in 1863, replacing the original gristmill built in 1842. Henry Ford lived nearby in Dearborn as a child and sometimes passed by it on his travels with his father along Ann Arbor Trail. He later bought it in 1918 and transformed it into a small automobile factory, still retaining its character.

Bike Shops

Cycle to Fitness: 10960 Farmington Rd., Livonia, MI 48150; (734) 266-8203; cycletofitness.com

D & D Bicycles and Hockey: 121 N. Center St., Northville, MI 48167; (248) 347-1511; ddbicyclesandhockey.com

Jacks Bicycle and Fitness: 24308 Michigan Ave., Dearborn, MI 48124; (313) 561-2560; www.jacksbikes.com

REI Northville: 17559 Haggerty Rd. (Haggerty and 6 Mile Rd.), Northville, MI 48168; (248) 347-2100; rei.com

Town and Country Bikes and Boards: 148 N. Center, Northville, MI 48167; (248) 349-7140; townandcountrybikeandboards.com

Trails Edge Cyclery: 232 N. Main St., Plymouth, MI 48170; (734) 420-1200; trails-edge.com

Blue heron in a marsh near Nankin Mills

The area's history goes even farther back, as the Nankin area was an original convergence of many Native American trails used by the Potawattomi, Ojibwa, and Ottawa tribes.

This is also the point where the roadway closes to traffic on Saturday during the warm months. For the next 6.5 miles it's vehicle free and often awash with walkers, runners, Rollerbladers, and cyclists of all ages. This is in part possible because there are no road crossings for that length except for a series of underpasses and one overpass.

The turnaround at the 17.0-mile mark, between Outer Drive and Ford Road, is rather nondescript. It's a wide-open area where you'll have to do a U-turn in the road. It is possible to go farther, though Ford Road is not recommended. There is a path, the Rouge Gateway Trail, that goes under Ford Road, then follows the backside of the Henry Ford Community College campus and the University of Michigan Dearborn campus. It also passes by the Henry Ford Estate Museum (not to be confused with the Henry Ford Museum across Michigan Avenue at Greenfield Village).

The Gateway Trail ends at Michigan Avenue in a small parking area with no clear directions to go any farther. Greenfield Village is only a stone's throw away to the southeast, but as yet there is no straightforward connection to

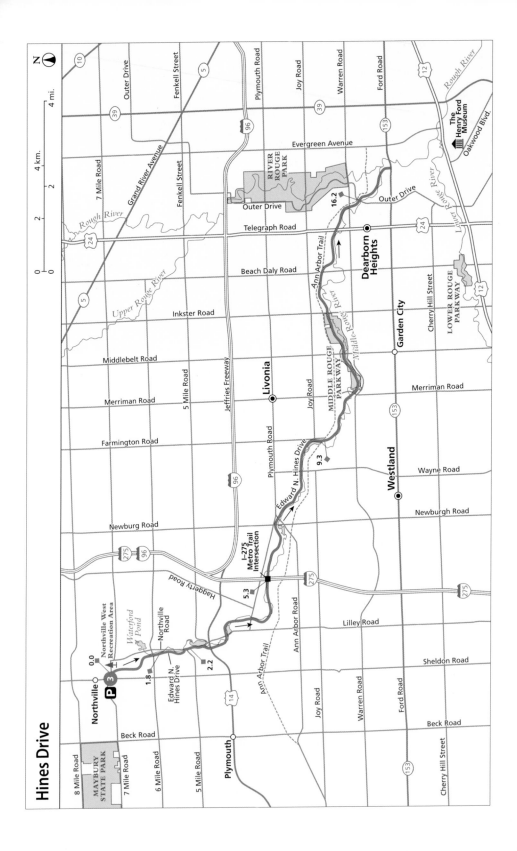

Hines Drive

it from this point. Michigan Avenue is a daunting proposition for cyclists to attempt to maneuver.

MILES AND DIRECTIONS

0.0 Leave the Northville West Parking Area and ride south.

1.8 Turn right onto Northville Road where it joins Hines Drive.

2.2 Veer right, staying on Hines Drive while Northville Road splits to the left.

5.3 Pass beneath the I-275 overpass and continue southeast on Hines Drive.

9.3 Past Ann Arbor Trail begins the stretch of Hines Drive that is closed to traffic on designated weekends in the warm months of the year.

16.2 Outer Drive is the end of the vehicle-free stretch of Hines Drive on designated weekends.

17.0 Hines Drive connects to Ford Road, and there's a nonmotorized pathway that goes beneath the Ford Road overpass, along the edge of the University of Michigan Dearborn campus.

34.0 Retrace pathway/return to trailhead.

RIDE INFORMATION

Local Events/Attractions
Be aware that the Henry Ford Estate Museum on the University of Michigan Dearborn campus is closed indefinitely for updating.
Henry Ford Greenfield Village and Museum: This is a good place to get a sense of regional history; www.thehenryford.org
Nankin Mills: Interpretive center with information on the cultural and natural history of the area; www.nankinmills.org.
Northville: Ride through the historic neighborhoods surrounding downtown Northville.

Restaurants
Edward's Cafe: 115 E. Main St., Northville, MI 48167; (248) 344-1550
Liberty Street Brewing: 149 W. Liberty St., Plymouth, MI 48170; (734) 207-9600
Tuscan Cafe: 150 N. Center St., Northville, MI 48167; (248) 305-8629

Restrooms
All along the route in the picnic/activity areas

4

Huron River Drive: Ann Arbor to Dexter

Huron River Drive is possibly the most heavily cycled recreational road in the Ann Arbor region, for good reason. It's a twisting, rolling ride along a scenic corridor beginning on the western edge of Ann Arbor. This is the gateway to most of the popular road rides outside of Ann Arbor. It's the go-to route for bike groups and individuals leaving town for quieter rural rides. It's also a complete ride experience in itself. It follows the Huron River Valley to the charming town of Dexter to the northwest. On the way it passes the calls of coxswains calling out to rowing clubs training on the river, the steep banks and carved ravines of Bird Hills Nature Area, the dramatic Barton Dam, two ornate iron bridges, sweeping riverine oxbows, and two Metroparks. It's forest lined, with a few houses dotted here and there, for nearly the entire length. You might imagine a river valley to be flat, but this scenic roadway has some short, dramatic climbs, and it rolls continually up and down with many twists and turns along the way.

Start: Barton Park parking area near the exit from M-14 on Huron River Drive

Length: 9.6 miles

Approximate riding time: 2 hours with stops

Best bike: Road or hybrid bike

Terrain and surface: Paved surface the entire length. There are few level areas, though the hills are short and for the most part not very steep. One hill is relatively steep, but also quite short.

Traffic hazards: This is a known recreational bike route, but there is only a small shoulder and caution is needed at all times. It gets moderate vehicular traffic most of the day, which increases for a short time during the rush hours. There is an occasional impatient driver, though this still doesn't deter a large number of cyclists from taking this route on a regular basis.

Things to see: Rowing groups in training on the Huron River, Barton Dam, Foster Bridge and Delhi Bridge (both iron, historic, and beautifully ornate), Delhi Metropark, Dexter-Huron Metropark, and much varied wildlife along the river

Maps: *DeLorme: Michigan Atlas & Gazetteer,* page 32; Huron-Clinton Metroparks Publications: Hudson Mills, Delhi & Dexter-Huron Map (pdf); Hike-Bike Trails Map (pdf); www.metroparks.com; USGS: Ann Arbor West Quad, Dexter MI Quad

Getting there by car: From downtown Ann Arbor, take Main Street (Business US 23) north 1.3 miles to Huron River Drive (turn left just before the on-ramp to M-14/US 23). Follow Huron River Drive underneath the highway for 0.3 mile to the Barton Parking area on the right. GPS: N42 18.123 W83 44.927

THE RIDE

This ride is popular for many reasons: it's close to downtown, it's hilly but not too hilly, it's scenic and the scene changes daily with the varying weather and the seasons, the river is often in sight and it's a pleasant view all along the way, it winds its way along from beginning to end, and it's short enough for a quick out-and-back workout or just a brief release from the bustle of life. It can be ridden fast and hard or it can be savored, and it fulfills either way.

Before hopping on the bike, stroll out on the long pedestrian bridge, adjacent to the parking area, that crosses the Huron River to Barton Nature Area (popular with birders) and look out on majestic views of the river often occupied by individual rowers quietly sculling on the placid water, or rowing teams from the University of Michigan or the local high schools, or look upon a scene teeming with birds flittering about. The bike ride begins with a sweeping cruise through a tunnel of trees on Huron River Drive with the river below on the right and the Bird Hills Nature Area with its high ridges and lush ravines on the left. In the late 1800s, Bird Hills was nearly entirely logged out and sat denuded of vegetation. This is hard to imagine as you look up at today's lush, mature, and diverse landscape. The city now owns about 162 acres of these hills, and it ranks as one of the most diverse parks in terms of native plant species in the city's Floristic Quality Assessment.

Within less than a mile will be a sightline upriver of the Barton Dam on the right. Barton Dam, constructed in 1912 to harness the river's power, was built by Detroit Edison Company and its engineer consultant Gardner

Coming over the rise near Delhi Metropark

Stewart Williams. It was the first in a series of dams constructed along the river by Detroit Edison, and this one in particular is an impressive sight. It's still in operation today. A short way farther along Huron River Drive, you'll pass the Barton Dam parking lot on the right, a meeting place of local bike groups and area paddlers. It's a short walk from here on a cinder path to view the dam close up and to walk across a metal grate walkway with views to the east, downriver, and west over Barton Pond and home of the Barton Hills Yacht Club, with small sailboats skimming over the water on warm summer days.

The next stretch of road will be one of the flattest anywhere along the route. You'll pass Maple Road with the Foster/Maple Road Bridge on the right. Built in the late 1800s, it's one of two metal truss bridges built in Michigan by the Wrought Iron Bridge Company of Canton, Ohio. (The Delhi Bridge, just up the road, was also built by the same company.) Over the bridge and up the hill is the community of Barton Hills. There's no town, but it is distinguished as the first Home Rule community in Washtenaw County, with its own charter. It was first built by Detroit Edison as an exclusive residential community for its company executives. Its population is just over 300, but it boasts the highest per capita income of any other location in Michigan. There are a few homes visible on the north side of the river and they are quite palatial.

Best Bike Rides Detroit and Ann Arbor

Continuing along Huron River Drive begins a long, graceful oxbow filled, at various times, with ducks, swans, great egret, blue heron, anglers, and paddlers, and if you take it slowly enough to look closely on a sunny day, lines of turtles on exposed logs on the river. It's not uncommon to see white-tailed deer here and in other places along the way. The pull-offs are small but worth the time to take a short break and ponder the activity and beauty of this natural wonder. This section takes on many different personalities at different times of day, with varying wildlife and magnificent reflections of the surrounding hills on the water.

Leaving the oxbow, and just beyond Wagner Road, you'll come across the first bridge crossing. Below it is Honey Creek, a tributary of the Huron. After that is a railroad track that carries local freight as well as riders on Amtrak from Detroit to Chicago. Take care in crossing, as this track is at an awkward angle to the road. At the bottom of the next hill is a bridge that crosses the Huron itself, and from here to Dexter the river will be on the left. Though it's hard to discern from the road, the Huron River has quite a history of small dams that powered mills all along the way. First there were sawmills, but later woolen mills, flour mills, paper mills, and cider mills. Their remnants are still visible in select areas along the river all the way to Dexter and beyond.

The road rises from here to crest above the Delhi Metropark across the river on the left. The top of this hill is the apex of the toughest climb on the return from Dexter, but for now enjoy the ride down. It's fast and sweeping. At the bottom of the hill and around a curve is the other wrought-iron bridge mentioned earlier, Delhi Bridge, on the left. It crosses the river into what was, in the mid-1800s, a thriving community with a grocery, a railroad depot, a schoolhouse, a woolen mill, a plaster mill, a sawmill, and two flour mills. When the mills left in the latter part of the 1800s, the village waned, but the bridge remains along with some of the houses. The Delhi Metropark on the other side of the river is worth a visit and a great place for a picnic break. It's part of the Huron-Clinton Metropark system that encircles the outer environs of Detroit along the Huron and Clinton Rivers, designed and initially implemented in the late 1930s and early 1940s as a greenbelt for outdoor recreational and educational activities. Delhi's 53 acres became a Metropark in 1957.

From here, the ride is a series of gently rolling hills through mostly tree-covered roadway with a scattering of houses tucked into the landscape and many views of the Huron River on your left. Watch for deer and wild turkey, though of course, they'll only appear when you aren't looking for them. There is a rather active intersection on this section to be aware of at Zeeb Road, at about the 6.6-mile point. Take care here. Beyond Zeeb there are some wonderfully graceful curves in the road. These curves, mixed with the tree canopy,

Bike Shops

Dexter Bike and Sport: 3173 Baker Rd., Dexter, MI 48130; (734) 426-5900; www.dexterbikeandsport.com

Great Lakes Cycling & Fitness: 2015 W. Stadium Blvd., Ann Arbor, MI 48103; (734) 668-6484; www.greatlakescycling.com

Midwest Bike & Tandem: 1691 Plymouth Rd., Ann Arbor, MI 48105; (734) 213-7744; www.midwesttandems.com

Performance Bike: 3059 Oak Valley Dr., Ann Arbor, MI 48103; (734) 769-0955; www.performancebike.com

REI Ann Arbor: 970 W. Eisenhower Pkwy., Ann Arbor, MI 48103; (734) 827-1938

Sic Transit Cycles: 1033 Broadway St., Ann Arbor, MI 48105; (734) 327-6900; sictransitcycles.com

Transition Rack: 217 S. Fourth Ave., Ann Arbor, MI 48104; (734) 214-9700; www.transitionrack.com

Two Wheel Tango: 3162 Packard St., Ann Arbor, MI 48108; (734) 528-3030; 4765 Jackson Rd., Ann Arbor, MI 48103; (734) 769-8401; twowheeltango.com

Wheels in Motion: 3400 Washtenaw Ave., Ann Arbor, MI 48104; (734) 971-2121; wheelsinmotion.us

will make it hard to believe you're in a relatively populated part of Michigan. At about the 8-mile point will be the second Metropark on the route, Dexter-Huron with 122 acres of land along the river. (There's still another Metropark along Huron River Drive, Hudson Mills, the largest of the three at over 1,500 acres, but it's a few miles beyond the turn-off at Mast Road for downtown Dexter.) Unlike Delhi Metropark, Dexter-Huron is not visible from the road. There's a short winding entrance road that leads to a couple of large picnic areas in a densely wooded park.

At this point the road rises gently almost all the way to the intersection at Mast Road. This is another busy and often confusing intersection, as there are five points coming together in an odd juxtaposition and a party store in the middle of it all with regular customer traffic going in and out. Take care here. Stay to the left, and when traffic clears, turn left onto Mast and cross the bridge (Mast Road becomes Central Street at this point).

You've just crossed the Huron River again, and on the right is the Historic Dexter Cider Mill, the oldest continuously operating cider mill in Michigan. On nice autumn weekends the lines to get a cider and dough-nut fix are serpentine. Take a right onto quiet Huron Street, then a left onto Broad. On both sides of the railroad tracks are historic buildings tied to rail transport, including the Dexter Mill, Dexter Lumber Company, and the charming train station. Nearly all of the buildings are restored and they're a beautiful gateway into the town of Dexter. Broad Street leads straight into the heart of downtown, with a pleasant sightline on the historic 19th-century three-story buildings the whole way. Dexter is a great place to hang out for a while with plenty of places to sit and relax, including benches in front of shops, around the centrally located clock tower, or in Monument Park around the corner on Main Street to the east with a large gazebo surrounded by a vernal landscape. The village has a popular bakery, a nice coffee shop, and some casual restaurants, all within close proximity that make hanging around and savoring the pace of small-town life very easy.

A short sidetrack down Main Street to the west goes under the railroad trestle and up a small climb to reveal Gordon Hall, sitting large and dramatically white, in an open field on the left. This was the home of the village's founder, Judge Samuel Dexter, built in the early 1840s. It is considered one of the best examples of the Greek Revival style of architecture in the state. It was also the birthplace of the judge's granddaughter, Katherine Dexter McCormick, who was a cofounder of the League of Women Voters.

MILES AND DIRECTIONS

0.0 Head northwest on Huron River Drive.

0.9 Barton Dam Parking Lot.

2.2 Maple-Foster Bridge on right.

4.0 Bridge over Huron River.

4.8 Delhi Bridge and crossing to Delhi Metropark on left.

6.6 Zeeb Road intersection. Continue on Huron River Drive, but take care here.

7.9 Dexter-Huron Metropark on left.

9.0 Turn left onto Central Street. Proceed with caution as this is a busy and confusing intersection. Cross the bridge.

9.1 Turn right onto Huron Street.

9.3 Turn left onto Broad Street.

9.6 Finish. Main Street, Dexter, Michigan.

Huron River Drive: Ann Arbor to Dexter

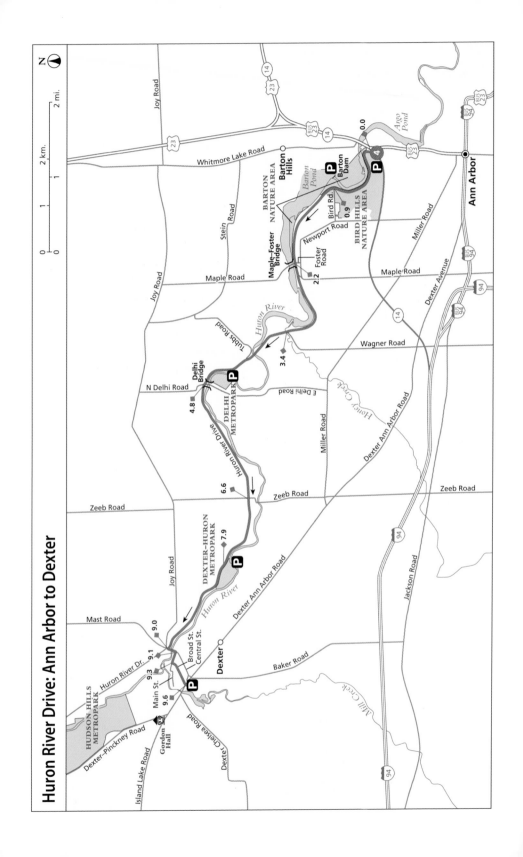

RIDE INFORMATION

Local Events/Attractions

Ann Arbor: There's something happening every weekend and usually even on weeknights in Ann Arbor during the warm months of the year. See arborweb .com for their calendar of events listings.

Dexter Cider Mill: Active and popular cider mill mid-August to mid-November. Wednesday to Sunday 9 a.m. to 5 p.m.; www.dextercidermill.com

Dexter Daze: This is an annual, early August community festival—since 1975—that features arts and crafts, local food, a parade, and free family entertainment. Downtown Dexter; www.dexterdaze.org

Dexter Farmers Market: A small farmers' market on Alpine Street with locally grown foods, along with arts and crafts. Open May through October, Saturday 8 a.m. to 1 p.m., Tuesday 3 to 7 p.m.; www.villageofdexter.org/general/farmers_market.htm

Restaurants

Ann Arbor: The list of Ann Arbor restaurants of all kinds is large and growing as I write this. I recommend looking up your favorite cuisine or finding a pub or cafe in Yelp (yelp.com). You'll be amazed at all the options.

Dairy Queen: The classic, downtown across from the park. Open every day, 11:30 a.m. to 9 p.m., March through October; 8041 Main St., Dexter; (734) 426-8647

Dexter Bakery: In the heart of downtown, this has been a popular local bakery for many years. Bakery items, sandwiches, soups, and beverages; 8101 Main St., Dexter; (734) 426-3848; www.thedexterbakery.com

Dexters Pub: Pizza, soups, and sandwiches; beer and wine; 8114 Main St., Dexter; (734) 426-1234

Joe & Rosie Coffee & Tea: A favorite among cyclists, this coffee shop offers a variety of coffee drinks, smoothies, and sandwiches. Seating inside in a charming wood-floored, brick-walled room, or outside looking out over the center of the downtown; 8074 Main St., Dexter; (734) 253-2344

Red Brick Kitchen & Bar: Pleasantly rustic and often busy with pub fare, beer, and wine; 8093 Main St., Dexter; (734) 424-0420; www.redbrickkitchen.com

Restrooms

Mile 4.8: Delhi Metropark

Mile 7.9: Dexter-Huron Metropark

Mile 9.0: Dexter Party Store (portable toilet alongside store, open to public)

Dexter–Chelsea–Patterson Lake

This route takes you into two small, charming towns worth exploring and wends its way along some beautiful rolling countryside. This route wanders through the heart of recreational Southeast Michigan that includes the Pinckney Recreation Area.

Start: Downtown Dexter at the intersection of Main and Broad Streets

Length: 32.6 miles

Approximate riding time: 2–4 hours

Best bike: Road bike, hybrid

Terrain and trail surface: Paved roads with varying shoulder widths

Traffic and hazards: M-52 north out of Chelsea is busy, but it also has a very wide shoulder offering a nice separation between bikes and cars. North Territorial Road is often busy with fast-moving traffic and minimal shoulder. Ride this short section with caution. Stay single file when riding with others on this road.

Things to see: Well-kept small towns, farmland, historic farmsteads, woodlands, marshes, wildlife

Maps: *DeLorme: Michigan Atlas & Gazetteer*, page 32

Getting there by car: From I-94 take exit 167 at Baker Road and head north 3 miles into downtown Dexter. Parking is available in lots downtown and on neighborhood side streets. GPS: N42 20.302 W83 53.320

THE RIDE

Dexter was originally known as Mill Creek Settlement when it was settled in the 1820s. Its name changed in 1830 to Dexter for its prominent founder, but the waterway that runs through the village, Mill Creek, still retains the name. Mills were the early settlers' economic lifeblood in the region, and Dexter had

The Chelsea Railroad Depot was built in 1880 along the Michigan Central Railroad.

all kinds of mills: a sawmill, cider mill, gristmill, and woolen mill. The cider mill still exists, on Central Street adjacent to the Huron River, and is a very popular spot in the fall.

The area around Mill Creek has recently been upgraded with a boardwalk, a newly reconstructed bridge, and environmental improvements. Dexter itself has numerous restored downtown buildings and a pleasant core streetscape from which to sip a coffee and prepare for the ride ahead.

Head west on Dexter-Chelsea Road, one of the main routes of the popular Ann Arbor Touring Society and the Velo Club, often lined with groups of cyclists on weekend mornings. If you're out on one of those mornings, watch for fast peletons sweeping by you on their way to the deep, rolling recesses of the county.

A few miles outside of Chelsea, after passing a series of farmsteads, you'll come to a small light industrial complex at Lima Center Road with a majestic series of connected grain silos (mile 4.5). Though it needs a new coat of paint, it's still quite awe inspiring as it rises out of the rural landscape. Carefully cross the double set of railroad tracks (flats are not uncommon) and continue on the rolling roadway to Chelsea.

While in Chelsea, you can load up on more coffee, get a bite to eat, or just sightsee and journey on. Once your culinary vibes have been satisfied, roll north out of town on M-52. It's a busy highway at times, but it also has a generous shoulder. Turn right onto Werkner Road.

Though you'll basically stay on this road all the way through the small village of Unadilla, it changes name a few times. The ride to North Territorial Road curves and rolls through a mix of farmland and rural residential areas. The road name changes to Island Lake after a curve to the right at mile 11.1. After a short climb the road swings left and becomes Stofer Road. A mile up is North Territorial Road. At the intersection is North Lake Country Store, a good place to replenish with snacks and drink if needed.

Cross North Territorial and the road is now named Hadley Road. This is where the ride character changes significantly. Plummet down the long, sweeping hill past North Lake and up the next hill, and you now have a sense of the terrain for the rest of the ride. This is rolling countryside. The houses thin out and the terrain becomes the dominant feature. The shoulder of the road is narrow, but traffic is relatively light and respectful for the most part. This area is filled with lake and marsh views, and constantly rolling and winding roadways.

Bike Shops

Aberdeen Bike & Outdoors: 1101 S. Main St., Chelsea, MI 48118; (734) 475-8203; aberdeenbike.com
Dexter Bike and Sport: 3173 Baker Rd., Dexter, MI 48130-1103; (734) 426-5900; www.dexterbikeandsport.com

Turn left at the stop sign at Kaiser Road (mile 16.7) and right 300 feet ahead onto Unadilla Road. Unadilla has a small party store and an adjacent park with an outhouse. Cross Portage Creek and head north out of town.

Take a right at the T onto Doyle Road. Doyle Road, which later becomes Patterson Lake Road, is a roller coaster through a dense forest. If you like tree-lined rides, you'll be thrilled along this section. Mile 18.9 crosses Livermore Creek, which is part of a picturesque marsh area that leads into Patterson Lake to the south.

Continue your up-and-down trek to Patterson Lake Road (mile 20.2) and turn right (south) onto Glenbrook Road for more rolling terrain and winding pavement. Glenbrook becomes Hankerd Road (mile 22.9), and it all splits right down the heart of a series of lakes and marshes as well as through Potawatomi mountain bike trail country in the Pinckney Recreation Area. For those who like to hike, bike, ski, ride horseback, or boat, be glad that this area was probably far too rough and marshy for farming. The contiguous Pinckney and Waterloo State Recreation Areas take up about 31,000 acres of land and comprise the largest park in the Lower Peninsula.

Hankerd Ts into North Territorial Road. Turn left. Though not the busiest stretch of North Territorial, traffic moves quickly and there's very little shoulder to speak of. Fortunately, it's only a short stretch of the ride. Pedal east to Dexter Townhall Road and turn right (south). Though the shoulder is still

Bucolic highlights in the surrounding countryside

narrow, there's less traffic. You're no longer in the recreation area. This returns to scenic farmland, scattered subdivisions, and houses lining the road.

Turn east onto Island Lake Road and enjoy the continued views across the still actively tilled farmland. It gradually becomes more populous and residential as it draws nearer to the village of Dexter. Cross under the train trestle and up the hill and you're back in town.

MILES AND DIRECTIONS

0.0 From the intersection of Broad and Main Streets, head west, over the bridge at Mill Creek.

0.2 Turn left onto Dexter-Chelsea Road (if you go under the train trestle, you're going the wrong way). Follow the initial curves then along the long straight stretch of road toward Chelsea.

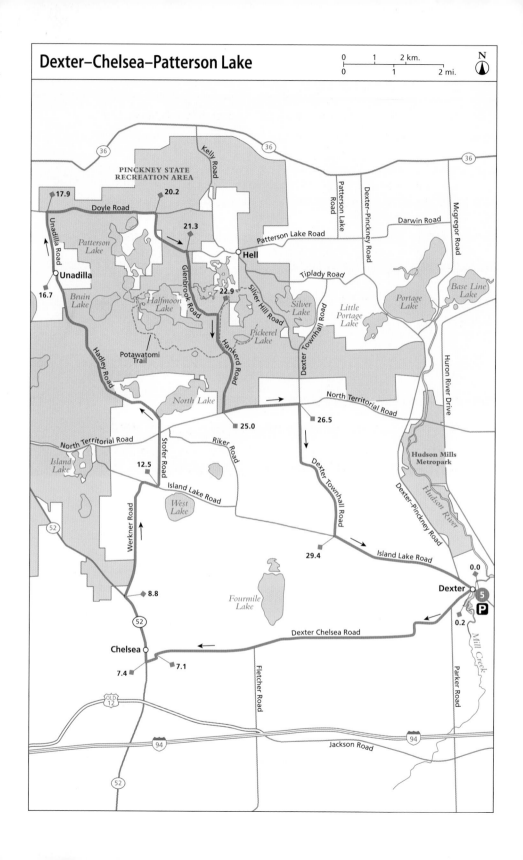

Dexter–Chelsea–Patterson Lake

PINCKNEY STATE
RECREATION AREA

Kelly Road

36 · 36 · 36

17.9 · 20.2

Doyle Road

Patterson Lake Road

Patterson Lake Road

Darwin Road

Dexter-Pinckney Road

Mcgregor Road

Unadilla Road

Patterson Lake

21.3

Hell

Unadilla

16.7

Bruin Lake

Halfmoon Lake

22.9

Glenbrook Road

Silver Hill Road

Tiplady Road

Silver Lake

Little Portage Lake

Portage Lake

Base Line Lake

Pickerel Lake

Potawatomi Trail

Hankerd Road

Dexter Townhall Road

Huron River Drive

Hadley Road

North Lake

North Territorial Road

26.5

North Territorial Road

25.0

Riker Road

Hudson Mills Metropark

Island Lake

Stofer Road

12.5

Island Lake Road

Dexter Townhall Road

Dexter-Pinckney Road

Hudson River

Werkner Road

West Lake

52

29.4

Island Lake Road

0.0

Dexter

5

P

0.2

8.8

Fourmile Lake

52

Chelsea

Dexter Chelsea Road

Mill Creek

7.4 · 7.1

OLD 12

Fletcher Road

Parker Road

94 · 94

52

Jackson Road

7.1 At the stop sign turn left, riding up and over the railroad tracks, then take the first right onto Jackson Road.

7.2 Turn left onto East Street, then a block over to Middle Street. Turn right onto Middle.

7.4 Turn right at the light onto Main Street/M-52.

8.8 Turn right onto Werkner Road. From this point to North Territorial Road, this route takes on two more names though it's the main roadway the entire way: a short stretch on Island Lake Road, and then onto Stofer Road. To make it even more complicated, beyond North Territorial it goes from Hadley Road to a jog on Kaiser Road, then onto Unadilla Road before coming to Doyle Road (deep breath).

12.5 Cross North Territorial Road and continue on Hadley Road.

16.7 Jog left onto Kaiser Road, then right onto Unadilla Road.

17.9 Turn right onto Doyle Road.

20.2 The main paved road swings right and becomes Patterson Lake Road.

21.3 Turn right onto Glenbrook Road.

22.9 The main paved road swings right and becomes Hankerd Road.

25.0 Turn left onto North Territorial Road. This is sometimes a busy roadway with fast-moving cars. What's more, there is minimal shoulder width. If riding with others, ride single file and stay to the right.

26.5 Turn right onto Dexter Townhall Road.

29.4 Turn left onto Island Lake Road.

32.1 Go straight on Island Lake Road, under the railroad trestle and back into downtown Dexter.

32.6 Arrive back at beginning.

RIDE INFORMATION

Local Events/Attractions
See Ride 4, Huron River Drive

Restrooms
Mile 0.2: There's a porta-potty in the back of the lot at the A&W on the corner.
Mile 16.8: There's a porta-potty in the park next to the party store in Unadilla.

Chelsea is often the destination and/or social stopover for cyclists on weekend rides. Its 19th-century character is still a prominent feature of the charming commercial center and its surrounding neighborhoods. It's the home of Jiffy Mix (you can't miss the white complex at the northwest edge of town), a prominent clock tower that's part of the historical redbrick Glazier Stove Company buildings, a sweet old railroad station, and the actor Jeff Daniels (who's definitely not a piece of architecture). Daniels runs the Purple Rose Theater on Park Street.

Chelsea is a good pre- or post-ride stop, and it's adjacent to some of the finest natural areas in the state, the Waterloo and Pinckney State Recreation Areas. This ride will take you pleasantly through the first of these, and beyond, through majestic farmland, over rolling glacial terrain, and past lakes, marshes, and woodlands often teeming with wildlife.

Start: Downtown Chelsea

Length: 30.4 miles

Approximate riding time: 2–3 hours

Best bike: Road

Terrain and trail surface: Paved rural roadways over rolling hills

Traffic and hazards: There is not much of a shoulder on any of these roads, though traffic is relatively light

Things to see: Ride through the Waterloo Recreation Area with hilltop views, marshes, farms, and woodlands

Maps: DeLorme: Michigan Atlas & Gazetteer, page 32

Getting there by car: From I-94, take exit 159 heading north on M-52 1.8 miles into downtown Chelsea. Parking is available throughout the town. Make sure to park in a spot that gives you enough time to complete the ride. There are time limitations in most of the lots downtown. There is also on-street parking in the neighborhoods. GPS: N42 19.085 W84 01.239

THE RIDE

Head west out of downtown Chelsea on Middle Street. The ride away from downtown takes you among well-cared-for homes, many well over a century old. At the end of Middle Street, take a sharp right onto Cleveland Street, go over the railroad tracks, and take a sharp left onto Cavanaugh Lake Road. To the left is the expansive Chelsea Retirement Community. To the right, a wide-open farm field. The pastoral countryside of rural Washtenaw County is now yours to feast upon.

From this point to just east of Pierce Road, the roadway is relatively flat with perhaps a gentle roll. Below Pierce it pitches up sharply and from that point west it will repeat this steadily rolling character, mile after mile. If you're out to train, it's great for building leg muscles. If you're out for the scenic beauty, the hills, farmsteads, marshes, woodlands, and gentle curves in the road will give you plenty to savor.

At mile 4.4 there's a great view over Cavanaugh Lake. There's also a small picnic area well situated to soak up that view. Just ahead is a wide marsh where the road is occasionally covered with water during spring thaws. The next few miles put the legs to the test with a series of biting rollers, but the scenery is just as dramatic, so you get fit while soaking in the beauty of the countryside. At some point the road becomes Harvey Road (through no fault of your own). Between Loveland and Clear Lake Roads, along a sweeping downhill curve, Pond Lily Lake (mile 6.6) will appear on the right. This is a very large marsh area with lake aspirations, often filled with wildlife and color. The inspirational view is followed by a stern uphill climb to Clear Lake Road.

Turn right onto Clear Lake Road and you're at the pinnacle of this ride. I can't say it's all downhill from here, not by any means, but there is a beautiful sweeping downhill for the next 1.5 miles to Clear Lake Park. The park has picnic tables, a beach, and nice views over the lake. It's a good stop for a snack break.

Back on the road, take a left at Trist Road a short way up at mile 9.0. Continue on the rolling terrain to mile 10.3, where the main road you're on becomes Seymour Road, but you want to stay on Trist by taking a right at the Y.

This is a great section of the ride. The road is narrow but quiet, and it twists like roads in small quaint villages. It even passes a road named Wild Turkey Drive. What more could you want?

It Ts into Mt. Hope Road. Take a right. The area opens up with farm and marshland on both sides of the road. A short way ahead at mile 12.7 is Reithmiller Road. Turn right. This is another road that's light on traffic but heavy with enjoyment. The road begins in mostly wooded cover, then opens

Downhill on Clear Lake Road

up to large farm fields and a sizable marshland area. At mile 14.5 is a parking area on the left to stop and enjoy the view over the wide-open field. I once came across a guy here with a large assortment of photo and video equipment. He'd come in from Cornell and spent the morning getting footage of a bird that nests in these fields. "One of the few habitats left in the country for this particular species," he said.

Bike Shop

Aberdeen Bike & Outdoors: 1101 S. Main St., Chelsea, MI 48118; (734) 475-8203

Ahead on the right is the commanding Saint Jacob Evangelical Lutheran Church, standing in quiet white relief against the expansive openness that surrounds it. Roll down the hill, across the stream, and up the gradual rise to more farmland and scattered houses until you reach Waterloo Munith Road. Turn right and take this into

Best Bike Rides Detroit and Ann Arbor

Foundations of the past

the small enclave of Waterloo. There's a party store for replenishment at the corner of Clear Lake and Waterloo Roads.

Stay left on Waterloo Road and get ready for more rolling terrain. This section of the ride is relatively enclosed by an overhead canopy of trees as it sweeps through a part of the Waterloo Recreation Area. The glacial topography is a noticeable feature. Again, exertion in natural beauty.

Climb the last hill, just past Clark Lake Road, to M-52 at mile 22.8. Turn right and enjoy the long downhill heading toward Chelsea. If the wind's at your back, this can be quite an ego booster as you plummet at top speed.

Chelsea–Waterloo

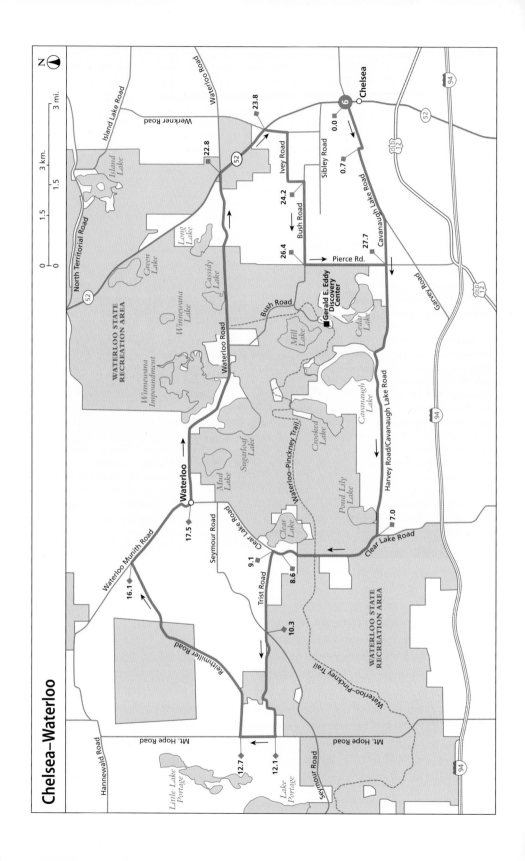

6

Don't get too carried away, though. There's a sharp right on Werkner Road at mile 23.8. It's possible to ride straight south and come into Chelsea a little over a mile ahead, but you would miss some more excellent roads that wind west of town.

Take Werkner to Ivey less than 0.5 mile up. Take another right. Ivey heads west, then south. The view opens to majestic and well-tended farms. Cross over Mill Creek and take a right at the T onto Bush Road.

The rolling, open farmland of Bush Road changes to woodland and marsh on Pierce Road (the Pierces, by the way, were some of the earliest and most prominent settlers in the Chelsea area back in the early to mid-1800s). Tucked deep in the forest to the west a short way is the Black Spruce Bog Natural Area, a national natural landmark. It's not accessible by bike, but by foot from the nearby Gerald E. Eddy Discovery Center farther west on Bush Road. It's all well worth the time to check out.

Take a left at Cavanaugh Lake Road. This should look familiar. It's the road you headed west on at the outskirts of Chelsea. It's also a nice reentry into town, farmland leading to a short jog over a railroad track and back through a well-kept Victorian-era neighborhood on Middle Street. Just in time for a coffee or a well-deserved meal.

MILES AND DIRECTIONS

0.0 Head west from the Main and Middle Street intersection.

0.7 The road takes a short jog, crosses the railroad tracks, and heads out Cavanaugh Lake Road.

7.0 Take a right onto Clear Lake Road.

8.6 This is the entrance into Clear Lake Park (right).

9.1 Take a left at Trist Road.

10.3 The road splits at this point with Trist Road going straight and Seymour Road going left. Go straight on Trist.

12.1 Turn right onto Mt. Hope Road.

12.7 Turn right onto Reithmiller Road.

16.1 Turn right onto Waterloo Munith Road.

17.5 At the intersection in Waterloo, go straight on Waterloo Road.

22.8 Go right onto M-52.

23.8 Go right onto Werkner Road at blinking yellow light.

24.2 Turn right onto Ivey Road.

25.1 Turn right onto Bush Road.

26.4 Turn left onto Pierce Road.

27.7 Turn left onto Cavanaugh Lake Road and follow this back to downtown Chelsea.

30.4 Arrive back at beginning.

RIDE INFORMATION

Local Events/Attractions
One Helluva Ride: A long-running and well-organized century ride (with other distances as well) that courses through western Washtenaw and eastern Jackson Counties. Run by the Ann Arbor Bicycle Touring Society; www.aabts.org
Purple Rose Theater Company: A playhouse run by the actor Jeff Daniels; 137 Park St., Chelsea, MI 48118; (734) 433-7782

Restaurants
Back to the Roots: 115 S. Main St., Chelsea, MI 48118; (734) 475-2700
Common Grill: 112 S. Main St., Chelsea, MI 48118; (734) 475-0470
Zou-Zou's: 101 N. Main St., Chelsea, MI 48118

Restrooms
Mile 4.4: Cavanaugh Lake across the road from the picnic area
Mile 8.7: Portable toilet at Clear Lake Park

Parker-Fletcher Route

This is a route for those who are comfortable riding alongside fast-moving traffic in limited lane widths. Even at that, it's a relatively popular road ride for cyclists in the area. It's a visual feast, whether it's viewing an expansive farmstead with grazing animals or waving cornfields with hawks soaring overhead, filtered panoramas of tree-lined lakes, or lowland marshes filled with statuesque egrets or herons. The topography rolls continuously, seldom overly steep or long, but continuously enough that you feel the tug of the effort on your legs mile after mile. This is rural riding at its bucolic best.

Start: Brauer Preserve, on Parker Road between Ellsworth and Waters Roads

Length: 15.5 miles

Approximate riding time: 1.5–2 hours

Best bike: Road bike or hybrid

Terrain and trail surface: Paved road

Traffic and hazards: This is a busy route in some sections, particularly Parker and Pleasant Lake Roads. There is no bike lane anywhere along this ride. Vehicles move fast (45 to 55 mph).

Things to see: Marshlands with swans, heron, egret, and other wildlife; rolling hills; expansive farmlands and farmsteads; a small residential community; a couple of large lakes

Maps: *DeLorme: Michigan Atlas & Gazetteer,* page 32

Getting there by car: From I-94 take exit 167 onto southbound Baker Road 0.3 mile to Jackson Road. Turn right onto Jackson and go 1.1 miles to the light at Parker Road. Turn left onto Parker and go 3.7 miles to the Brauer Preserve County Park. Parking area on the right. GPS: N42 14.245 W83 53.793

Fletcher Road shed

THE RIDE

Exit the Brauer parking lot and turn right (unless it's the second time you've ridden this; in that case, turn left and ride it in reverse. It's great either way). At mile 0.3 you'll pass between a couple of ponds. The road sits perched above them, offering great views of the varied marsh vegetation and the bird life. At mile 0.7 is a steep, yet relatively short, pitched climb to a plateau that will pass Ellsworth Road and lead to Pleasant Lake Road, with a wide swing west just beyond the 2.0-mile mark. From here to Fletcher Road will be a series of long rollers with expansive views of farmsteads, pasturelands, and Pleasant Lake itself. On the way you'll go through the tiny hamlet of Fredonia, which sounds like the name of a small country in a Marx Brothers movie, but it's actually the location of a cluster of houses, a party store, a restaurant, and Freedom Township Hall.

Head north on Fletcher Road and the level of traffic should decrease

Bike Shops

Aberdeen Bike & Outdoors: 1101 S. Main St., Chelsea, MI 48118; (734) 475-8203

Dexter Bike and Sport: 3173 Baker Rd., Dexter, MI 48130; (734) 426-5900; www.dexterbikeandsport.com

Two Wheel Tango: 4765 Jackson Rd., Ann Arbor, MI 48103; (734) 769-8401; twowheeltango.com

considerably. Not that Pleasant Lake Road is heavily trafficked, but Fletcher is less so. There are more rolling hills and farm fields and, at the 8.5 mile mark at Waters Road, the beautiful old Zion Evangelical Lutheran Church and cemetery dating back to the mid-1800s. Marking the rich German heritage of this part of the county, services were held exclusively in German until the 1930s.

Continue on to a wide jog west at mile 9.4 then north once again until reaching Scio Church Road at mile 10.1. Turn east and continue the loop through the countryside. At mile 12.0 is Sutton Lake on the left. By now you're probably realizing that, though this part of Michigan is by no means mountainous, this is not the flatlands either. This part of the region was carved by glaciers that shifted back and forth for centuries, leaving dips and knobs on

Parker-Fletcher Route

Parker Road pond

the landscape evidenced by the gentle hills and lowland marshes everywhere you look.

At the corner of Parker and Scio Church Roads at mile 14.4 is one of the most prominent of these marsh areas. The intersection was placed smack in the middle of this marsh. Sections of this roadway are underwater in the wet seasons of the year. The marshes, when filled with water, are often teeming with herons, egrets, swans, ducks, and other wildfowl. The road shoulders in this often busy intersection are narrow and the gravel shoulders are as well. Take care as you enjoy the bird watching.

Turn south onto Parker and pedal the remaining mile back to the Brauer Preserve. The entire 15.5-mile loop is complete.

MILES AND DIRECTIONS

0.0 Turn right from parking area onto Parker Road.

2.2 Swing right onto Pleasant Lake Road.

6.4 Turn right onto Fletcher Road.

10.1 Turn right onto Scio Church Road.

14.4 Turn right onto Parker Road.

15.5 Turn right into the Brauer Preserve parking lot.

Best Bike Rides Detroit and Ann Arbor

Clear Lake–Huttenlocker

This is a quiet ride through prime countryside in the region. It touches along the outer edges of Waterloo State Recreation Area and wanders through wide-open farmsteads separated by dense forests and colorful marshlands teeming with wildlife. It also passes by the Waterloo Farm Museum, a restored and re-created 19th-century farm that offers a glimpse into farm life in the early settlement days. The paved roads have relatively little traffic. For all these reasons, this area is popular wandering ground for local bike clubs.

Start: Begin and end in Clear Lake Park parking area

Length: 15.8 miles

Approximate riding time: 1–2 hours

Best bike: Road bike

Terrain and trail surface: Paved country roads

Traffic and hazards: The shoulders are narrow and traffic can move fast on these roads, though for the most part traffic is light.

Things to see: Woodlands, marsh areas, farmsteads, Waterloo Farm Museum, wildlife, gently rolling hills. Clear Lake Park has a beach on the lake and picnic facilities.

Maps: *DeLorme: Michigan Atlas & Gazetteer*, page 31

Getting there by car: From I-94 take exit 153, the Clear Lake Road exit, and head north. Drive 2.8 miles to Clear Lake Park. Turn right into the park entrance and park in the designated parking lot. GPS: N42 19.953 W84 09.178

Leave Clear Lake Park and turn right onto Clear Lake Road. Continue past Trist Road and up to the highest elevation of the day. Though the route rolls up and down quite a bit, since this is a glacially shaped area of the state, the hills on this particular ride are relatively gentle, with only a couple of short exceptions. The view to the right is a long one over Clear Lake and beyond that forest then marshland.

The road turns more distinctly north at mile 1.3, and the marshland changes to farm fields leading into the small crossroads of Waterloo. There's a party store on the right at the intersection for supplies. Turn left at the intersection onto Waterloo-Munith Road. Follow this rolling road past small farms first, then past Riethmiller Road the views expand over larger farmsteads with defining hedgerows of trees. Pass through a woodland copse at mile 4.2 and emerge to see a restored historic farmstead ahead on the left.

Waterloo Farm Museum (www.waterloofarmmuseum.org) is a partially restored and partially re-created 19th-century farmstead. It's open 1 to 5 p.m. Friday, Saturday, and Sunday and is designed to give a good depiction of what a typical farm family's life was like in the mid- to late 1800s. There are special events held here periodically throughout the year. Visually, it's quite stunning along this dogleg in the road, with all the carefully maintained buildings: the farmhouse, outbuildings, and barns.

Bike Shop

Aberdeen Bike & Fitness: 1101 S. Main St., Chelsea, MI 48118; (734) 475-8203; www.aberdeenbike.com

The road enters into a lush forest with the canopy arching over the road until it reaches Parks Road at mile 5.3, where you turn right, staying on pavement. Hannewald Road straight ahead turns to dirt. Parks and Waterloo-Munith are one until the next intersection, where Waterloo-Munith takes a 90-degree left turn. Take that turn.

Ride through the midst of large farm fields that lead to a sizeable marsh until arriving at the left turn onto Huttenlocker Road at mile 7.8. Enjoy more farm views on this quiet road for the next mile, then take a left onto Hannewald Road (paved in this section). Hannewald leads to Mt. Hope Road, where you'll swing right, heading south.

Mt. Hope leaves the farm fields for a shaded forest lining both sides of the road, with a scattering of houses and some marsh areas. Watch for wildlife,

A restored 19th-century farm on Waterloo-Munith Road

8

such as wild turkey, hawks, and the ubiquitous red-winged blackbird with its trill filling the air. The views open up after passing Reithmiller Road, with grazing cows often part of the scene.

Take a left onto Trist Road at mile 12.5. This small, twisting road leads along the northern rim of the Waterloo State Recreation Area (on the right), so plentiful trees are the order of the day on this segment. It's an easygoing, ever-weaving ride up and down hill, though more up than down, to Seymour Road, where you'll climb more heartily up to the sometimes busier part of Trist. All is relative here, however, so busy is often still reasonably quiet.

Continue straight on Trist and back to the T at Clear Lake Road, where you'll take a right. Within 0.2 mile turn left into Clear Lake Park and you'll be

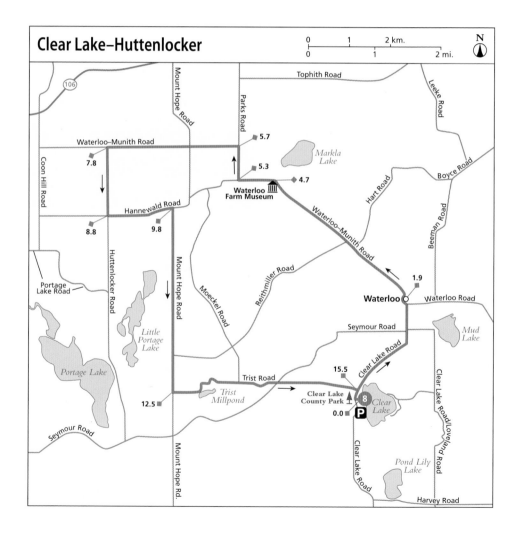

back where you started. The park offers a nice beach for swimming after a good ride, and places to picnic on the ridge with great views over the water.

MILES AND DIRECTIONS

0.0 Park in Clear Lake Park and turn right onto Clear Lake Road.

1.9 Turn left onto Waterloo Road at the Waterloo intersection.

4.7 The Waterloo Farm Museum is on the left.

5.3 Stay on the paved Waterloo Munith Road.

5.7 Turn left and continue on Waterloo Munith Road (Parks Road goes straight).

7.8 Turn left onto Huttenlocker Road.

8.8 Turn left onto Hannewald Road.

9.8 Turn right onto Mt. Hope Road.

12.5 Turn left onto Trist Road.

15.5 Turn right onto Clear Lake Road.

15.8 Take another left into Clear Lake Park.

RIDE INFORMATION

Restrooms
Start/Finish: Porta-john at Clear Lake Park

Gregory–Munith

The beginning of this ride follows the same route as the Ann Arbor Bicycle Touring Society's yearly 100-mile One Helluva Ride. We'll miss Hell altogether, but only because the route goes west and Hell is farther east. Rest assured, though, you can get there from here.

The point is, the touring society includes this area in its now famed ride because these are great paved roads to wander over on a bike. They're still relatively low in traffic volume, and the scenic backdrop is far more heavenly than hellish, especially if you like riding through rolling countryside.

Start: Parking lot at a small municipal park in the heart of Gregory alongside the Lakelands Trail

Length: 45.2 miles

Approximate riding time: 3–5 hours

Best bike: Road bike

Terrain and trail surface: Paved roads over mostly gently rolling hills

Traffic and hazards: Most of the roads on this route are not heavily traveled, but neither do they have wide shoulders. Some traffic moves quickly on these roads.

Things to see: Farmsteads, forests, wildlife, long scenic views over open countryside, pleasantly rolling roads

Maps: *DeLorme: Michigan Atlas & Gazetteer*, pages 31, 32

Getting there by car: From the I-96/M-52 interchange at exit 122, head south 10 miles to M-36. Turn left onto M-36 and follow it 7.5 miles to the village of Gregory. The parking area is in the small park on the west side of the road next to the Lakelands Rail Trail. GPS: N42 27.614 W84 05.080

Adams Road near Stockbridge

THE RIDE

Ride north out of Gregory on M-36 to Dexter Trail (mile 0.5) and turn left. Though the route is mostly over gently rolling roads, this early phase of the ride on Dexter Trail puts the climbing legs on alert. None of these hills are long, but they have a steep enough pitch to get you breathing hard. Fortunately, the long ranging views out over the farm fields will give you something to focus on other than the work you're doing.

A short way past Dutton Road, the road climbs to the highest point on the entire ride, then tilts down until it reaches Brogan Road. From that point on, the route climbs gently and descends gently throughout. The only other extreme, if you can call it that, will be the scenic beauty of the countryside.

After Brogan, the fields will still be there, but they'll be broken up by forested areas, and the road will slip through sections of tree-lined canopy up to M-52 (Stockbridge Road). The town of Stockbridge is only 1.5 miles south.

Cross M-52 and ride to Adams Road at mile 6.8 and turn left. Follow this past the fields and through another line of trees, with a large forested area on the left and over the Polliwog Drain to Morton Road. Turn right, then left onto Heeney a short way up. Take note of the drain crossings dotted along the way, often indicated by a line of trees and vegetation carving its own squiggly line through the otherwise open landscape.

Heeney swings west at mile 8.5, then passes Derby Cemetery, Jacobs Drain, and Pickett Drain before reaching Parman Road. Turn left onto Parman and ride past a colorful marsh and a series of farms to Baseline Road. This is the same Baseline Road that becomes 8 Mile Road many miles to the east, the northern property line for the city limits of Detroit. As its name implies, it's also the baseline used in the survey of Michigan in the early 1800s. The original baseline and meridian crossing points are only a few miles west of this point. The ride will get closer yet, though the actual historical marker is landlocked, surrounded by private property, though a designated state park.

But first, turn left, pedal to Musbach Road, then turn right. Continue on through this patchwork quilt of a landscape (from the sky that's the pattern), past Territorial Road, to the outskirts of Munith at Plum Orchard Road. There is a party store to replenish supplies on the southeast corner. After that, head west on Plum Orchard Road. It's busy at times, and there is trucking traffic as well, but it also has a wide shoulder. Ride this to Fitchburg Road (mile 16.9) and turn right.

Follow Fitchburg Road north. You're still watching for drains, right? Portage River Drain is on this road and you don't want to miss that, do you? Turn left onto Territorial Road with a small cluster of residences near the intersection on the west side. Back in the early settlement of the country many roads were labeled "Territorial." Most have been changed since, but this was a stubborn one and kept the name intact. Take this to Bunkerhill Road at mile 20.2 and turn right. (Don't many of these roads sound like great place names for a film on early American independence? Fitchburg, Bunker Hill, Dexter Trail. Names right out of the early American plat book.)

Bike Shops

Aberdeen Bike & Fitness: 1101 S. Main St., Chelsea, MI 48118; (734) 475-8203; www.aberdeenbike.com
Dexter Bike & Sport: 3173 Baker Rd., Dexter, MI 48130; (734) 426-5900; www.dexterbikeandsport.com

Continue north and Gee Farms, a large plant nursery, is on the left as you near the next intersection at Baseline Road. In season there's also an open-air market with fruits, ice cream, and baked goods. Turn left onto Baseline. This very quickly swings north again on Williamston Road. Pass East Fitchburg Road, not to be confused with the north-south Fitchburg Road, and ride to Decamp Road at mile 24.9. There's a party store on the southwest corner. If you haven't stopped anywhere for refreshments up to this point, you may want to stop here. There are still over 20 miles to go and this is the last store on the route.

Resume the northward route where the landscape transitions from wide-open fields into more forested surroundings with occasional marshlands. Eventually, Williamston Road swings east and merges with Ewers Road, then starts to curve north again. Before completing the left-hand curve, take a right and stay on Ewers Road at mile 27.6. A short way ahead Ewers Ts into Lienhart Road. Turn left. Lienhart takes a curve to the east and becomes Ewers once more. This is a rolling, sweeping stretch of road that passes under tree canopies and past extensive marsh areas, and eventually a small enclave of houses before coming to the confluence of Parman Road and Dexter Trail. Turn left onto Dexter Trail and follow this to Carter Road (Dexter Trail will continue on westward, to the left). Turn right.

Carter Road traffic moves at a good clip, but traffic is generally light. The expansive views over these wide-open spaces are quite dramatic. Take a right at Dietz Road (mile 34.6). The drama continues as you swing left at Swan Road, then cross M-52 once more. Turn right onto Brogan Road, which you'd crossed early on in your adventures farther south. This takes you to M-36. Turn left.

M-36 is a major rural connector road, hence busy at times, though in general it's pretty moderate. There isn't a designated bike lane, but the shoulder is reasonably wide and the landscape views remain a pleasant mix of farm fields, woodlands, old farm buildings and houses, a well-cared for scattering of residences, and trees along the roadway.

At mile 42.0 you'll pass through the small farming community of Plainfield, once a favorite crossroads and camp area for Native Americans and now a cluster of houses. Continue southeast to a point where the road takes a sharp left (mile 43.5), then an even sharper right. This is all still M-36. Soon you'll pass Dexter Trail and be back on the section of road from which you began this journey. Gregory appears just beyond this. There is a party store as well as a small grocery store in Gregory for any post-ride snacks or refreshments.

MILES AND DIRECTIONS

0.0 Leave the parking lot in Gregory heading north on Gregory Road.

0.5 Turn left onto Dexter Trail.

6.8 Turn left onto Adams Road.

7.8 Turn right onto Morton Road, then a short way up, left onto Heeney Road. Heeney Road curves west a little way beyond that.

11.1 Turn left onto Parman Road.

12.9 Turn left onto Baseline Road.

13.6 Turn right onto Musbach Road.

15.9 Turn right onto Plum Orchard Road.

16.9 Turn right onto Fitchburg Road.

17.9 Turn left onto Territorial Road.

20.2 Turn right onto Bunkerhill Road.

21.1 Turn left onto Baseline Road. The main road then swings around to Williamston Road.

27.6 Turn right onto Ewers Road.

28.1 Turn left onto Lienhart Road and it shortly turns right once again onto a continuation of Ewers Road.

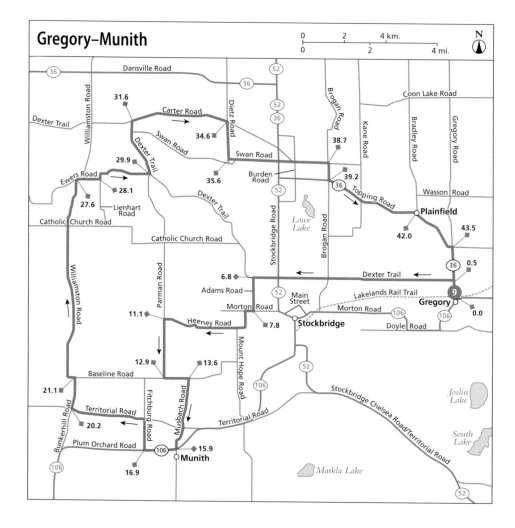

29.9 Turn left onto Dexter Trail.

31.6 Turn right onto Carter Road.

34.6 Turn right onto Dietz Road.

35.6 Turn left onto Swan Road.

38.7 Turn right onto Brogan Road.

39.2 Turn left onto M-36.

42.0 Stay on M-36, swinging right through Plainfield.

43.5 Stay on M-36, swinging left on the main roadway, then jog right on M-36 / Gregory Road.

45.2 Return to the center of Gregory and the parking area.

RIDE INFORMATION

Local Events/Attractions
Gee Farms: Large nursery with a farm market; 14928 Bunkerhill Rd., Stockbridge, MI 49285; (517) 769-6772

Restrooms
Start/Finish: Porta-potty at the park, in season

Active farms along the way

Saline–Clinton

There's a slow and steady elevation gain of over 200 feet on this ride, but it takes 27 miles of gradual rolling ascents to get there. What's more prevalent are the steady, gradual ups and downs through scenic farmland, as well as passing through the historic village of Clinton.

Saline is named for a well-known salt deposit that attracted Native Americans and early settlers from miles around to gather it for trade and to cure meat.

Start: Begin in a small public parking lot in Saline on the south side of Henry Street near the heart of downtown

Length: 40.7 miles

Approximate riding time: 3–4 hours

Best bike: Road bike

Terrain and trail surface: Gently rolling along most of the route, to hilly on Schneider Road. Traffic can get busy along Ann Arbor-Saline Road to Brassow Road, but that's really the most hazardous area the entire way. Maple Road has a generous bike lane for a good long section.

Traffic and hazards: Traffic is relatively low for the most part, though there is very little shoulder, and the traffic moves quickly. Traffic on Ann Arbor-Saline Road.

Things to see: Downtown Saline and Clinton, majestic barns, farmsteads, rolling countryside

Maps: *DeLorme: Michigan Atlas & Gazetteer,* page 32

Getting there by car: From US 23 take exit 34 onto westbound US 12/ Michigan Avenue and go 5.3 miles to Williams Street in Saline. Turn left and go 1 block to Henry Street. Turn right and go 0.1 mile to the public parking area on the left. GPS: N42 09.968 W83 46.761

Arkona Road farm

THE RIDE

Head west on Henry Street through the residential streets of Saline to where it Ts into Monroe Street. The large Oakland Cemetery is opposite. Turn left and head south out of town. Though this will be the primary road you'll follow for the early part of this ride, be aware that it changes names a number of times along the way. Note that by the time you get to your eventual turn toward Clinton at mile 9.0, the last road name will be Britton Highway. Between Monroe Street and Britton Highway it will become Macon Road, Jordan Road, Arkona Road, Goodrich Road, and Hack Road. One primary road, many names.

Cross the Saline River while still in town, then ride out past Johnson Road and the remnants of the now-abandoned small Saline Airport. From here on, the tour of farm country begins, with panoramic views that scan for miles over exposed fields. Along with dairy and sheep farms, you'll pass fields covered in alfalfa, corn, soybeans, and wheat, among many other specialty crops. The other feature is the rural architecture: numerous barns and other farm buildings, many over a century old. Because of the open views, these buildings feature prominently in the landscape.

Take the turn west onto Clinton-Macon Road and pass the small residential community at the crossroads with Macon Highway (yes, the same one you were on earlier that took a turn that you didn't take because it becomes a dirt road). There's a small party store here for refreshments if needed. Continue the journey through farm country on the rolling roadway, arriving in the outskirts of Clinton at a T on Tecumseh Street. Turn right.

A short way up at mile 16.0 is a gas station party store with snacks. A half mile from there is Michigan Avenue (US 12), once the Sauk Trail where the Native Americans hiked for miles single file to reach their destinations. Compare that to the wide and fast-moving traffic route today that connects Detroit with Chicago (and all the way to Aberdeen, Washington, if you're feeling footloose). It's been superseded by I-94, but it's still an often-used roadway with a long history.

North of US 12 the road name changes to Clinton Road . It passes through farmland dotted with some of the most interesting barns in the county, particularly on the right at mile 19.1 and farther up opposite Wilbur Road at mile 19.9. Besides the grain fields, there are also herds of sheep to keep an eye out for in this area up to Austin Road.

Turn right onto Austin and find that the road pitches up considerably for the next mile or so. It curves and rolls until the turn left onto Schneider Road at mile 25.3. The road climbs steadily again after Bemis Road, past the dramatic Bethel Church (built by German settlers in the area in 1909) and cemetery at the intersection on Bethel Church Road.

Roll up and down the hills (mile 27.2 is the high point of this ride at 1,045 feet above sea level) past another old Catholic cemetery tucked into the trees at Heiber Road and on to Pleasant Lake Road. Turn right. Traffic moves fast along Pleasant Lake, so take care and stay to the right. Weave past cattle farms and corn fields until the road swings sharply left where Parker and Pleasant Lake Roads converge for a short period. Curve right (east) at mile 30.7 and stay on Pleasant Lake Road. The road continues to roll through farm country until it reaches Ann Arbor–Saline Road at mile 35.8.

Bike Shops

Tree Fort Bikes: 1866 Whittaker Rd., Ypsilanti Township, MI 48197; (734) 484-9999; www.treefortbikes.com
Ypsilanti Cycle: 116 W. Michigan Ave., Ypsilanti, MI 48197; (734) 482-7881; ypsilanticycle.com

Turn right onto the busiest road of the entire route. This is a major connection between Ann Arbor and Saline, as its name implies, and the shoulder is skimpy. Fortunately it's a short though necessary connection to Brassow Road at mile 36.3. Turn left at Brassow and follow it to Maple Road. Turn right. Maple is a major connection to Saline as well, but it has bike-lane-width shoulders, making for a more comfortable ride.

Follow this past Woodland Drive and the Saline Middle School on the right. Continue on to Clark Street at mile 39.8 and turn right. Take this to the T and turn left onto Harris Street. Take Harris back across Michigan Avenue, then a block up to Henry Street. Turn right and a short way up on the left is where you began this journey.

MILES AND DIRECTIONS

0.0 Leave the parking area, turning left onto Henry Street.

0.3 Turn left onto Monroe Street. This main road changes names a number of times before reaching Clinton-Macon Road: Macon Road, Jordan Road, Arkona Road, Goodrich Road, Hack Road, and Britton Highway. They're all the same main road south.

9.0 Turn right onto Clinton-Macon Road.

15.9 Turn right onto Tecumseh-Clinton Highway.

16.5 This is the main intersection in downtown Clinton.

21.9 Turn right onto Austin Road.

25.3 Turn left onto Schneider Road.

28.4 Turn right onto Pleasant Lake Road.

30.8 Turn right to continue east on Pleasant Lake Road.

35.8 Turn right onto a short stretch of Ann Arbor-Saline Road. This can be a very busy section of road with minimal shoulder. Ride with caution.

36.3 Turn left onto Brassow Road.

37.3 Turn right onto Maple Road.

39.8 Turn right onto Clark Street.

40.1 Turn left onto Harris Street.

40.5 Turn right onto Henry Street and go a short way up the street to the parking area on the left.

40.7 Arrive back at starting point.

RIDE INFORMATION

Local Events/Attractions

Many of Saline's downtown buildings have been beautifully restored to their historic brick roots. The neighborhoods near downtown also have some nice historic character.

Restaurants

Saline Downtown Diner: Fresh homemade food in the heart of historic downtown. Breakfast and lunch. 131 E. Michigan Ave, Ste. D; (734) 316-2343; www.salinedowntowndiner.com

Mac's Acadian Seafood Shack: Fish, sandwiches, and beverages in a nicely restored historic building downtown. Lunch and dinner. 104 E. Michigan Ave; (734) 944-6227; www.macsinsaline.com

DIRT ROADS AND BIKE PATHS

. . . .

DIRT ROADS

Southeast Michigan offers something that isn't found everywhere: great dirt roads to pedal over (rides 11–19). Washtenaw and Oakland Counties in particular have mile after mile of interconnected dirt roads, with low traffic volumes and beautiful countryside. In some cases the dirt roads cross into other jurisdictions as well, offering nearly endless options for routes. While some counties paved most of their roadways through the years, Washtenaw, Oakland, and a few others put their money elsewhere, continuing to maintain, but not to pave, many of their back roads.

This is a boon to the cyclist. Some of the most beautiful bucolic rides in the region are down these quiet country lanes. It's not that you don't have to heed vehicular traffic—it still exists and it can move quickly, even on these roads—but it's far less daunting than many of the busy paved roads in the region.

The routes laid out are only a few of the options available to the intrepid cyclist. Take a ride and you'll notice more dirt roads branching off from the one you're on. Sometimes they lead to a paved road, but often they continue on to another network of dirt roads.

Some cyclists take their road bike on the dirt roads. It's possible, though I'd recommend at minimum a 28mm tire width due to potholes and large stones that seem to arise at the most awkward and unavoidable moments. But don't be put off by the unique and varied riding surface. If you've never tried it, it might take a little getting used to. You'll want to take turns in a more upright position, for instance, so the wheel doesn't slide out, but since you already know how to ride a bike, it's just a change of style, not a whole new thing. Cyclocross bikes are ideal for these conditions, and even hybrid and mountain bikes work great.

What you'll find is a variety of conditions from sandy to gravelly to smooth as pavement, sometimes all within a short distance of one another. Be prepared and stay relaxed and the ride can be very enjoyable. What you often get on dirt roads is more time to enjoy the view; you'll get deeper into the countryside, many of the hills are hillier, and you'll have time to savor the surroundings since vehicles won't be your main concern. With a region so full of them, it's one more way to expand your horizons.

BIKE PATHS

Bike paths (rides 20–31) are often called trails, even in their titles, but I call them paths to differentiate from mountain bike trails, of which there are plenty in Southeast Michigan. The pathway has become an art form in this region. They're all over and they often interconnect. And if they don't interconnect, they may do so soon. There's a dedicated group of people in conservancies, state agencies, and rail-trail organizations who are working diligently to create not only a regional network but also a statewide and even national network of pathways. For further information on the planned Michigan network of pathway connections, go to www.michigantrails.org, the website of the *Michigan Trails & Greenways Alliance*. They update all kinds of information about pathways and trails in the state, plus there are map finders that will locate pathways near you.

On top of that, there are individual groups who work to maintain and expand specific pathways. These often have their own websites, with current updates, such as that of the I-275 Metro Trail group (I-275.michigantrails.org).

In any event, these bike routes are some of the most popular of all places to cycle. They often go from town to town, or they go from highly populated urban areas to quiet rural areas on a dedicated cycling/walking route. The only contact with vehicles is at road crossings. They're very comfortable for those who feel intimidated riding in traffic. They're also, with only a few exceptions, relatively flat, as they often follow old abandoned rail lines. This is great for those days when hills don't call to you, for those who find steep inclines too challenging or downright pesky, and for families with small children.

There is nowhere in Southeast Michigan where a bike path is far off. If you've never tried one, you may be surprised how unique and enjoyable they are to ride. For those of you who ride them regularly, there's probably something in the works to expand your path into the wider network, so you'll have more places to explore. For an added plus, I've seldom found anywhere with such a large number of friendly people. Smiles and waves are standard behavior. That tells you something right there.

Additional bike paths worth exploring in the region

Lower Rouge River Trail, Canton; 4 miles one way; GPS: N42 16.818 W83 27.972

This is a wide crushed-gravel path that winds through the Rouge woodlands, occasionally crossing back and forth over the river on beautifully designed new bridges. It connects to the I-275 Metro Trail near Michigan Avenue.

Wadham Avoca Trail, Port Huron; 9.9 miles one way; GPS: N42 58.973 W82 32.328

This is a beautifully wooded trail that becomes more rural the closer it gets to the small town of Avoca. There's also a magnificently restored railroad bridge that crosses Mill Creek at mile 8.2. It's paved for the first 3.1 miles, then it becomes well-packed cinder.

Falling Waters Trail, Jackson; 10.7 miles one way; GPS: N42 12.470 W84 26.359

The trail starts on the outskirts of Jackson and heads west, though there is a section of paved trail going east almost to downtown. Be aware that if you do try to get to downtown, the path doesn't go all the way there and you'll have to navigate through residential streets at some point. Going west, though, is very straightforward. The highlights are the Lime Lake Causeway beginning at mile 5.7, including benches along that stretch and a swimming area, the rural setting, and the small town of Concord 0.5 mile beyond the parking area at the western end of the path. There are sections of path with canopies of trees overhead, marshlands to observe wildfowl, and long views over farm fields.

West Bloomfield Trail, Arrowhead Road to Telegraph, West Bloomfield; 5.4 miles one way; GPS: N42 34.074 W83 23.586

Beautifully wooded trail with some great marsh and lake views. This is a very popular trail, active at all times of day and especially on weekends. There are a few dangerous road crossings, particularly at the 2.5- and 4.5-mile marks, both at Orchard Lake Road. There are even commercial areas with cafes if you want to make it leisurely.

Before venturing forth by bike, take a walk onto the footbridge that reaches across the Huron River. The various crew clubs, including University of Michigan's Crew Team, practice along this stretch of water. Sculls glide sleekly beneath the bridge and up or down the river at a deceptively brisk pace.

This ride is close to downtown Ann Arbor yet reaches quickly into the countryside where it feels miles from any urban area. It's hilly, as it passes through the glacially shaped area of the county. It starts in a river valley, shortly climbs out of it, then fans out on quiet dirt roads that pass wide-open farm fields and historic farmsteads, through forested areas, winds along the edges of marshlands supporting wildlife, by properties preserved for farming or as open space in perpetuity, and alongside the richly vegetated banks of the Huron River.

There's a lot to see and experience within a short radius of Ann Arbor. It highlights one of the area's strengths: the ability of a relatively populated region to retain its close connection to its farming roots and the natural world.

Start: Park in the Barton Nature Area parking lot along Huron River Drive

Length: 25.4 miles

Approximate riding time: 2–3 hours

Best bike: Cyclocross or hybrid

Terrain and trail surface: Rolling dirt roads with occasional gravel. The ride begins and ends along a paved stretch of Huron River Drive.

Traffic and hazards: There is minimal shoulder on Huron River Drive and the road surface can be rough in places. Traffic moves briskly, but this is generally recognized as a major bike route and the cars are accommodating for the most part. Part of Webster Church Road is paved, with a similar traffic situation. There's less traffic on the dirt roads, but there are some busy crossroads, North Territorial Road in particular.

Things to see: A lush river, glacial terrain, farmland, wildlife (often white-tailed deer), marshlands, forests

Maps: *DeLorme: Michigan Atlas & Gazetteer*, page 32

Getting there by car: From downtown Ann Arbor, take Main Street (Business US 23) north 1.3 miles to Huron River Drive (turn left just before the on-ramp to M-14/US 23). Follow Huron River Drive underneath the highway for 0.3 mile to the Barton Nature Area Parking lot on the right. GPS: N42 18.123 W83 44.927

THE RIDE

Ride west on Huron River Drive. The first 2 miles are on this sweeping, tree-lined, paved section of roadway. It's a major bike route for individuals and groups in the area. On the left is Bird Hills Nature Area, a tall, forested natural bluff with a series of ravines leading down toward the river. On the right is the Huron River, the major water resource in the area.

There are nice views of Barton Dam off to the right at mile 0.7. The dam parking lot is across from Bird Road at mile 0.9 (this is another public parking option if the Barton Nature Area parking lot is full). The road parallels the river and railroad tracks on the right after this point. Barton Pond, created by the dam, is the large body of water to the right as well. On warm days this is dotted with sailboats, and there are times when it's also filled with bobbing swans, ducks, or geese.

The road arcs to the Foster Bridge on Maple Road at mile 2.2. Built in 1876, this is one of two metal truss bridges existing in Michigan. It was restored in 2003. It's also a one-lane bridge where traffic, including bicycles, crosses on a first-come, first-cross basis. When it's your turn, take it slowly enough to enjoy the beautiful views up- and downriver. Once over, take the Y in the road to the left. This leads away from the river valley, which means an ascent up Maple Road. It climbs to Landsdowne Road, then drops for a short distance. Get the momentum going here because there's one more ascent to Stein Road. Though not the only hills on this ride, these will be the longest and steepest climbs of the day.

Take a left onto Stein Road. Watch for deer, often in large herds. They roam from field to field in large groups in this area. Though sometimes considered a traffic nuisance due to their sheer numbers, they're also fascinating to see as they graze en masse. They're also skittish if you get too close, so don't be surprised if they suddenly disappear.

Stein is a mix of open fields and hedgerows, small farms and residences. You might even spot a cyclist or two in this area, as it's relatively close to Ann

Barn windows, Scully Road

Arbor and a popular dirt road riding area. Stein Ts into Joy Road. Turn left. Joy is one of the roads in the region that stretches from Detroit out through the metropolitan area and all the way to the village of Dexter, not far west of here. It was most likely named after a prominent Detroit attorney in the mid-1800s as part of Detroit Edison's labeling of the roads in the region in order to clarify where their power lines were routed.

There are wide-open, still-active agricultural fields on both sides of the road with the old, majestic Zeeb farm with its many outbuildings on the right. Turn right onto Jennings Road at mile 5.1. This Ts into Northfield Church Road. Turn left and a short way up, the road goes right (north) and becomes Jennings once again. A short way after that, at mile 6.1, turn left onto Farrell Road. Farrell rolls along more farmland to the intersection at the paved Webster Church Road. On the left is a cemetery and the historic Webster United Church of Christ built in 1835 and listed as the oldest building in continuous use in Washtenaw County.

Turn right onto Webster Church Road and ride to North Territorial Road. This is a very busy roadway with fast-moving traffic. Cross with care. The other side of the road becomes dirt once again. It swings right and left past farms and houses, where it Ts into Valentine Road at mile 9.8. Straight ahead through the trees is Independence Lake. Turn left. Follow Valentine to Merrill Road and turn right.

This begins a long, very gentle ascent to Walsh Road at mile 11.2. Turn left and get ready to roll. The full extent of Walsh Road is quite a roller-coaster ride. This route touches on part of that, but it reveals the dramatic character even in this short mile-long stretch. It descends to a rich marsh (watch for an egret or a heron), then steadily ascends to Scully Road. There are farms and houses all along the way, but there's also a thick tree cover alongside the road. It's a very popular road among dirt road cycling aficionados.

Turn left at Scully. The road drops past large farm buildings worth slowing down for, passes Valentine Road, then rolls up and down on the tree-lined route, where it once again crosses North Territorial Road. Scully rolls past another marsh where birds are known to congregate, as is often obvious by the increase in the avian vocal social networking. This rises up to Gregory Road. Turn right, arriving at a crossroads with Zeeb Road in just over 0.5 mile. On the right is a llama farm, and usually there are numerous llamas milling about the yard or near the barn doing whatever llamas do.

Turn left onto Zeeb Road. Follow this to Farrell Road at mile 16.1 and turn left. This follows another hilly, farm-laden, tree-lined section of roadway. Note that some of the land in this area is preserved forever as farmland. This is due to a series of preservation programs set up in the region in order to save land for agricultural use or for use as open space.

Return to the intersection with Webster Church Road and keep going on Farrell. This will re-track a section that you rode on the way out. Turn right at Jennings Road, take the short left jog in the road that becomes Northfield

Bike Shops

There's no shortage of bike shops in Ann Arbor.
Great Lakes Cycling & Fitness: 2015 W. Stadium Blvd., Ann Arbor, MI 48103; (734) 668-6484; www.greatlakescycling.com
Midwest Bike & Tandem: 1691 Plymouth Rd., Ann Arbor, MI 48105; (734) 213-7744; www.midwesttandems.com
Performance Bike: 3059 Oak Valley Dr., Ann Arbor, MI 48103; (734) 769-0955; www.performancebike.com
REI Ann Arbor: 970 W. Eisenhower Pkwy., Ann Arbor, MI 48103; (734) 827-1938
Sic Transit Cycles: 1033 Broadway St., Ann Arbor, MI 48105; (734) 327-6900; sictransitcycles.com
Transition Rack: 217 S. 4th Ave., Ann Arbor, MI 48104; (734) 214-9700; www.transitionrack.com
Two Wheel Tango: 3162 Packard St., Ann Arbor, MI 48108; (734) 528-3030; 4765 Jackson Rd., Ann Arbor, MI 48103; (734) 769.8401; twowheeltango.com
Wheels in Motion: 3400 Washtenaw Ave., Ann Arbor, MI 48104; (734) 971-2121; wheelsinmotion.us

Church Road, and turn right back onto Jennings at mile 18.4. Turn left when you reach Joy Road and right when you reach Stein Road.

Partway up Stein, at mile 20.2, Tubbs Road Ts into Stein. Take Tubbs to the right. This is a tight, thickly forested, twisting ride down a long hill. As a word of warning, it does have sections of loose gravel, and near the bottom there's a sharp right turn where the gravel may be the loosest. Some of the turns are blind as well, with an occasional car. Now that you have the warnings, just take it easy, stay to the right, and enjoy the descent. It's a real treat.

At the bottom, Tubbs meets paved Huron River Drive. Turn left onto Huron River Drive, cross the bridge over the Huron River, and pedal up a long, gentle hill to the railroad tracks. Cross carefully, as they run at an angle across the road. Cross another bridge, this time over Honey Creek, then past Wagner Road and begin pedaling along the river oxbow.

The oxbow usually has a wildlife performance on show. There are days when it's lined with stark white egrets all along the opposite side of the river. Often turtles are sunbathing on logs jutting out of the water, swans are sitting on nests waiting for their signets to hatch, and kayakers are floating down the river fishing or taking photographs.

Soon Foster Bridge reappears on the left, and you've rejoined a section of Huron River Drive that began the route. Return past Barton Pond and Dam and Bird Hills Nature Area to the parking lot at Barton Nature Area. If you feel like you need more exercise, there are some nice hikes through both Bird Hills and Barton Nature Areas. If replenishment is in order, downtown Ann Arbor is just a 5-minute drive to the east on Main Street.

MILES AND DIRECTIONS

0.0 Start in the small parking lot for Barton Nature Area. Head west along Huron River Drive.

2.2 Turn right onto Maple Road and cross Foster Bridge.

2.3 Once over the bridge, swing left to continue on Maple Road. It becomes a dirt road halfway up the hill.

3.3 Turn left onto Stein Road at the crossroad.

4.6 Turn left onto Joy Road.

5.1 Turn right onto Jennings Road.

5.8 Turn left for a short jog on Northfield Church Road

5.9 The road swings right back onto Jennings Road.

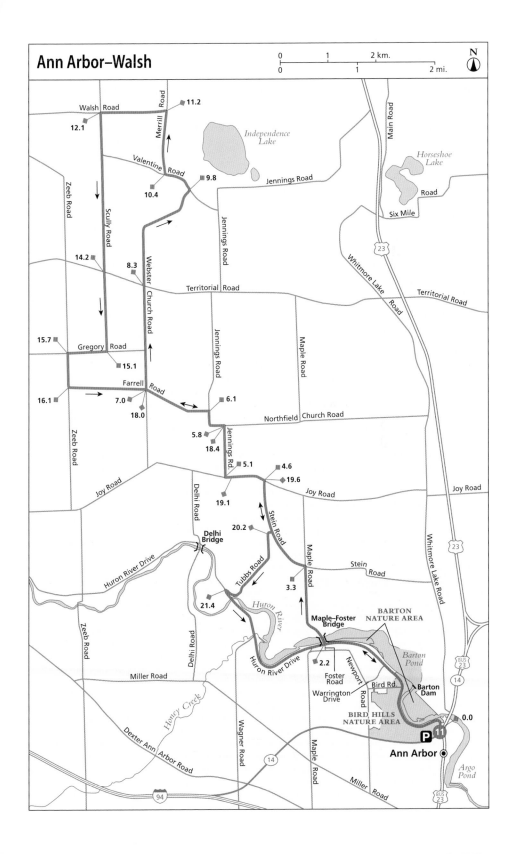

0   1   2 km.

0   1   2 mi.

N

Walsh   Road
12.1

Merrill   Road
11.2

Independence
Lake

Horseshoe
Lake

Valentine   Road
9.8
10.4

Jennings Road

Main Road

Road

Six Mile

Zeeb   Road

Scully   Road

23

14.2
8.3

Webster   Church   Road

Territorial   Road

Jennings   Road

Whitmore   Lake   Road

Territorial   Road

15.7
Gregory   Road
15.1

Jennings   Road

Maple   Road

16.1
Farrell   Road
7.0
18.0
6.1

Northfield   Church   Road

5.8
18.4

Jennings Rd.

5.1
4.6
19.6

Joy   Road

Joy   Road

Joy   Road

19.1

Zeeb   Road

Delhi   Road

Stein   Road

20.2

Delhi
Bridge

Huron River Drive

Huron   River

Tubbs   Road

Maple   Road

Stein   Road

3.3

23

21.4

Maple–Foster
Bridge

BARTON
NATURE AREA

Barton
Pond

Delhi   Road

Huron River Drive

2.2

Foster
Road

Newport   Road

Bird Rd.

Barton
Dam

BUS
23

14

Miller   Road

Warrington
Drive

BIRD HILLS
NATURE AREA

0.0

Honey Creek

Wagner   Road

14

Maple   Road

Dexter Ann   Arbor Road

P

11

Ann Arbor

Miller   Road

BUS
23

Argo
Pond

94

6.1 Take a left onto Farrell Road.

7.0 Turn right onto the paved Webster Church Road.

8.3 Cross North Territorial Road. This is a busy road with fast-moving vehicles. Cross with care. Once over, Webster Church Road turns to dirt.

9.8 Turn left onto Valentine Road.

10.4 Turn right onto Merrill Road.

11.2 Turn left onto Walsh Road.

12.1 Turn left onto Scully Road.

14.2 Cross North Territorial Road once more.

15.1 Turn right onto Gregory Road.

15.7 Turn left onto Zeeb Road.

16.1 Turn left onto Farrell Road.

18.0 Turn right onto Jennings Road, then swing around the curve for another short jog on Northfield Church Road.

18.4 Turn right, continuing on Jennings Road.

19.1 Turn left onto Joy Road.

19.6 Turn right onto Stein Road.

20.2 Turn right onto Tubbs Road.

21.4 Turn left onto Huron River Drive and return to the parking lot.

25.4 Finish.

RIDE INFORMATION

Local Events/Attractions

There's something happening every weekend and usually even on weeknights in Ann Arbor during the warm months of the year. These are often listed in annarbor.com.

Restaurants

The list of Ann Arbor restaurants of all kinds is large and growing as I write this. I recommend looking up your favorite cuisine or finding a pub or cafe in Yelp (yelp.com). You'll be amazed at all the options.

Ellsworth–Waters

It's a big rectangular ride, which sounds stiff and geometric, but for some reason the route offers enough variety, both in terrain and in changes in the landscape, that the geometry is softened by the beautiful details.

There is a benefit to the rectangle. If, for whatever reason, you decide to shorten the route, every north-south road facing in all along the ride will take you to the other side of the rectangle (either Waters or Ellsworth Roads), where you can enjoy the benefits of the experience with fewer miles logged. And every one of those mile-long road segments is worth exploring.

This is countryside with a capital C. It passes through large tracts of farmland with some excellent rural architecture, past marshes teeming with wildlife, through shady woodlands, and over some of the more scenic hills the area has to offer. These 19.8 miles offer a great hill workout for those looking for that kind of experience, or a scenic day out for those who take it at a more easygoing pace. And it's not too far from Ann Arbor. You could drive a lot farther away for this kind of thing, but in this case it's right nearby if Ann Arbor is home base. (You can ride your bike to it if you're so inclined. Many do.)

Start: Park at the Brauer Preserve County Park

Length: 19.8 miles

Approximate riding time: 1.5–3 hours

Best bike: Cyclocross, hybrid, mountain bike

Terrain and trail surface: Mostly dirt roads over gently rolling to steeply hilly terrain

Traffic and hazards: Depart and return along a short section of busy roadway with minimal shoulder

Things to see: Farmlands, marshes, rolling terrain, wildlife, livestock, forests

Maps: *DeLorme: Michigan Atlas & Gazetteer,* page 32

Getting there by car: From I-94 take exit 167 onto southbound Baker Road 0.3 mile to Jackson Road. Turn right onto Jackson and go 1.1 miles to the light at Parker Road. Turn left onto Parker and go 3.7 miles to the Brauer Preserve County Park. Parking area is on the right. GPS: N42 14.245 W83 53.793

THE RIDE

Depart the Brauer Preserve parking lot and head south (right) on Parker Road. This paved segment of road can be busy at times with fast-moving traffic. Even at that, it's a popular bike route because of the rolling terrain and scenic beauty of the countryside. This is readily apparent within 0.3 mile as the road rolls past marshland on either side. Look for herons, egrets, and other wildlife standing stalwart in the water.

Climb a rise to Ellsworth Road at mile 0.8 and turn right. This is the start of a repeated series of rolling hills, none long, but some rather steep with racy downhill dashes and lactic acid–inducing uphill climbs. The payment for this exertion is a close connection with a constantly varying farmland and forest landscape, past 19th-century barns, forested marsh areas, grazing sheep, flocks of wild turkeys, panoramic views over rolling farm fields, and arching woodland enclosures.

Pace yourself. This is the biking version of lather, rinse, repeat. Either pedal hard down the hills and let momentum carry you partway up the next rise, or just keep an even pace and a nice low gear on the uphills and the scenic rewards will keep coming at you.

Nearing the spired St. Thomas Church and cemetery at Haab Road, look back over your right shoulder at the expansive rolling field. Sometimes there will be grazing sheep, but even if there aren't, this is a million-dollar view and it's yours for free. This is why we ride. The road begins a gentler roll as it passes Schneider, Rentz, and Lima Center Roads. After this, it descends to a curve, hiding a long, arching climb to Schmitz Road.

Bike Shops

Great Lakes Cycling & Fitness: 2015 W. Stadium Blvd., Ann Arbor, MI 48103; (734) 668-6484; www.greatlakescycling.com
Two Wheel Tango: 4765 Jackson Rd., Ann Arbor, MI 48103; (734) 769-8401; twowheeltango.com
Wheels in Motion: 3400 Washtenaw Ave., Ann Arbor, MI 48104; (734) 971-2121; wheelsinmotion.us

Ellsworth Road barn

Mt. Hope Cemetery comes up on the right as the road rolls on a long and well-deserved downhill to a T at Fletcher Road. The major hills of the day have been scaled. The road will continue to go up and down, but much more gently than the segment of Ellsworth just ridden.

Take a right onto the paved Fletcher Road. This is a relatively quiet segment of the route and the only other paved section besides the busier Parker Road.

The ride wouldn't be complete without a few cows. Keep your eyes open so you don't miss this exceedingly rare animal in its natural habitat. If a smile lifts the corners of your mouth, they've done their job.

At the intersection with Waters Road is the Zion Lutheran Church, both the old and new buildings. The old brick church is a beautiful example of one of the early churches in the area. Turn right onto Waters and pass St. Johns Church, a more humble, though still fascinating, reminder of the region's history. There may be horses lazily grazing in the field on the right.

The trade-off for fewer steep hills on Waters Road is a more open feel than that on Ellsworth. Waters is one large blanket of wide-open views over corn, soybean, and hayfields, punctuated by forest edges in the distance, hedgerows, and select, mature solo white oak and hickory trees. And maybe a cow or two.

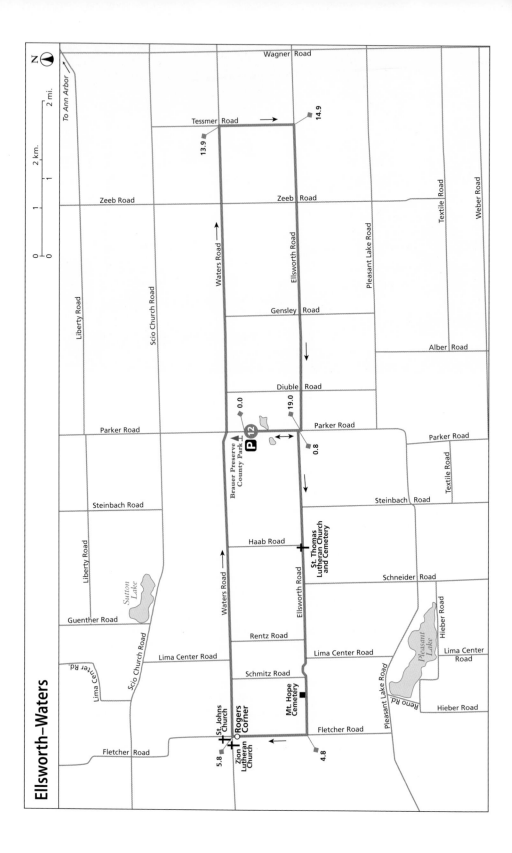

Ellsworth–Waters

At mile 8.2 there's a small barn outbuilding lined with mulberry trees alongside the road that I'm partial to. But there are other barns and farmsteads along the way that replenish those of us in need of our countryside fix.

Cross Parker Road at mile 9.9 and continue on into a more rural-residential section of the ride. Farms still dominate, but they're rimmed with residential developments and single houses in more abundance than the landscape to the west. The road climbs gently, at times indiscernibly, as it passes Zeeb Road and on to Tessmer Road at mile 13.9. Turn right.

Tessmer offers a nice coast-worthy downhill (often dotted with locals out on a walk or bike ride) to a short uphill that Ts into Ellsworth Road. The farm theme spreads out before you on much of this return segment. The crossroads will all have familiar names now as you work your way back to the paved Parker Road. Take a right onto Parker and roll downhill then onto the short, gentle ascent that returns you to Brauer Preserve. If you need a short walk, the preserve leads back on a two-track dirt road, along working farm fields to a pond, around to other fields, through a forest, and back on the two-track.

MILES AND DIRECTIONS

0.0 Leave the Brauer County Park parking area and turn right onto Parker Road.

0.8 Turn right onto Ellsworth Road.

4.8 Turn right onto Fletcher Road.

5.8 Turn right onto Waters Road.

13.9 Turn right onto Tessmer Road.

14.9 Turn right onto Ellsworth Road.

19.0 Turn right onto Parker Road.

19.8 Turn left into the Brauer parking lot.

RIDE INFORMATION

Local Events/Attractions
Brauer County Park has a short hiking trail to a pond, around working fields and through a small section of forest.

Manchester–Bethel Church

This hilly dirt-road route begins and ends in Manchester and is one of the hilliest areas of Washtenaw County, though most of the hills are gently rolling. There are a few sections with sharp but short climbs and one long, fast downhill.

The area is mostly filled with farms and wide-open farm fields: field crops, cattle, horses, and sheep.

After the ride, check out the village of Manchester. It has many historic buildings right around downtown that have been beautifully restored. In particular, look for St. Mary's Church laden in fieldstone on the west side of town at Macomb and Main Streets. The entire downtown area is worth a wind-down walk.

Start: Chi-Bro Park, 209 Ann Arbor St. (M-52), Manchester, MI

Length: 24.1 miles

Approximate riding time: 1.5–2.5 hours

Best bike: Cyclocross, hybrid, mountain bike

Terrain and trail surface: Dirt roads and a short section of paved roads in Manchester and on Schneider Road

Traffic and hazards: You'll need a certain comfort level riding on gravel roads of varying quality, from loose to hard-packed gravel. The roads throughout are low-volume vehicular routes.

Things to see: Scenic ride through hilly farmland; long views over farm fields, historic barns, houses, and outbuildings

Maps: *DeLorme: Michigan Atlas & Gazetteer*, page 32

Getting there by car: From I-94 take exit 159 onto M-52 and head south 10.3 miles to Chi-Bro Park on the left at the edge of the village of Manchester. GPS: N42 09.101 W84 02.271

THE RIDE

Leave Chi-Bro Park through the back end (east side) on a gravel two-track. This becomes a tree-covered pathway that passes behind a series of houses. The pathway angles to Main Street. Continue east on the paved Main Street to Hibbard Street and take a left. This goes a couple of blocks to Parr Road. Take a right and begin the dirt road adventure. Town rapidly recedes as it gives way to farmland. Parr swings north and rolls gradually uphill to Bethel Church Road.

Bike Shop

Aberdeen Bike & Fitness: 1101 S. Main St., Chelsea, MI 48118; (734) 475-8203; www.aberdeenbike.com

Turn right onto Bethel Church. This is farm country. Long-ranging views of fields and various lines of hedgerows stretch out in all directions. This will be the general theme of nearly the entire ride, with changes in crops from corn to wheat to soybeans and a few open fallow fields dotted with shrubs, along with some farms devoted to livestock and horses. Basically, this is a breadbasket area of the region. What makes it great to ride through is its history, as many of the farmsteads have buildings that were built in the early settlement of the area, and the topography, which rises and falls repeatedly, offering varying vistas from one mile to the next.

The first major climb comes as you pass Esch Road at mile 3.5. This will take you to the highest elevation point of the ride. The descent is long, nearly to Eisman Road, where it begins a gentler roll for a long stretch. In autumn, the Alber Orchard, on the right at Eisman, opens its doors as a cider mill, and on weekend afternoons there's often a bluegrass band playing in the yard.

At mile 5.0 Bethel Church jogs around Silver Lake on the left, often covered in flocks of bobbing ducks and geese. Roll past Ernst Road with wide-open spaces spread before you. At mile 6.6 there's a small German cemetery, the St. Franziskus Kirche cemetery, established in 1858. The church was razed long ago, but the brick Italianate rectory, now a private home, is in view just west of the cemetery.

Continue past a farm with a large barnyard full of old tractors to Schneider Road. This is a sometimes busy four-way stop. Across the way is the majestic Bethel Church, another German congregation, established in 1840; the current church was built in 1909.

The area's German heritage continues with some farmsteads ahead. Pedal on and take a left at Steinbach Road. On the southwest corner is an old farmstead originally settled by a German family, as are two farms on Weber Road (first right).

Ernst Road, blue heron

Weber Road merges with Parker Road, then the two go their separate ways at mile 9.3. Turn right onto Parker and return to Bethel Church Road and take a left. Roll through more farmland and past an occasional wood copse to Grass Road (mile 11.8). Turn right, follow this to Saline Waterworks Road, and take another right. Saline Waterworks is a straight shot back through some of the most expansive farm field views of the entire ride. It Ts into paved Schneider Road. Turn left. This is probably the busiest traffic section of the route, though it's usually only moderately so. Take it to Bemis Road and turn right.

Bemis offers an entirely different character than that found in the rest of this route. For the next 2 miles the narrow road will wind and undulate dramatically through dense forestland and past houses and, yes, still more farmland. It's a major change of landscape and terrain from the wide-open farmsteads passed so far. Enjoy the hills. They will tax the muscles to a degree. They aren't overly long, but they are relatively steep and they do repeat a few times. The views down slope into the forests are beautiful.

By Ernst Road the terrain has leveled off somewhat. Turn right and take Ernst to Pfaus Road. Turn left onto Pfaus and prepare for a whole different rural experience. On the left at mile 19.1 is a shoe tree, a massive oak festooned with hundreds of shoes, top to bottom. Once you've finished your photo shoot of the shoe tree, ride the long downhill to Eisman Road and take

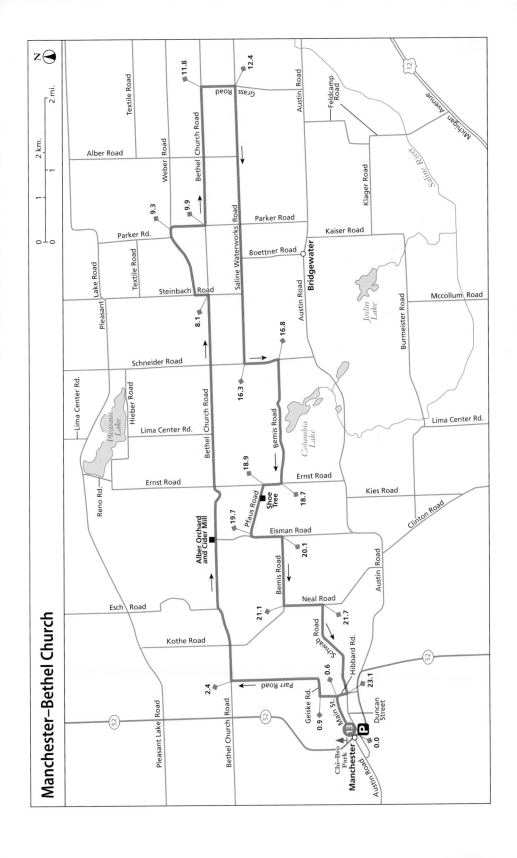

Manchester–Bethel Church

a left. The farm on the northeast corner was settled by the Alber family, the same family as those at the Alber Orchard you passed earlier on Bethel Church Road at Eisman.

Take a right back onto Bemis Road at mile 20.1. Perhaps the name Bemis is synonymous with the word "hill" because after crossing a small stream the road pitches up sharply for a short way, then levels off before reaching Neal Road. Take a left onto Neal, then a right onto Schwab and enjoy the last mile of countryside as it passes between a marsh and forest area. You know you're within the city limits when the dirt road makes an abrupt transition to even pavement and housing developments at mile 22.9. This is now Duncan Street. Take Duncan to Hibbard, and turn right. Ride that to the stop sign at Main, and turn left. This should look familiar, as it's the road you started out on.

Find the pathway that leads back to Chi-Bro Park at mile 23.7. If you miss it, take Main to the M-52 intersection. Turn right and climb a short way up the hill to the park entrance.

MILES AND DIRECTIONS

0.0 Leave Chi-Bro Park on the two-track leading from the east side of the parking lot.

0.3 Merge onto Main Street heading east.

0.6 Turn left onto Hibbard Street.

0.9 Turn right onto Geiske Road (begin dirt road).

1.1 Swing north onto Parr Road.

2.4 Turn right onto Bethel Church Road.

8.1 Turn left onto Steinbach Road.

8.3 Turn right onto Weber Road.

9.2 Turn right onto Parker Road.

9.3 Turn right, continuing on Parker Road.

9.9 Turn left onto Bethel Church Road.

11.8 Turn right onto Grass Road.

12.4 Turn right onto Saline Waterworks Road.

16.3 Turn left onto Schneider Road.

16.8 Turn right onto Bemis Road.

18.7   Turn right onto Ernst Road.

18.9   Turn left onto Pfaus Road.

19.1   Shoe Tree.

19.7   Turn left onto Eisman Road.

20.1   Turn right onto Bemis Road.

21.1   Turn left onto Neal Road.

21.7   Turn right onto Schwab Road.

22.9   Manchester City limits. Return to paved road.

23.1   Turn right onto Hibbard Street.

23.3   Turn left onto Main Street.

23.7   Find two-track path to the right leading back to Chi-Bro Park (easy to miss), or continue on to the four-way stop at M-52.

24.1   Turn right onto M-52. Turn right into Chi-Bro Park a short way up the hill.

RIDE INFORMATION

Local Events/Attractions
The Manchester Chicken Broil: Held in mid-July every year since 1954, this is a popular event in the area. There's music and there are activities, but mostly there's chicken; www.manchesterchickenbroil.org.
Downtown Manchester: Take a walk through downtown Manchester with its many beautifully restored historic buildings.

Restrooms
Start/finish: Porta-potty at Chi-Bro Park

Sharon Area

The Sharon area is known for its natural beauty and glacially carved topography. The route laid out mixes vast, open farmsteads with densely wooded natural areas. And of course there are hills. They're not too big or too small, and you get to go down as many as you go up. It's worth it.

Start: Sharon Hills Mountain Bike Park parking lot

Length: 20.3 miles

Approximate riding time: 1.5–3 hours

Best bike: Cyclocross or hybrid

Terrain and trail surface: Mostly dirt road with a few miles of paved road segments

Traffic and hazards: Though the paved roads are not heavily trafficked, they have narrow shoulders and speeds in the 50s. The dirt roads can be rough in some areas.

Things to see: Sharon Mill, beautiful rolling countryside with expansive farms and quiet woodlands

Maps: *DeLorme: Michigan Atlas & Gazetteer,* pages 31, 32

Getting there by car: From I-94 at exit 159, head south on M-52 7.2 miles to Pleasant Lake Road. Turn right onto Pleasant Lake Road and follow it 3.2 miles to Sharon Hollow Road. The parking area is on the left at the apex of the roadway curve. GPS: N42 10.946 W84 05.614

THE RIDE

The ride begins from a mountain bike park parking lot, but it's not a mountain bike ride. It's a dirt road/paved road ride through some prime countryside, over 20 rolling miles of relatively quiet back roads. There are two short paved

Lammon Road

segments; the first comes at the start. It heads downhill on Sharon Hollow Road right away. At the bottom of the hill is Sharon Mill on the River Raisin, originally the site of a sawmill in the 1830s, then a gristmill. It was rebuilt in 1928 by Henry Ford and became a cigar lighter factory. It's now restored as a public park area owned by the Washtenaw County Parks & Recreation Commission. It's a charming spot to check out either during the ride or just after.

Continue up a pointed climb, not long, but it will get the legs working, especially this early in the ride. At Sharon Valley Road take a quick left, then a quick right, continuing south on Sharon Hollow Road. This is open farm country.

Take a right at Buss Road (mile 2.4). The farm panoramas continue for another 1.5 miles, until the road arcs left and the road feels as if it narrows, but really it's heading into a long allee of trees as the forest closes it in and the road rolls and twists a bit more.

Turn right onto Pierce Road (mile 5.3) and head north. Cross back over the River Raisin at mile 5.8. River Raisin got its name from the early French explorers due to the plentiful wild grapes that grow along its banks. *Raisin* is the French word for grape.

The road passes into a large natural area all the way to Sharon Valley Road. This is all part of the Sharonville State Game Area. Sharon Valley Road, a short jog in the route, is paved and it runs through more dense forest canopy. Turn left at Prospect Hill Road and back onto dirt. It will live up to its name as you immediately climb a long hill. Both sides of the road are still part of the Game Area and densely wooded.

Turn left at Lammon Road, a mile-long downhill run in a quiet setting. Savor this. Take a right onto Fishville Road. The natural forestland continues as does the Game Area. Fishville then takes a dogleg left, then right again and opens up to farm fields to the west.

There's another transition from dirt to pavement onto Curtis Road. This is a quiet road but with little shoulder. It returns to dirt as you swing left back onto Prospect Hill Road. The road curves east for a short way, then it Ts into Jacob Road. Turn left and look for the stone barn on the right at mile 14.2. It's one of those humble architectural wonders you occasionally stumble over on rides like this.

Continue to Washburn Road and take a right. After crossing Sharon Hollow Road, there's a slight uphill jog followed by a climb for the next mile. The rewards for any climb on this route are great. Turn right at Sylvan Road and prepare for downhill nirvana. But as you begin your zooming descent, be aware that at mile 17.2 the roadway splits, with Wingate on the left and Sylvan on the right. You want to stay on Sylvan. Every map

Bike Shop

Aberdeen Bike & Outdoors: 1101 S. Main St., Chelsea, MI 48118; (734) 475-8203

I've seen makes it look like Sylvan goes straight. It doesn't. It's a definite right. Take it. This is a winding, beautiful descent through the forest. Somewhere it's rated a category 5 climb, one of the few in the region, and you have the luxury of going down it. Watch for cars on the turns, stay to the right and all will be well. Enjoy the marsh about halfway down on the right. It's in a deep bowl.

At the bottom is a right turn onto Trolz Road (mile 18.2). Follow this flat stretch to the curve left onto Sharon Hollow Road and pedal easily to the short jog at Easudes Road. Stay left on Sharon Hollow and find yourself back where you began your journey.

MILES AND DIRECTIONS

0.0 Leave the Sharon Mills Mountain Bike parking area and head south onto Sharon Hollow Road.

1.1 Jog left onto Sharon Valley Road, then right, back onto Sharon Hollow Road.

2.4 Turn right onto Buss Road (dirt).

5.3 Turn right onto Pierce Road (dirt).

6.9 Turn right onto Sharon Valley Road (paved).

Sharon Area

7.4 Turn left onto Prospect Hill Road (dirt).

8.5 Turn left onto Lammon Road (dirt).

9.5 Turn right onto Fishville Road (dirt).

11.5 Turn right onto Curtis Road (paved).

12.8 Turn left onto Prospect Hill Road (dirt).

13.1 Prospect Hill swings east and becomes Kendall Road (dirt).

14.1 Turn left onto Jacob Road (dirt).

14.6 Turn right onto Washburn Road (dirt).

16.6 Turn right onto Sylvan Road (dirt).

17.1 Stay to the right and continue on Sylvan Road. Be careful, because Wingate looks like the main route here. You don't want to miss out on this winding section of Sylvan. Watch for oncoming vehicles on the blind curves.

18.2 Turn right onto Trolz Road (dirt).

19.3 Trolz Road swings south and becomes Sharon Hollow Road (dirt).

20.1 Take the right jog onto Easudes Road, then turn left, back onto Sharon Hollow Road.

20.3 Return to the parking area on the right.

RIDE INFORMATION

Local Events/Attractions
Manchester is a charming small town nearby. There are antiques shops and places to eat, and it's just a nice town to walk around as part of your day out.

Restrooms
Mile 0.4: Down the hill at Sharon Mill (in season)

North Lyndon–Embury

This is a teasingly short ride in one of the most beautiful natural areas in Southeast Michigan. It's almost cruel to head out and then return so soon. It's like tasting a delicacy that doesn't even come close to filling you up—it just leaves you yearning for more. But that's not a bad way to approach some rides. This one will have you wanting to come back and explore the area more. Savor the moments.

This area has some excellent mountain biking and some great hikes as well, with long boardwalks that stretch over picturesque marshlands. You'll want to check all that out on another day. The Pinckney-Waterloo Trail also crosses through this area. It's recreation paradise. Be warned.

Start: Park Lyndon North off North Territorial Road

Length: 11.3 miles

Approximate riding time: 1 hour

Best bike: Cyclocross, hybrid, mountain bike

Terrain and trail surface: Dirt and paved roads

Traffic and hazards: North Territorial traffic moves quickly with almost no road shoulder. Steep downhill on Embury Road. Major road crossings at M-52.

Things to see: Forests, lakes, wildlife, farmsteads

Maps: *DeLorme: Michigan Atlas & Gazetteer,* page 32

Getting there by car: From I-94 at exit 159, head north on M-52 through Chelsea 7.4 miles to North Territorial Road and turn right. Follow North Territorial 1.1 miles to Park Lyndon North. Turn left into the parking lot. GPS: N42 22.812 W84 03.710

THE RIDE

Leave the parking lot and turn left (east) onto North Territorial Road. This is not known as one of the great roads to ride a bike on in some sections, but this area is hilly, relatively quiet, and quite scenic. Traffic does move at a good clip, however, so take care.

Ride 0.4 mile to Embury Road and turn left. On the map, Embury is a straight line, seemingly nondescript. In truth, it's one of the most beautiful roads in the region. It's relatively narrow, it has some great hills, or maybe a better way to put it is repeated rises and falls. There are just enough gentle curves to make you wonder what's up ahead. It's also covered by a wooded canopy nearly the whole way, and when it's not, there are marshlands to enjoy. Embury is enticing.

Possibly the most challenging part of the ride will be rolling down the first hill. It's not the drop, though it is a rapid descent. The real challenge will depend on the condition of the road. There are times when it's reasonably hard-packed, and that makes things easy. But if it's in its soft loam phase, it can be a bit squirrely to ride through. Take it at a moderate pace and stay relaxed and things should work fine. At the bottom is a tamarack marsh, well worth the adventurous descent to see. The soft architecture of the trees and the surrounding wildflowers can be an amazing display at various times of year. Of course, you now have to climb up and out of the lowland, but you came out for exercise, right?

Bike Shops

Aberdeen Bike & Outdoors: 1101 S. Main St., Chelsea, MI 48118; (734) 475-8203; aberdeenbike.com
Dexter Bike and Sport: 3173 Baker Rd., Dexter, MI 48130; (734) 426-5900; www.dexterbikeandsport.com

Midway down the road is the Waterloo-Pinckney Trail crossing. This is part of the Pinckney State Recreation Area. At this point, even along the road, you're totally immersed in a dense oak-hickory forest with various woodland plants on the small hummocks and down in the lower marsh areas. It's one of those places where you'd expect to hear legends about woodland creatures (hobbits, elves, dwarves, that kind of thing). Though the forest is in close to the narrow road, it's also possible to see into it as well and enjoy the roll of the glacial terrain.

Near the end of Embury is a small parking area on the left that leads down to Sullivan Lake. On the right side of Embury is a sizable working farm.

Embury Road

Around the corner on Joslin Lake Road is South Lake off to the left with some nice sight lines down its length.

Continue to Boyce Road and take a left. At the 3.6-mile mark is a bridge crossing over a large marsh. This is the lowland connection between South Lake (just passed) and Joslin Lake just beyond sight to the north. This whole area is covered in marshland, making it great habitat for the wildlife that inhabit the area. It's a nice overlook spot.

Beyond this, as you leave the state recreation area, the character begins to change. The land opens up to reveal farm fields and scattered houses. Trees still line the road, but the feeling is much more open. The road rolls, but gently. After crossing M-52 at mile 5.5 the rural character continues.

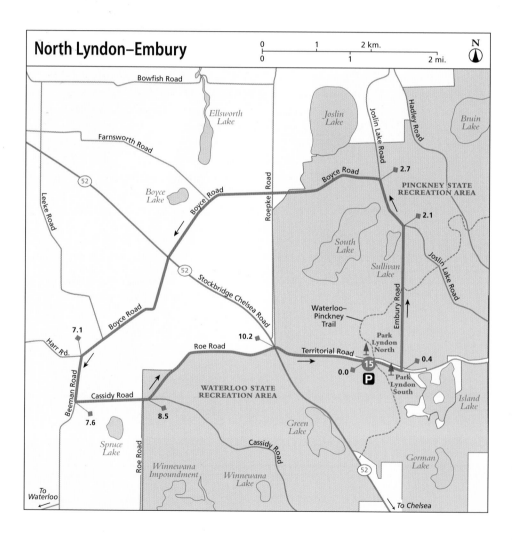

North Lyndon–Embury

Arc left onto Beeman Road, and the road narrows slightly and the trees become predominant again. Turn left (this should be called the Left Turn Ride) onto Cassidy Road. Though this section has some residences along the way, the character returns somewhat to that of the more forested rec area, especially where it turns onto Roe Road. Cassidy continues to the right and it's quite a nice ride through the forest, but that's for another time. Take that left onto Roe Road. It's a relatively flat ride through the woods, then there's a section of open fields once more.

Nearing M-52 again, the road rises up considerably. Climb to the highway and cross over and you'll shortly be rewarded with both pavement and a long downhill on North Territorial Road. This section of North Territorial is sweeping, rolling, and densely wooded. It's a very pleasant place to ride a bike. If Park Lyndon North was at the base of this hill, all would be easygoing with a big smile. How often do all the stars line up that well, however? After crossing the short causeway between the ponds in the hollow on either side of the road, the road grants you one last biting climb. Take a left when you get near the top and enter the park. There's a covered shelter with plenty of picnic tables and a few grills as well if you want to cap the ride off with a picnic barbecue.

MILES AND DIRECTIONS

0.0   Leave the parking area and turn left onto North Territorial Road.

0.4   Turn left onto Embury Road.

2.1   Turn left onto Joslin Lake Road.

2.7   Turn left onto Boyce Road.

7.1   The road splits at this point, with Boyce Road turning to the right and Beeman Road going straight as the main road. Follow onto Beeman.

7.6   Turn left onto Cassidy Road.

8.5   Turn left onto Roe Road.

10.2 Cross M-52 back onto North Territorial Road. This is a busy main road with fast-moving traffic. Cross with care.

11.3 Arrive back at Park Lyndon North.

RIDE INFORMATION

Restrooms
Start/Finish: Park Lyndon North parking area

Holly Recreation Area and Environs

Many sections of Oakland County continue their historic tradition as a major recreation outlet for the Detroit Metro region. Oakland County is dotted with extensive recreation areas set aside for public use, intertwined with residential properties. Add to this the glacial moraine that's left behind a corrugated landscape, rich with low marsh areas, ponds, and small lakes, among jutting peaks, and it makes for a region lined with natural areas and wildlife mingling in amongst the development.

Much of this ride combines all of the above, a rolling tableau of scenic beauty in an ever-growing region. The hills aren't excessively long, nor are they inordinately steep, but the steady pulse of up and down will help keep your fitness up. That said, the natural surrounding beauty will distract you from the work you're doing. This is a region where hundreds of riders at all levels join in on organized group rides due to the sheer enjoyment of pedaling over these back roads.

Start: Holly Recreation Area State Park parking area

Length: 33.5 miles

Approximate riding time: 2–4 hours

Best bike: Cyclocross or hybrid

Terrain and trail surface: Dirt roads over rolling hills

Traffic and hazards: Downhill dirt section on Jossman Road has a sharp, often loose gravel curve between Grange Hall and Perryville Roads on a fast downhill. Short section of busy paved road on Grange Hall between Brandt and Bird Roads.

Things to see: Farmsteads, old farm buildings, fields, marshes, ponds, lakes, natural wooded areas

Maps: State of Michigan DNR–Holly Recreation Area: www.michigandnr
.com/parksandtrails/details.aspx?id=459&type=SPRK; *DeLorme:
Michigan Atlas & Gazetteer*, page 41

Getting there by car: From I-75 at exit 101, head east on Grange Hall
Road for 1.5 miles. Turn right onto McGinnis Road and go 0.8 mile to
state park entry road on the right. Pass entry station and take the first
right. Follow the road 0.2 mile to the Heron Lake parking area. Michigan
State Park Passport or day pass required for park entry. GPS: N42 48.712
W83 31.499

THE RIDE

Begin at Heron Lake parking lot. It's a nice place to start, with a large rest-
room/changing facility, a beach, picnic areas, a concession stand, and great
views over the lake. Head north through the park entrance roads, take a left at
the entrance gate, and a right onto McGinnis Road heading east. The densely
wooded recreation area is on both sides of McGinnis as it gently climbs to
Wildwood Road. After Wildwood it winds through the recreation area land for
a while, with houses and open fields interspersed.

Turn north (left) onto Jossman Road and dive back into a thick forest that
arches over the road, opening up to a large active field on the right approaching Grange Hall Road. The road descends rapidly after Grange Hall. This is a
coasting dream, but keep in mind that there's a sharp left turn in the road at
mile 3.8. The road surface can be rough at times and it's a blind turn, so take
it easy, stay to the right, and all should keep the bike upright. The descent
continues to mile 4.1, where there's a sharp right turn and a speed reducing
uphill, though the instructions on the previous turn should still be retained.
There's a sizable marsh pond area to the left worth eyeing carefully for wildlife.

The short climb is followed by another, less precipitous descent to the left
at Perryville Road past Phipps Lake and continuing on to another left at Barron Road and a quick jog right that resumes as Perryville Road. And . . . another
short, steep climb. This again begins a long, rolling descent through an open
marsh area on each side of the road to Van Road at mile 7.6. Turn right.

Continue rolling through the now-thematic recreation/residential area to
the Y with Groveland Road. Keep to the left as Groveland and Van join for a short
distance. Turn left at mile 9.3 and stay on Groveland as it passes by another
marsh (what else?) and continues its gentle descent to Horton Road. Turn right
onto Horton and prepare for a massive transition into new jurisdictional lands
at mile 10.4. There's no way to get ready for the dramatic transcendence from

Oakland into Genesee County, but at the line, green stays, ah, green and fields become, well, more fields. In other words, the landscape theme changes little and the bucolic setting is sustained. But if riding in Genesee County has always been a dream, then this is the golden moment. Savor it because after Horton Road turns right and heads east past wide-open farm fields and Van and Thayer Roads, it takes another right turn onto Jossman Road and reenters Oakland County at mile 13.8.

The road begins a slow, rolling ascent on the tree-lined Jossman to Perryville Road at mile 15.6. This is the crossroads that took you west earlier, but this time turn left and head east, downhill to Brandt Road. Turn right onto Brandt. Since the turn off Jossman onto Perryville, much of the surrounding land is state wildlife area. Nearly all the dense forest to the right is public hunting land.

Grange Hall Road in this area is a busy paved roadway. There's a good-size shoulder, but watch for fast-moving traffic as you turn left on this short jog over to Bird Road. Turn right onto Bird and enjoy the spiky climb and the series of rolls that follow. Bird takes a jog to the right as it meets Glass Road, then a jog left again. Continue to Bald Eagle Lake Road and turn left. Climb and then descend a twisting, forested road to where it opens out onto a view left of built-up Bald Eagle Lake.

> ## Bike Shops
> **Cyclefit & Snow Sports:** 1006 N. Leroy St., Fenton, MI 48430; (810) 750-2348; cycle-fit.net
> **Kinetic Systems Bicycles:** 60 S. Main St., Clarkston, MI 48346; (248) 625-7000; kineticsystemsbicycles.com

Turn right onto Allen Road and take a steady ascent, turning right onto Reese Road. Follow this to Oak Hill Road. Jog left, then a quick right, continuing on Reese headed south. The hill tops out near a horse track through the trees on the left. That was the last sizable hill of the route. The rest of the ride back follows a gently rolling series of lefts and rights—Rattalee (r), Ellis (r), Knox (l), Bridge Lake (r), Kier (l), Jossman (r), Bald Eagle Lake (l), Wildwood (r), McGinnis (l)—and back to the park entrance, and from there to the Heron Lake parking area. Be aware at mile 29.1, where the main road swings right and becomes Oak Hill Road, go straight, continuing on Jossman Road. It's a pleasant roll through tree-covered roads, along marsh areas, and past fields and houses knit in among the trees.

Horton Road barn and sheds

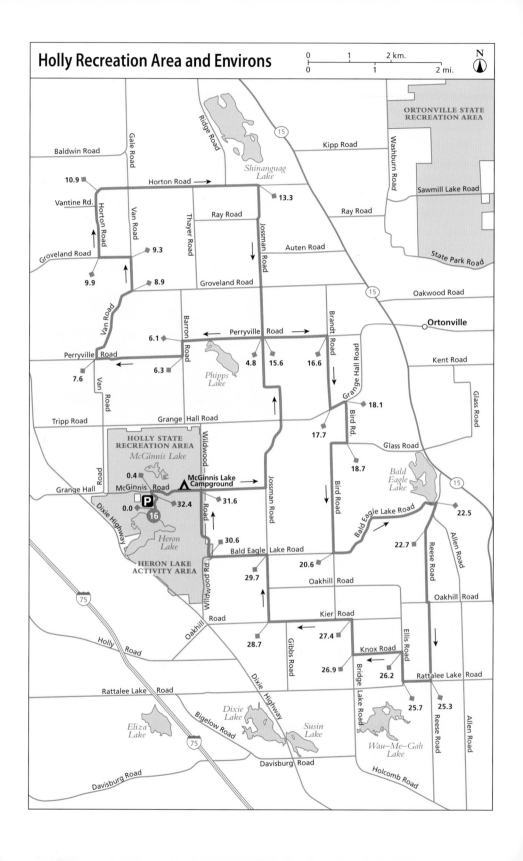

MILES AND DIRECTIONS

0.0 Leave the Heron Beach parking area and wind out past the entrance to the park.

0.4 Turn right onto McGinnis Road.

2.3 Turn left onto Jossman Road.

4.8 Turn left onto Perryville Road.

6.1 Turn left onto Barron Road.

6.3 Turn right onto Perryville Road.

7.6 Turn right onto Van Road.

8.9 Turn left onto Groveland Road.

9.3 Turn left onto Groveland Road (Van Road continues straight).

9.9 Turn right onto Horton Road.

10.9 Swing right as Horton Road continues east.

13.4 Turn right onto Jossman Road.

15.6 Turn left onto Perryville Road.

16.6 Turn right onto Brandt Road.

17.7 Turn left onto Grange Hall Road. Grange Hall is paved and sometimes busy. Cross with care.

18.1 Turn right onto Bird Road.

18.7 Turn right onto Glass Road. This is a short jog that returns south on Bird Road.

20.6 Turn left onto Bald Eagle Lake Road.

22.5 Turn right onto Allen Road.

22.7 At the Y in the road, keep right, turning onto Reese Road.

24.1 The road takes a jog left onto Oak Hill Road, then right back onto Reese Road.

25.3 Turn right onto Rattalee Lake Road.

25.7 Turn right onto Ellis Road.

26.2 Turn left onto Knox Road.

26.9 Turn right onto Bridge Lake Road.

27.4 Turn left onto Kier Road.

28.7 Turn right onto Jossman Road. Be aware at mile 29.1, where the main road swings right and becomes Oak Hill Road, go straight,

29.7 Turn left onto Bald Eagle Lake Road.

30.6 Turn right onto Wildwood Road.

31.6 Turn left onto McGinnis Road.

32.4 Turn left into the entrance to the state park and follow the road back to the Heron Lake parking area.

33.5 Arrive back at the parking area.

RIDE INFORMATION

Local Events/Attractions
Back 40 Challenge: An organized group ride in October each year with distances from 10 to 66 miles; www.flyingrhinocc.com/back-40-challenge
Michigan Renaissance Festival: August–September; www.michrenfest.com

Accommodations
Michigan Department of Natural Resources, Holly Recreation Area: There's a 144-site campground in the Holly Rec Area at McGinnis Lake, plus a few available cabins; www.michigandnr.com/parksandtrails/details .aspx?id=459&type=SPRK

Restaurants
The French Laundry: 125 Shiawassee at Adelaide, Fenton, MI 48430; (810) 629-8852; www.lunchandbeyond.com

Restrooms
Start/Finish: Heron Lake beach parking area

Ortonville Recreation Area and Environs

This area is part of that Oakland County ethic to intersperse recreational land in amongst the farmland and residential enclaves. It's wonderfully glacial, with rolling hills and small lakes and marshes scattered about the region.

There's an interesting transition going on in this area, with residential properties increasing as farmland gets purchased for housing, but there's still plenty of farming going on. That, along with the recreation areas and natural features, helps the area retain its rural, wooded character.

This route winds through all of that. It offers a good workout or a good respite from the busy world, or both, as it touches that need to be close to forests, remember where our food comes from, and, if we're lucky, see a few large wild birds fly over our heads as we pedal down the road.

Start: Big Fish Lake Park

Length: 19.6 miles

Approximate riding time: 1.5–3 hours

Best bike: Cyclocross, mountain bike, hybrid

Terrain and trail surface: Dirt road, mix of packed, fine, and rough gravel. A couple of short sections of paved road. The ride ranges from relatively flat, to rolling, to long hilly sections. Some climbs are steep.

Traffic and hazards: Relatively quiet on the dirt roads. Leaving and returning from Big Fish Lake Park, there is a section of paved road, Hadley Road, where faster-moving traffic is present, but there is a comfortable shoulder on this 0.3-mile stretch.

Oakwood Road at mile 5.7 is paved, has little shoulder, and fast-moving traffic for about 0.5 mile. It turns off onto Leece Road (actually straight) at mile 6.2. Leece is once again a dirt road. Transitions from paved to dirt roads can be gravelly. Potholes and some washboard sections on dirt roads.

Things to see: Deer, heron, egret, dense forests, farm fields, working farms, lakes, ponds

Maps: *DeLorme: Michigan Atlas & Gazetteer,* page 41

Getting there by car: From I-75 take exit 91 heading north on Ortonville Road (M-15) 8.2 miles to Oakwood Road. Follow Oakwood 3.1 miles to Hadley Road and turn left. Take Hadley 1.3 miles to the entrance to Big Fish Lake Park on the right. Follow the entrance drive 0.5 mile to the parking area. A Michigan Recreation Passport or day pass is required. GPS: N42 53.112 W83 23.740

THE RIDE

Big Fish Lake Park has a panoramic view of the lake and a sizeable parking area. The road out of the park is paved, as is Hadley Road. Take a left onto Hadley at the park entrance. The surroundings are marshlands and farm fields.

Turn right onto Sawmill Lake Road, past a line of single-family homes that transitions to large fields. A short way past Honert Road the surroundings change to forestland. This is the Ortonville Recreation Area. The dense stand of trees on both sides of the road creates a tunnel-like effect. Though the road doesn't narrow, it feels like it does. It also begins to descend and keeps descending after the turn onto Sands Road (mile 3.0). This is a very fun, winding descent, but watch for cars around the blind curves.

Take a left onto State Park Road and begin ascending. Bloomer 3 mountain bike trail is on a side road off State Park Road at mile 4.4. This is not to be confused with Bloomer Park in Rochester. This is a trail all its own on a trailhead up the drive a short way. There are park cabins that can be rented back there as well. Continuing on State Park Road, the climb rises to a point where it emerges from the forest, opening back up on farm fields, then past Honert Road to a right turn onto Oakwood Road.

Oakwood is a paved road without much of a shoulder, and it can be busy at times. You'll only be on it a short way as Oakwood swings west and you'll go straight onto the dirt Leece Road. Leece descends to a T at Hummer Lake Road with Truax Lake straight ahead. Turn left. This leads to an intersection with Hadley Road. They join for a very short stretch, then Hadley turns north. In each case, keep heading east. The road rolls up and down for a while, passing through a wooded residential area until it reaches Sashabaw Road at mile 8.2.

Canopy over Big Fish Lake Road

Turn left, joining with Sashabaw for a short way as the road swings back east, then Sashabaw turns north and Hummer Lake continues east, then arcs south as it passes Hummer Lake itself. Once beyond the lake, the road resumes its eastward path. Farm fields, then forest, replace the houses on the north side of the road.

At Hurd Road (mile 10.2) turn left. Wide-open farm fields predominate in this section, with a smattering of houses here and there. It's apparent, especially past Oakwood Road, that this area is transitioning from farm country to residential, but there are still remnant farm buildings that remain even as the land is acquired for houses. And the working farms have maintained many of those magnificent farm buildings.

Turn left onto Davison Lake Road for a very pleasant ride down a quiet section of tree-lined road that comes to a refreshing terminus (turn, actually) looking over Davison Lake. Follow the road to the left as it becomes Connell Road and take it to a right turn onto Big Fish Lake Road at mile 13.4. The road takes a series of sharp right and left turns through an area that continues the tree-lined residential area theme. There's a short detour down a Davison Lake access road to the right at mile 13.8 if you want more connection with that lake. It will take you a little over 0.1 mile to a spot with a view out over the lake. A short break may not be a bad idea because there's going to be some climbing coming up shortly.

Bike Shops

Kinetic Systems Bicycles: 60 S. Main St., Clarkston, MI 48346; (248) 625-7000; kineticsystemsbicycles.com
Main Street Bicycles: 5987 26 Mile Rd., Washington, MI 48094; (586) 677-7755; mainstreetbicycles.com
Paint Creek Bicycles: 27 E. Flint St., Lake Orion, MI 48362; (248) 693-9620; paintcreekbicycles.com

Continuing on to the T in the road where it meets Silver Birch Road (though in essence it stays Big Fish Lake Road), take a right. There's a magnificent view between houses out over Big Fish Lake as you're perched on a bluff high above it. You might even be able to spot your car in the parking lot far to the other side.

The road goes up a very gentle rise, then down a short drop to a point where it rises with a bit more vigor. This is one of the longer, steeper hills on this ride. Pick a pace and either motor or putter up it. This tree-lined esplanade is one of the special places on the ride, so whatever you do, don't close your eyes and miss it.

Once over the top it descends to Hadley Road. Cross Hadley and savor your reward for that previous climb, a long descent down the mostly forested

Fox Lake Road. Pass the equestrian camp on the right and then, guess what? You get one more chance to put those climbing legs to good use. Motor or putter once more to Honert Road and take a left, still climbing, with the forest on the right and the emergence of farm fields on the left.

Pedal to Sawmill Lake Road and take a left, returning on a road you were riding earlier as you headed out on this adventure. At Hadley Road take another left and then right, back into the Big Fish Lake Park entry drive.

MILES AND DIRECTIONS

0.0   Leave Big Fish Lake parking lot.

0.6   Exit Big Fish Lake Park and turn left onto Hadley Road.

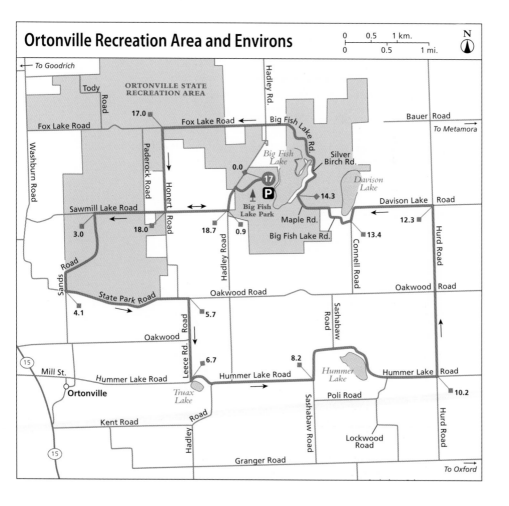

0.9 Turn right onto Sawmill Lake Road.

3.0 Turn left onto Sands Road.

4.1 Turn left onto State Park Road.

5.7 Turn right onto Oakwood Road.

6.2 Go straight onto Leece Road (dirt).

6.7 Turn left onto Hummer Lake Road.

6.9 Stay to the left as Hummer Lake Road merges with Hadley Road.

7.2 Go straight on Hummer Lake as Hadley swings north.

8.2 Turn left onto Sashabaw Road/Hummer Lake Road.

8.8 Go straight on Hummer Lake Road as Sashabaw Road swings north.

10.2 Turn left onto Hurd Road.

12.3 Turn left onto Davison Lake Road.

13.2 Swing left onto Connell Road.

13.4 Turn right onto Big Fish Lake Road.

14.3 Turn right onto Silver Birch Road. The name morphs into Fox Lake Road.

15.7 Cross Hadley Road.

17.0 Turn left onto Honert Road.

18.0 Turn left onto Sawmill Lake Road.

18.7 Turn left onto Hadley Road.

19.0 Turn right into the entrance to Big Fish Lake Park and follow the road back to the parking area.

19.6 Arrive back at starting point.

RIDE INFORMATION

Restrooms
Start/Finish: Big Fish Lake Park

Lake Orion–Metamora

There are places along the way that really do look like northern lower Michigan. It's hard to keep telling yourself that you're in heavily populated southeast lower Michigan. The hills are a constant and some are a challenge, though none are very long. The roads are tree-covered most of the time, creating a tunnel effect in some areas. It's almost architectural, like going through a natural hallway, ever-changing, vibrant, and full of life.

Besides the plentiful natural features all along the way, the wildlife, and the rolling glacial terrain, there are horse farms. This is horse country. There are signs posted periodically along the way to remind you of this, but you don't need them to know. Horseback riders may pass you, or horse-drawn buggies. Horse farms are all over the place, with names like Win A Gin and Shenanigans Farms. Horse farms mean plentiful acres of pastureland, wood fences defining the slope of the land, and majestic barns and outbuildings.

Start: Bald Mountain North Parking Lot

Length: 31.5 miles

Approximate riding time: 2–4 hours

Best bike: Cyclocross, mountain bike, hybrid, wide tire bike with knobby tread

Terrain and trail surface: Dirt roads, rough to hard packed

Traffic and hazards: Soft loam or large gravel on some roads; downhills can be tricky with rocks or with washboard effects at times; traffic is light

Things to see: Horse farms, birds (blue herons, egrets, sandhill cranes, hawks), farm fields, woods, tunnel-of-tree effect on some roads, ponds, lakes, streams

Maps: DeLorme: Michigan Atlas & Gazetteer, pages 41, 42

Getting there by car: From I-75 head east at exit 81, then swing around the exit ramp and head north (right) on Lapeer Road. Follow Lapeer for 2.1 miles to Silverbell Road. Turn right onto Silverbell and go 2.4 miles to Adams Road. Turn left onto Adams and go 3.6 miles to Stoney Creek Road. Turn right onto Stoney Creek for a short 0.1-mile jog to Harmon Road. Turn left onto Harmon and take it 0.5 mile to the Bald Mountain parking lot on the left at the intersection with Predmore Road. GPS: N42 46.974 W83 11.817

THE RIDE

Head east out of the Bald Mountain parking area on Predmore Road. In this section, the roadway is richly wooded because it follows alongside the Bald Mountain recreational area. Even occasionally busy Lake George Road a mile up follows the edge of Bald Mountain rec area. Up the road a short way farther on the right is Addison Oaks County Park. Woods are the theme of this ride, even when riding past the numerous homes and horse farms all along the way. In the 19th century this part of the region was targeted as the bucolic recreational outlet for the urban areas nearby, and that still stands today, as indicated by its many parks and recreational options.

Turn west onto Drahner Road. As the roadway narrows and twists, the sense of diving deep into the countryside increases. Within a mile is the Saint Benedict Monastery tucked into a natural setting on the left and Hosner Road on the right. Turn onto Hosner and drop downhill. To this point it's been a gradual 100-foot uphill climb for nearly 4 miles. The downhill drops back that 100 feet in 1.5 miles. That sets the theme for the rest of your ride, a rolling series of mostly gradual (with only a few exceptions), yet relatively continual, ups and downs through the natural settings of the area.

You'll cross the Polly Ann Trail at mile 5.1. This is an abandoned rail line that's become a recreational rail-trail, one of many in Michigan. This can be another day's ride (this flat rail corridor is a nice contrast to the abundant hills in the area). Watch for egrets in the pond on the right just past the rail-trail. Their plumage is in stark contrast to the rich greens and browns of their surroundings, and they're common in this area.

Ride north to Ray Road and turn left. The road becomes a densely tree-covered lane and soon swings left down a rapidly sweeping descent that arcs to the right. Stay right as you zoom past Ballantyne Road (stay on Ray). At the bottom is a large marsh on the left. Keep an eye out for more wildlife.

Take a right onto Delano Road. This section can be a sandy uphill climb, depending on the time of year. If so, it will be the only part of the ride that's a

Hosner Road egrets

challenge to ride through, so bear with it for a short way and you'll rise out of it by the time you get to Noble Road. The reward is a ride through a beautiful tree-lined trough with scenic glimpses of open fields on each side.

Continue along the steadily rolling, relatively narrow road just beyond Oakwood Road, where you'll begin a general descent for the next 4.5 miles. This section to Rock Valley Road at mile 11.7 is tree-lined with open fields on both sides. If you're lucky, you'll pass a group in the midst of horseback riding lessons at one of these farms.

The view off to the northwest at the turn onto Rock Valley Road is a sweeping panorama just before climbing a very short hill, then resuming your long descent in a more densely wooded portion of the route. Near the intersection with Barber Road is the small, peaceful Rock Valley Cemetery.

Continue to the T at Gardner Road and turn right onto a more open area surrounded by fields, and as you ride forth, keep telling yourself that you're just at the edge of the Detroit Metropolitan Area.

Turn right onto Brocker Road and put on your climbing legs. The next mile up to Barber Road will take some resolve, then after a short respite another uphill effort. It's not overly steep or long, but you will notice that things have changed topographically. But with a good attitude and an eye for beauty, you'll enjoy every pedal stroke because this is a gorgeous part of the ride. Once the road swings onto Casey Road, the reason for coming here will be all too apparent. This is one of the most dramatic tunnel-of-tree segments of backcountry roadway in the area.

Casey swings east after the dramatic tunnel and opens somewhat on a gently rolling, bucolic stretch of road that leads to Haven Road (actually, Haven seems to have an identity crisis, as it's labeled plural, Havens, and singular depending on the map you're using—and sometimes both on the same map). Take a right, south, and continue along more gently rolling roadway than that found in the first half of the ride, but this too has some pleasant twists here and there.

At mile 24.0 the road follows a curving lake edge with excellent views out over the water. Like many of the lakes in this area, there are wide marshy edges that welcome wildlife, so keep your eyes focused on finding some interesting birds, or listen for their calls.

A short way ahead, the road turns west onto Noble Road, then south again onto Curtis Road. At mile 25.8 you'll cross the Polly Ann Trail once more. Less than a mile ahead is Shoup Road (mile 26.4). Turn right. This is a short connection over to Lake George Road. Lake George Road is sometimes busy, with fast-moving traffic, but the good thing is it's a wide road, so there's plenty of space to pass.

It's a steady uphill climb to Drahner Road. At this point things might look familiar. This is where you turned west on your way out. Keep going straight south on Lake George. Across Drahner, the land on your left is Addison Oaks County Park, a popular park in the region. There's a daily fee for entrance to those who don't live in the county.

At Predmore Road turn right (west, mile 30.5) and continue back the way you came. When you reach Harmon Road, the Bald Mountain parking lot is directly across the road.

Bike Shops

Main Street Bicycles: 5987 26 Mile Rd., Washington, MI 48094; (586) 677-7755; mainstreetbicycles.com
Paint Creek Bicycles: 27 E. Flint St., Lake Orion, MI 48362; (248) 693-9620; paintcreekbicycles.com
Stoney Creek Bike: 58235 Van Dyke Rd., Washington, MI 48094; (586) 781-4451; stoneycreekbike.com

MILES AND DIRECTIONS

0.0 Leave the parking lot and head east on Predmore Road.

1.0 Turn left onto Lake George Road.

2.8 Turn left onto Drahner Road.

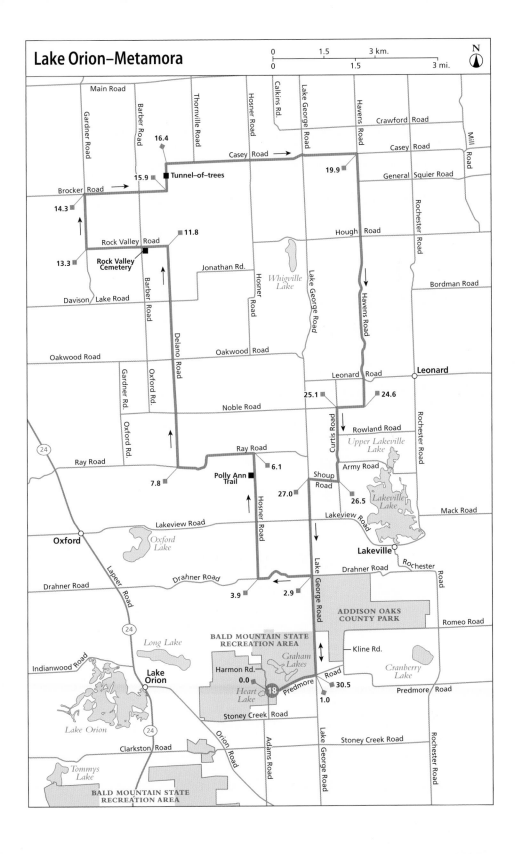

Lake Orion–Metamora

3.9   Turn right onto Hosner Road.

6.1   Turn left onto Ray Road.

7.8   Turn right onto Delano Road.

11.8   Turn left onto Rock Valley Road.

13.3   Turn right onto Gardner Road.

14.3   Turn right onto Brocker Road.

15.9   Brocker Road swings left onto Casey Road.

16.4   Casey Road turns east.

19.9   Turn right onto Haven Road.

24.6   Turn right onto Noble Road.

25.1   Turn left onto Curtis Road.

26.5   Turn right onto Shoup Road.

27.0   Turn left onto Lake George Road.

30.5   Turn right onto Predmore Road.

31.5   Cross Harmon Road into the parking lot.

RIDE INFORMATION

Local Events/Attractions
The town of Lake Orion is a charming nearby historic village with nice shops and places to eat.

Petersburg–Monroe

These are long, straight, flat country roads with panoramic views over expansive farm fields of corn and soybeans. There are long trains and you can see them from afar. And there are drains carving through the fields all over the place.

The "mountain" is at Ida Center Road on the bridge crossing over US 23. It's about the only significant elevation change you'll come across on this ride. Flat is beautiful. Truly.

Start: In a small parking area on the east side of Teal Road, near Lulu Road in the Petersburg State Game Management Area

Length: 28.8 miles

Approximate riding time: 2–3 hours

Best bike: Cyclocross or hybrid

Terrain and trail surface: A combination of paved and dirt road sections

Traffic and hazards: Very narrow shoulders on the paved roads. Traffic is light to moderate on most of these, but it does move quickly.

Things to see: Farmland and wide-open spaces on quiet back roads

Maps: *DeLorme: Michigan Atlas & Gazetteer*, pages 24, 25

Getting there by car: From US 23 take exit 13 headed west on Ida West Road 0.4 mile to Summerfield Road and turn left. Take Summerfield 2.0 miles to Lulu Road and turn right. Follow Lulu 1.4 miles to Teal Road and turn left. The parking area is 0.2 mile ahead on the left. There are other parking spots in the State Management Area on Teal and Lulu Roads if this one is full. GPS: N41 52.723 W83 41.785

THE RIDE

Park in one of five small parking areas in the management area. Two are along Teal Road and three are on Lulu Road. This is a state game area, so they are probably most popular during the fall hunting season, and it might be hard to find a spot.

Head south on Teal Road. This is a paved section with marsh and forest land on either side for the next 0.5 mile to Bacon Road. Turn right onto Bacon Road, the first dirt section of road.

Perhaps more than any other route in this book, this one goes back and forth a number of times between paved and dirt segments of roadway. It's also one of the flattest, since it's in the ancient glacial floodplain. That's partly why it's such good farmland. The soil is rich. But that mix of dirt and pavement can also be compared to a renowned relatively flat road race in France between Paris and Roubaix. So let your imagination fly. Southeast Michigan with an accent.

Not that you need to let the imagination do much work on this ride. If you're a fan of farm fields as far as the eye can see in all directions, this is your ride. It really is impressive to see so much agricultural land spread out before you. And one thing you'll notice is that there are drainage ditches crossing the road and running straight on through the fields on a steady basis and ranging over the entire ride. If they weren't there, the farmland would return to marshland all over.

Bacon Road comes to Todd Road at mile 2.0. Turn left (east). By the way, you've already crossed a series of drains and the ride is only beginning. You're back on pavement. Take a right onto Summerfield a mile up and get ready for the toughest climb of the day. Bow your head and dig deep as you go up and over the US 23 interchange. In 0.2 mile you'll rise 12 feet. (You'll cross US 23 once more on the return, so prepare for another "grueling" uphill struggle!) Actually, except for areas closer to the Detroit River and the rail-trails, most of the routes in this book roll through hilly glacial terrain. This is one of the exceptions, and as enjoyable and scenic as hills can be, this is a nice contrast.

Of course, one thing that wide-open roads offer is unfettered access of wind. Consider that as you pace yourself through the ride. If the going seems awfully easy, there's a chance that it's because the wind's at your back. Conversely, if it seems tough going on the way out, it should be mostly smooth cruising on the way back.

Turn left onto Tunnicliff Road just past the interchange. A KOA campground is on the left. Continue to Wells Road and turn left (north). This is a return to a dirt road. Take this to Todd Road (mile 4.8) and go right. Todd turns to pavement at Kruse Road at mile 5.4. At this point, the farmland views begin

Lehr Road

in earnest. From here on, the views will vary mainly by crop and farm building styles. You can't tell as easily from the road, but from an aerial view the plentiful drains run mostly at a diagonal, southwest to northeast, through the fields. They're all headed to Lake Erie a short way east. It creates quite a pattern.

Take Todd to Geiger Road (mile 9.8) and turn left and back onto dirt. Within 0.5 mile the Richardson Cemetery is on the left off in the middle of a field, anchored by a mature lone oak tree.

Take a right at the paved Lulu Road at mile 11.8. Follow this to the T at Minx Road and turn left. Minx takes a short left/right jog at Hubbard Road, then runs up to Albain Road. Go right at Albain and then left at mile 14.5 onto Lehr Road. Lehr is designated a seasonal road, but it's probably passable most of the year by bike. It's one of the most distinct roads on the route because it seems to be more a farm cut-through than an official road. It's the farthest extent of the ride and well worth checking out because it's so quiet and yet so wide open. Part of it skirts a small woodland on the right, and the rest is farm fields. I watched a red-tailed hawk circle overhead for quite a while without any distractions.

Take a left onto Saum Road. This begins the return ride. Take a left at Martell Road and a right at Darby Road (mile 17.0). From just before the turn onto Darby there was one drain, and you'll cross two more on Darby, with one more between them on the left. Counting drains could be a game on this ride.

Swing around to Albain Road and take a right (west). Albain is paved and though relatively light with traffic, it will probably be the busiest of all the roads on this route. Like most roads in this area, there's very little if any shoulder. Lewis Avenue is a mile ahead, and if you need refreshments, the village of Ida is to the right, less than a mile up. Otherwise, continue the next mile to Jackman Road (mile 20.2) and turn left. Take a right onto Lulu Road and continue west. Lulu is paved all the way to Secor Road (mile 23.1), where it turns to a mile-long dirt segment for the last time on this route.

Take a left at the T, Wells Road, and ride to the next right at Ida Center Road (mile 25.2) where you'll turn right. Here comes the last climb of the day. Crank up and over US 23 once more and roll down the other side to Summerfield Road and turn right. Turn left at Lulu Road (mile 27.2) and pedal back into the state game area. Turn left at Teal Road and the parking lot is just up ahead on the left.

MILES AND DIRECTIONS

0.0 Leave the parking area and turn left onto Teal Road.

0.7 Turn right onto Bacon Road (dirt).

2.0 Turn left onto Todd Road (paved).

3.0 Turn right onto Summerfield Road (paved). Cross the overpass at US 23.

3.6 Turn left at Tunnicliff Road (paved).

4.4 Turn left onto Wells Road (dirt).

4.8 Turn right onto Todd Road (dirt for the first mile, then paved).

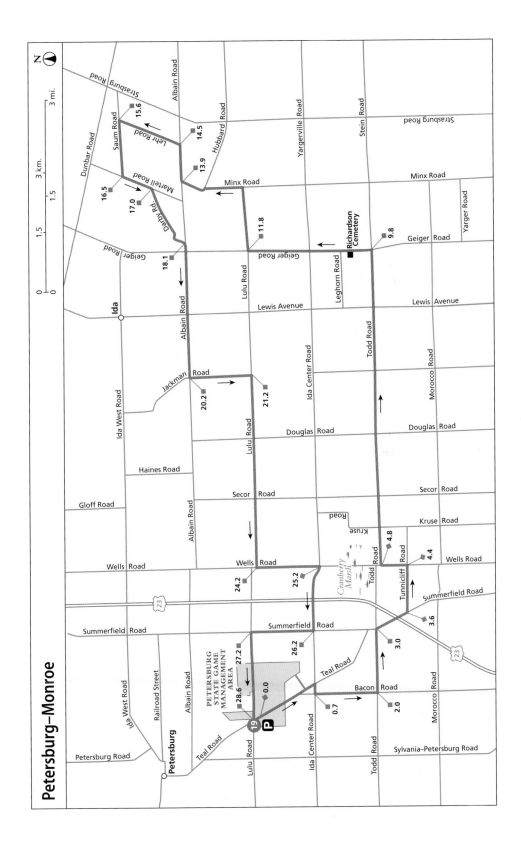

Petersburg–Monroe

9.8 Turn left onto Geiger Road (dirt).

11.8 Turn right onto Lulu Road (paved).

12.9 Turn left onto Minx Road (dirt).

13.5 Jog left, continuing on Minx Road.

13.9 Turn right onto Albain Road (paved).

14.5 Turn left onto Lehr Road (dirt).

15.6 Turn left onto Saum Road (dirt).

16.5 Turn left onto Martell Road (dirt).

17.0 Turn right onto Darby Road (dirt).

18.1 Turn right onto Albain Road (paved).

20.2 Turn left onto Jackman Road (dirt).

21.2 Turn right onto Lulu Road (paved, except for mile-long dirt section between Secor and Wells Roads).

24.2 Turn left onto Wells Road (paved).

25.2 Turn right onto Ida Center Road (paved). Cross US 23 on the overpass.

26.2 Turn right onto Summerfield Road (paved).

27.2 Turn left onto Lulu Road (paved).

28.6 Turn left onto Teal Road (paved).

28.8 Turn left into the parking area.

RIDE INFORMATION

Restaurants

There are places to get supplies and refreshments in the villages of Ida and Petersburg, as well as in Monroe.

Monroe was where General George Armstrong Custer spent his childhood years, and the historic displays are worth a visit.

Border-to-Border Trail:
Ann Arbor to Ypsilanti

This is a scenic, tree-lined linear park that follows the general route of the Huron River. It cuts through major park systems, connects two primary urban areas, and rims the edge of a couple of major college campuses.

The Border-to-Border Trail, or B2B, is an extension of what was once known as the Huron River Bikeway, a 12.5-mile bike path proposed in 1977. It took 11 more years to implement the first 1.5-mile stretch along the river between Fuller Road and Gallup Park. It's now a valued recreational/commuter connection between Ann Arbor and Ypsilanti (Ypsi) that has occasional interaction with vehicles along the roadways. It's still expanding with new or updated segments on a regular basis.

The entire trail currently extends from Bandemer Park in Ann Arbor to North Hydro Park at the eastern tip of Ford Lake in Ypsilanti. There are segments getting built in the Dexter area, though they are still detached from the main Ann Arbor/ Ypsi path. The route south and east from Depot Town in Ypsi is still a work in progress. It's possible to ride the route through some eastside Ypsi neighborhoods and along a path that parallels Grove Street near Ford Lake. The intent is to someday have a continuous bike path from the county border in southeast Washtenaw and follow the general course of the Huron River to the northwest border. Hence, border to border. As in the rest of the state, there are probably plans to connect it to a much broader trail link in the future.

The route laid out here extends from Bandemer Park to Ypsilanti's Depot Town mainly because they are two strong destination points on the most clearly developed sections of the current trail. Ypsi's Depot Town offers a number of options for food and refreshment, and it's a historically interesting, well-restored small urban focal point in the region.

Start: Bandemer Park, Ann Arbor, for a ride to Depot Town in Ypsilanti

Length: 21.7 miles round-trip

Approximate riding time: 1.5–3 hours

Best bike: Road, hybrid, or cyclocross

Terrain and trail surface: Paved path, irregular surface occasionally, some roadways and city streets

Traffic and hazards: Major road crossings and some sections on moderately busy roadways. Pedestrians and Rollerbladers also use this path and it can get busy on the weekends with all the various users, especially in the Gallup Park area. Numerous driveway entries, busy road crossings.

Things to see: Long scenic stretches of the Huron River, particularly in Argo and Gallup Parks in Ann Arbor; the imposing University of Michigan Hospital perched on a hill; the St. Joseph Mercy Hospital; the edges of the Eastern Michigan University Campus; and historic Depot Town in Ypsilanti

Maps: B2B Trail: bordertoborder.intuitwebsites.com/Maps.html (the maps are getting somewhat out of date); *DeLorme: Michigan Atlas & Gazetteer*, pages 32, 33

Getting there by car: From M-14 at exit 4, descend to Whitmore Lake Road and take a left and an immediate right into the entrance to Bandemer Park. Cross the bridge over the Huron River and follow the road back to the parking area. GPS: N42 18.075 W83 44.715

THE RIDE

The path begins at Bandemer Park and dives into a densely tree-lined and curvilinear paved pathway alongside a popular disc golf course in the adjacent woods. It pops out on an open area often bustling with activity, as it's the home base for the Ann Arbor Rowing Club, the U-M Crew Team, and local high school crew teams. There's a BMX bike course tucked in on the left as well. Watch for pedestrians crossing to the docks at mile 0.4, sometimes with long sculls (not skulls, as that would be a different story altogether) on their shoulders.

Note: The B2B signage for this pathway is small and sometimes hard to distinguish from all the other signs and street furniture distracting your attention. Look for the small green signs not much larger than a paperback book scribed with B2B. There are other, larger trail markers about the height of an adult with maps and other information, but there are fewer of these. The small signs are what you'll depend on to keep on the pathway.

Follow the path east to where Argo Pond opens up on your left. On warm weekend days this is often bustling with crew teams, kayakers, and canoeists all enjoying the river. Continue to where it turns left over the Argo Dam. This is a narrow crossing. It is possible to ride across, but that depends on the activity at any given time, as it has anglers and walkers using it as well.

Once over, the path Ys, with the left-hand path leading to Argo Canoe Livery, a popular city-run boat rental and launch area. There's also a small, seasonal concession stand. You'll take the path to the right that extends along a newly developed series of rapids and small falls called the Argo Cascades. At the end of the cascades causeway, swing right, down a slope path that leads under the Broadway Bridges and onto a wooden section of the path. Keep in mind that wet wood is extremely slippery for bike tires, so proceed with care when wet. This is a short bridge that leads back onto a stretch of paved path along the riverside, known eponymously as Riverside Park.

The next section of the pathway connections can be confusing, so the following are detailed directions.

Take the path to Maiden Lane and turn right onto the sidewalk that leads over the bridge. On the other side, look for the small B2B sign that directs you left across Maiden Lane. Push the pedestrian crossing button for the signal, as this is a very active multilane crossing. Once across, ride down the north side of Fuller Road. Follow this downhill and past Fuller Park (and the pool) until you cross the river once more. Just beyond this is Cedar Bend Drive, where you'll turn right and cross Fuller Road. There's a pedestrian crossing button here as well that's very useful, as traffic can be both fast and busy.

Once over, turn left onto the pathway (with driveway crossings) and follow it uphill to the end of the parking lot on the right and take a right turn away from Fuller Road (mile 2.3). This leads along the edge of Mitchell Field, around a curve and over a small wooden bridge onto the Gallup Park section of the pathway. This is one of the most popular park paths in the city of Ann Arbor and the beginning of the original 1.5-mile path built in 1988. It was the culmination of years of planning and advocacy for bike paths in the region. The natural beauty and the views of the river are stunning from here to Geddes Dam just beyond the underpass at US 23. This, like the Argo area, is very popular on the weekends, with an assortment of walkers, runners, Rollerbladers, and other cyclists.

Beyond Gallup Park Drive (with a bridge crossing on the left), there are a number of options to explore other aspects of the park. But for now, keep going straight across the drive and along the path. Cross under the Huron Parkway bridge and continue to one of the picnic areas in the park at mile 4.1. This is often active with families and small children (and even geese on the path), so take it easy through here. Keep to the left and ride between the river and the railroad tracks. The views across the river are up a lush hill. Part of that greenery is the Concordia College campus. Pass under the US 23 bridge to Geddes Dam.

Take a left at Old Dixboro Road that crosses the dam, and climb the hill to the first right onto Dixboro Road. Take the path over the bridge to Huron River Drive. Here there's a double crossing of the roadway, first straight, then left. There are more pedestrian buttons here to aid with these busy roadway crossings. After the second crossing, take an immediate right (your only choice) and climb the pathway up the hill.

At mile 6.1 the pathway splits. You can go either straight or left. Going straight leads along the roadway until it comes to Mcauley Drive, at which point you'd take a left on the path. The preferred route is not to go straight and instead to take the left at the split. This leads along the top of the river bluff and away from traffic and driveway entrances. There is a lookout spot with a river/woodland view and benches at mile 6.4 if you take the preferred inner bluff path. Eventually the paths converge at mile 6.7, along Mcauley Drive.

Mcauley Drive is a large ring road around St. Joseph Mercy Hospital. The path follows the outside of this road with many driveway crossings along the way. This eventually swings back around to a crossing at Huron River Drive once more. You're now entering the Ypsilanti realm of your ride, and it changes dramatically with the strong presence of Eastern Michigan's sports complexes on the perimeter of the EMU campus. The largest of all is Rynearson Stadium, where the EMU football team plays.

Follow the pathway straight (south) across a series of driveway entrances until you reach the rail-trail bike path at mile 8.1. Turn left onto the path and enter a dense tree-lined section of the trail that's a major student connection between main campus and the recreation complexes.

At the first street crossing, Cornell Road, take a left and ride down to Huron River Drive once more. This section of the pathway is really less a bike path and more a sidewalk connection around campus. It's wide, but it currently has many poorly graded driveway crossings that are not conducive to a smoothly flowing bike route. Much of the route from this point until Frog Island Park at mile 10.5 are basically cut-throughs around campus that are both confusing and not overly bike friendly. Pay careful attention to the pathway signage and take care with pavement changes and traffic flow as you negotiate this area.

Turn right onto the pathway along the south side of the road and follow it past a series of roughly cut and sometimes busy campus driveways to Ann Street (mile 9.7). Take a right onto Ann and ride to St. John Street, where there's a short jog in the road. Stay on Ann until you reach Ford Avenue. Take a left onto Ford and follow it 2 blocks to Adams Street, where you go right. Take this a block over to Forest Avenue and go left. Cross Huron Street, then one last time over the Huron River to Market Place and go right. Frog Island Park is on your right. You've done it!

Just down the street on the left is the historic freight house (1878). Straight ahead to Cross Avenue puts you in the heart of Depot Town. The original Depot is gone, but the historic buildings from the mid- to late 1800s are still there, and the small commercial area exudes 19th-century charm. Across River Street is the Ypsilanti Automotive Heritage Museum housed in the last Hudson car dealership. The Food Co-op is just across the tracks to the south. There are other shops and restaurants to check out on Cross Street. Nearby Riverside Park, just across the river on the south side of Cross Street, is often active with events in the warm months. It will also get you right down alongside the river.

Trail sign

When you're ready, return past the freight house and north on Market Place. The return trip is basically a backtracking of the route you came down on, except for a short section at the beginning near the EMU campus. There are a series of one-way streets that require a route variation for a few blocks.

Take a left onto Forest Avenue and over the river to Huron Street. Turn right onto Huron Street and left a block up at Adams Street. Huron is a wide main road, often busy with traffic, so take precautions while crossing over for the left turn. Huron is a one-way street along here.

Go another block to Jenness Street and turn right. Take a left at St. Johns Street. Cross Lowell Street and continue on to Ann Street. At this point the ride returns to Ann Arbor along the same route that you came down on.

MILES AND DIRECTIONS

0.0 Begin in the Bandemer Park parking area. Head south on the bike path. Pass the staging area for the crew teams in the area, cross over Argo Dam, and ride past the Cascades.

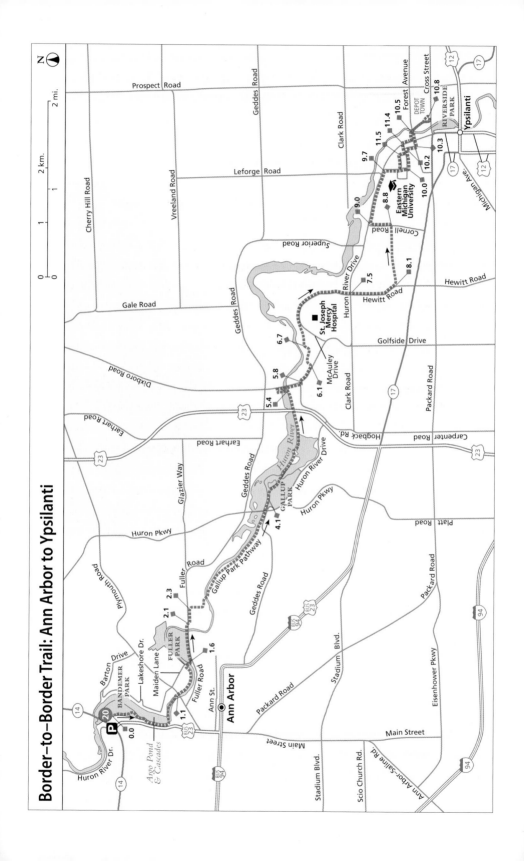

Border-to-Border Trail: Ann Arbor to Ypsilanti

1.1 After the Cascades, the path takes a sharp right rather than straight to Swift Street. Take that right and go under the Broadway Bridge, then through Riverside Park.

1.6 Turn right at Maiden Lane and cross the bridge over the Huron River.

1.7 Turn left at the signalized intersection. There are helpful pedestrian crossing signals here.

2.1 Cross Fuller Road at Cedar Bend Drive, then turn left on the other side of Fuller and pedal uphill.

2.3 Turn right onto the trail and follow it as it winds its way back over the Huron River, then on to Gallup Park. Continue straight on path, crossing Gallup Park Drive, under Huron Parkway.

4.1 Stay to the right through the play area and continue west under the US 23 overpass to Geddes Dam.

5.4 Turn left at the dam and cross the river.

5.5 Do a U-turn onto the pathway that crosses back over the Huron River.

5.8 Cross twice at Huron River Drive (straight first, then left), then climb the hill on the pathway.

6.1 Look for where the path goes left. Take the left (the path actually splits at this point and comes back together a short way ahead).

6.7 The path reunites. Continue west on the path adjacent to Mcauley Drive.

7.5 Cross Huron River Drive and continue straight (south) past the stadium complex.

8.1 Swing left onto the rail-trail pathway.

8.8 Turn left onto Cornell Road.

9.0 Turn right onto the path adjacent to Huron River Drive.

9.7 Turn right onto Ann Street.

10.0 Take Ann Street to where it Ts into Ford Avenue. Turn left onto Ford Avenue.

10.2 Turn right onto Adams Street.

10.3 Turn left onto Forest Avenue. Cross Huron Street, then take the bridge over the river.

10.5 Turn right onto the path at Market Place.

10.8 Turn left onto Cross Street in the heart of Depot Town. Circle the block and turn left into the parking lot, returning to Market Place and heading back up the street.

11.1 Turn left onto Forest Avenue and cross the bridge once more.

11.2 Turn right onto Huron Street.

11.4 Turn left onto Jarvis Street. Take care, as Huron Street can be busy at times.

11.5 Turn right onto Jenness Street, then left onto St. Johns Street.

11.7 Rejoin the route at St. Johns and Ann Streets and head back to Bandemer Park in Ann Arbor along the same way you came.

21.7 Arrive back at Bandemer Park.

RIDE INFORMATION

Local Events/Attractions
Both Ann Arbor and Ypsilanti have events nearly continuously on the weekends and even on weeknights during the warm summer months. See arborweb .com for their calendar of events listings.

Restaurants
Corner Brewery: This is a local brewpub with bar food. Very popular spot with locals; 720 Norris St., Ypsilanti, MI 48197; (734) 480-2739
Sidetrack Bar and Grill: Beer and burgers in a charming, popular setting alongside the tracks that will put you back 100 years; 56 E. Cross St., Ypsilanti, MI 48198; (734) 483-1035

Restrooms
Start/Finish: Bandemer Park
Mile 0.9: Argo Canoe Livery
Mile 1.9: Fuller Park
Mile 2.2: Mitchell Field
Mile 3.6: Gallup Park Canoe Livery

Clinton River Trail

In this world it doesn't hurt to be well-connected. Many people's careers take flight due to their acquaintance with a network of associates. Bike paths are no different. This path is an excellent example. It is a major spine to other path tributaries. It runs through some major suburban sections of metro Detroit, and many other paths either tie into it, they eventually will, or they come close enough to make the link on relatively short segments of roadway.

The tributaries, or maybe they could be called cousins, include the Paint Creek, Polly Ann, West Bloomfield, Stony Creek, and Macomb-Orchard Trails. Macomb-Orchard is actually just a northern continuation of the Clinton River Trail (they combine to form one long, nearly 36-mile bike path). If the West Bloomfield Trail ever cleanly connects to the southern end of the Clinton River Trail, that will add over 5 more miles. (Actually, it does, but there's a gap on the Clinton River Trail that's quite glaring. You need to do a long, nearly 4-mile, roundabout ride on some busy roads to tie into the last southern 1.5 miles or so. The southern section is actually more a part of the West Bloomfield Trail than the Clinton River Trail.)

It's the Clinton River Trail that has a connection to all of these, except the Polly Ann Trail. Plus, it runs alternatingly through both active commercial areas and quiet woodlands. Though it slips through a very busy metropolitan area, you often feel so removed from all the commercial activity that it's easy to forget that the urban world is a stone's throw away.

Not that the path is removed from activity. It's very active, especially on weekends, but also during weekday mornings, afternoons, and evenings. It temporarily removes these users from all the traffic and commerce and worldly activity that hums outside its linear spine.

Start: Park in the designated parking area on the east side of Opdyke Road, midway between South Boulevard and Auburn Avenue

Length: 9.3 miles one way

Approximate riding time: 1–2 hours

Best bike: Hybrid, cyclocross, mountain bike, road bike with wider tires

Terrain and trail surface: Basically it's cinder in Rochester, gravel to the Auburn Hills border, and rough asphalt within the limits of Auburn Hills. In the Rochester section the lead-ups to the intersections are smoothly paved.

Traffic and hazards: Many road crossings, all well marked, though vehicular traffic doesn't usually stop for trail traffic, nor do the vehicles readily acknowledge bikes. The section of pathway through Auburn Hills is asphalt, but it's rough—disconcertingly so—to ride on.

Things to see: The quiet, meandering Clinton River, marshes, I-75 overpass (really, it's an interesting place to watch the world pass by below you), pleasant downtowns, tree esplanades lining the pathway, pull-offs to view the river or with descriptive placards explaining local history

Maps: Friends of the Clinton River Trail website: www.clintonrivertrail. org; Michigan Trails & Greenways Alliance–Michigan Trails Finder: www.michigantrails.org/map/viewer.php; *DeLorme: Michigan Atlas & Gazetteer*, pages 41, 42

Getting there by car: From M-59 take exit 39 onto Opdyke Road headed south. Go 1 mile to the Clinton River Trail parking area on the left. GPS: N42 37.616 W83 14.929

THE RIDE

Head northeast from Opdyke Road. Though you're immediately sandwiched between two residential areas, the vegetation is lush on both sides and your immersion into the separate linear park world has begun. Within 0.5 mile, the path rises up on a highway overpass and you find yourself over a very noisy, very busy, very wide stretch of road. This is I-75: Miami, Florida, at one end, Sault Ste. Marie, Michigan, at the other. Give yourself a minute, bridge top center, to savor this one. Warm beaches or rustic north woods. Talk about a network for your imagination to travel through. Once that sinks in, roll down the path and on toward Auburn Hills.

This is the section of pathway that has been paved with a very rough layer of asphalt. The surface is uneven and it can throw you off balance if you're not paying attention.

The surroundings are a bit more urban light industrial for a short period, but still lined with trees. Cross Squirrel Road, then on to Grey Road, where the path takes a bit of a jog on the edge of downtown Auburn Hills. Keep an eye on the signs for guidance around Auburn Hills Village Center.

More than many towns in the region, this area integrates the old and the new and gives a strong sense of the dynamic changes that have taken place as Detroit has expanded into the metro region. Settled in the 1820s and going through many iterations before becoming Auburn Hills in the 1980s, its modern character predominates, but there's also a peppering of historic buildings here and there to keep the area tied to its roots.

The path crosses Auburn Road, the main street at mile 1.6, alongside Juniper Street. Take a right onto the pathway once you've crossed, then pedal less than 0.1 mile to where the path swings left across from Cherryland Street. This returns to the world of the greenway. Continue through a mix of mostly modern commercial, manufacturing, and housing districts to mile 2.6, where there's a small exhibit on the left side of the path that describes the period when mastodons roamed the area. There's even a simulated mastodon bone bench on which to rest your own weary bones.

Just ahead, at Leach Road, there's a restroom and parking area. There's also a map box, one of many dotted along the route, often well-stocked with

Cyclists on the Clinton River Trail

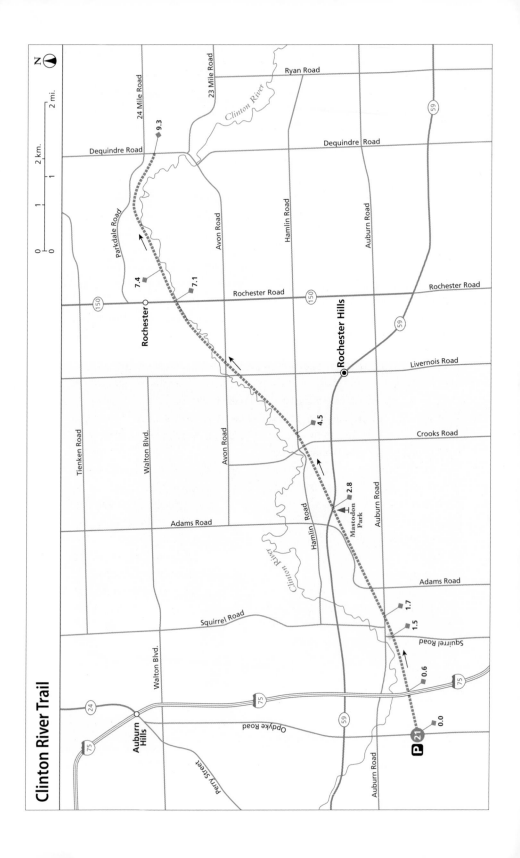

trail maps. On the east side of Leach Road the path splits into a Y. Stay to the right. Don't follow the path directly adjacent to Adams Road. Continue on to where the path goes under M-59, then past manufacturing and research facilities, which I know sounds less than appealing, but the surprise here is that the greenery along the path dominates the scene, not the surrounding land uses. And the path does find greener areas ahead as it passes Crooks and Hamlin Roads.

There's a bridge crossing a small stream at mile 5.0, which is a gateway into a part of the trail that gets reacquainted with the Clinton River. This is highlighted at mile 5.2 with a short detour on the left, implemented by the Rochester Rotary Club, that takes a swing into the woods on a narrow single-track trail that winds along the river's edge.

> ## Bike Shops
> **KLM Bike & Fitness:** 2680 Rochester Rd., Rochester Hills, MI 48307; (248) 299-0456; klmfitness.com
> **Rochester Bike Shop:** 426 Main St., Rochester, MI 48307; (248) 652-6376; www.rochesterbikeshop.com

Continue to Livernois Road, where there's another restroom on the east side of the road. The path takes a well-marked jog at Avon Road and passes over a wood bridge spanning the Clinton River at mile 6.2.

There's a large parking area at mile 7.0 between Diversion Street and the Rochester Road pathway underpass. There's also a nice pullover that descends to river level where you can take a break.

Cross another wood bridge at mile 7.4, and on the other side is the connection to the Paint Creek Trail on the left, headed north. You might notice trail use increases in this area, as it's in the heart of the city of Rochester. The Clinton River Trail continues east, passing a mostly forested riverine landscape on the right and residential areas on the left.

There's a small parking area with a bicycle self-fix-it station, including tire pump, at mile 7.7. The trail then enters into a tree-lined section, crosses a small bridge at mile 8.6, then a pond filled with bleached dead trees just beyond that to the left. The Clinton River Trail officially ends at Dequindre Road, but this is in name only. It continues on under a new moniker: the Macomb-Orchard Trail (also described in this book).

MILES AND DIRECTIONS

0.0 Park at the small lot on Opdyke Road. Head east on the path.

0.6 Cross over I-75 on the overpass.

1.5 The path cuts around the edge of downtown Auburn Hills.

1.7 Cross Auburn Road and take a sharp right, then a short way up, the path swings left, away from the road.

2.8 Restroom at Leach Road.

3.4 Go under M-59.

4.5 There's a jog in the path as it crosses Hamlin Road.

7.1 The path goes under Rochester's Main Street. There's a pull-off here for a break and to get close to the river.

7.4 Connection to the Paint Creek Trail.

7.7 There's a parking area with a fix-it station here.

9.3 Clinton River Trail ends and Macomb-Orchard Trail begins at Dequin-dre Road.

RIDE INFORMATION

Local Events/Attractions
Stony Creek Metropark is nearby. There is a bike path connection off the Macomb-Orchard Trail at 25 Mile Road.

Restaurants
Chomp: 200 S. Main St., Rochester, MI 48307; (248) 608-1054
Downtown Cafe: 606 N. Main St., Rochester, MI 48307; (248) 652-6680
Lipuma's Coney Island: 621 N. Main St., Rochester, MI 48307; (248) 652-9862

Restrooms
Mile 2.8: Along the trail at Leach and Livernois Roads

Hudson Mills Metropark

This short bike path is a very charming and varied pathway that is in the most westward park of the Huron-Clinton Metropark system. The Metroparks span a five-county stretch that basically rings the Detroit metropolitan area. Conceived in the early part of the 20th century, it expanded through the years through frugal land acquisition to comprise 13 parks beginning along Lake St. Clair to the north, then arcing around through Macomb, Oakland, Livingston, Washtenaw, and Wayne Counties, back to Lake Erie to the south.

There are plans in the works to connect the path in Hudson Mills Metropark to the town of Dexter to the south. Even without the connection, it's a pleasant way to enjoy the quiet rural open space along the Huron River. The loop on the east side of the river varies from a ride along open fields to a winding, majestic, tree-lined stretch alongside the river filled with maple, oak, and hickory trees. There are small wooden bridge crossings as well. The path then leads over the Huron River and on to the west side along a winding path following the river and through patches of rich marshland. (This is the section that is slated to continue on to Dexter.)

Hudson Mills is named for a sawmill built in 1827, followed by a gristmill in 1846. Some of the remnants of early mill activity are visible on the west bike path near the Huron River bridge crossing.

Start: Begin and end at the parking lot in the River Grove picnic area

Length: 6.5 miles

Approximate riding time: 1 loop takes about 0.5 hour

Best bike: Hybrid, road bike, mountain bike

Terrain and trail surface: Paved, well-maintained pathway with wooden surfaced bridges (slippery when wet)

Traffic and hazards: Occasional drive crossings; other bikers, hikers, dog walkers, Rollerbladers, and families strolling the area

Things to see: The Huron River, a tree-canopied pathway, open fields, marshlands, wildflowers, charming bridge crossings

Maps: Huron-Clinton Metroparks: www.metroparks.com; *DeLorme: Michigan Atlas & Gazetteer,* page 32

Getting there by car: From US 23 take exit 49 and head west on North Territorial Road. Continue 7.9 miles to the entry drive to the Metropark and turn left. Take the first right past the entry booth and park adjacent to the River Grove picnic area. All of the Metroparks require a daily or yearly pass. GPS: N42 22.989 W83 54.678

THE RIDE

Leave the River Grove picnic area heading west, down the hill on the bike path. Be aware that this can be a very popular place on warm weekends, and there are many pathway users: hikers, Rollerbladers, dog walkers, and so on. The Huron River and a small channel tributary appear straight ahead. This part of the trail is densely forested with a rich deciduous canopy that includes oak, hickory, and maple trees. In fall, the hickory trees are a brilliant yellow.

Cross the first wooden bridge, weave through a short section of forest that's basically on an island that's between two channels of the river, and cross the second bridge that leads to a long stretch of path that's nearly at river level. This is a popular launching area for canoes and kayaks, so keep your eyes out for these as they carve their way downstream.

The path draws close to the river at about mile 0.6 and gently curves along for another 0.5 mile until it begins to draw up and away from the river at mile 1.2. There's a long, easygoing rise until the trail starts to open up, with views looking down to the river on the right and over open fields on the left. Along the edges of the fields and through the forest is a popular disc golf course, and there will often be "golfers" with bags full of discs slung over their shoulders to tackle the challenges. The open fields to the left are also used as soccer fields. As with most Metroparks, there are many recreational activities taking place simultaneously.

Bike Shops

Aberdeen Bike & Outdoors: 1101 S. Main St., Chelsea, MI 48118; (734) 475-8203; aberdeenbike.com
Dexter Bike and Sport: 3173 Baker Rd., Dexter, MI 48130; (734) 426-5900; www.dexterbikeandsport.com

The river disappears from view on the right and is replaced by a picnic area with shelters and a restroom. There are five such areas within the park.

This segment of the pathway is wide open, with expansive views on all sides, and continues this way, for the most part, for the next mile. At mile 1.8

Dogwood spring flowers on the path along the river's edge

there's a path to the left that goes to the Activity Center. If you're looking for park information or something from the concession stand (seasonal), take a left. At mile 2.0 you'll cross the Activity Center/Park Office vehicle access drive.

Continue ahead and watch for grazing white-tailed deer in the fields, particularly in the early mornings and during twilight. Nearing the River Grove picnic area, take a right at mile 2.6, cross the road, and head north through a rolling section of path past the Rapids View picnic area. The trail splits at mile 2.9, with the left path going under the North Territorial Road bridge and the right path going across the bridge. Stay on the right path and cross over. The views downriver on the bridge are worth taking a few minutes to enjoy.

Once over the bridge look to the left for remnants of and information on the mill activity that took place during the early settlement of the area. The path then weaves south through a thickly forested area with periodic glimpses of the river off to the left. Watch also for fecund marshland with colorful marsh marigold, skunk cabbage, and various other wildflowers and native plants depending on the season.

The path comes to a turnaround at mile 4.5. Keep in mind that there are plans afoot to continue this path all the way to the village of Dexter, so the future may offer more adventure and greater connections to the area.

Return the way you came, crossing back over the Huron River and arriving at the T in the path at mile 6.5, where you turn right and find yourself back at the River Grove picnic area, with picnic tables, covered shelters, a restroom, and a good place to replenish after a good ride, with nice views through the trees and down the hill toward the river.

MILES AND DIRECTIONS

0.0 Leave the River Grove picnic area parking area and head west, down the bike path.

0.2 Cross the first bridge over the Huron River.

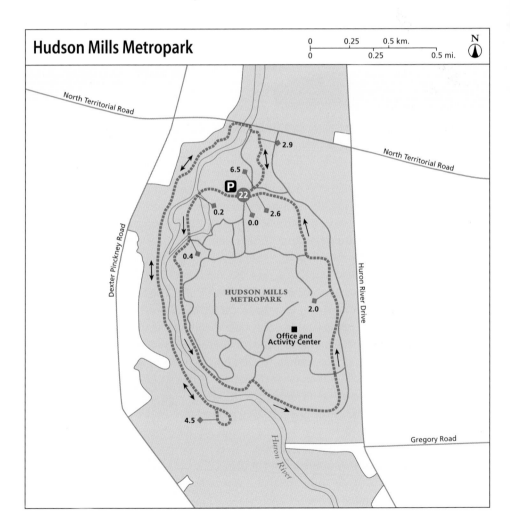

0.4 Cross the second bridge over the river. Follow the loop along the river then around to the other side of the park area.

2.0 Entrance drive to Park Office and Activities area.

2.6 Turn right, crossing the drive and heading off on the out-and-back sections of the pathway.

2.9 Stay to the right at the Y in the path and go over the bridge.

4.5 Loop around at the turnaround and return on the same path.

6.5 Turn right, cross the drive, and return to the start.

RIDE INFORMATION

Local Events/Attractions
Hudson Mills has events and activities year-round posted on their website, metroparks.com.

Restaurants
Concession stand open seasonally in the Activity Center. The village of Dexter is also nearby for more substantial fare.

Restrooms
In each of the five picnic areas

Huron Valley Rail Trail
and Lyon Oaks County Park Connector

This is part of a series of local, county, regional, and state trails that connect, or are slated to connect, into one another in this area. In this case the connections go well beyond this specified route: one deeper into Island Lake State Park, and another into Kensington Metropark and from there on to the town of Milford (all in this book). It's quite a web and offers a nice variety of riding options.

This path system leads out of South Lyon, eventually connecting to either Lyon Oaks County Park to the northeast or Island Lake State Park to the west.

Start: Volunteer Park south of South Lyon, accessed from Dixboro Road

Length: 10 miles, South Lyon to Island Lake State Park; 9.4 miles, South Lyon to Lyon Oaks County Park

Approximate riding time: 1–2 hours

Best bike: Road or hybrid bike

Terrain and trail surface: Paved bike path in mostly good condition throughout. It's mostly flat except for a hilly section along I-96 through an old landfill that's now a township park.

Traffic and hazards: Some roadway crossings, with those more heavily trafficked as you near Island Lake State Park.

Things to see: Numerous birds in lush marshlands, greenway parks along I-96, tree-lined tunnel-of-tree sections

Maps: Huron Valley Pathway: www.southlyonmi.org/1/223/rail_trail.asp; *DeLorme: Michigan Atlas & Gazetteer*, pages 33, 41

Getting there by car: From US 23 take exit 54 (southbound) or 54A (northbound) at 9 Mile Road. Head east on 9 Mile 4.8 miles and turn right onto Dixboro Road. Follow Dixboro for 0.4 mile and turn left into Volunteer Park. Follow the road back to the parking area. GPS: N42 26.514 W83 39.656

THE RIDE

Begin in Volunteer Park where there's plenty of parking. This section may not be known officially as part of the Huron Valley Trail. It's actually part of the South Lyon City Trails, but it's a good place to begin and it will take you nearly the full extent of the available pathway in the area. In the late 1800s, South Lyon was a busy railroad crossroads. Not all the railroads prospered through the years, leaving linear public open space winding through town, hence the prevalent bike path corridors. Our gain.

From the parking lot, roll down to the pathway running north-south along the full length of the east side of the park. Turn left. The trail does extend farther south, but only as far as 8 Mile Road, though the short wooded section is a pleasant short ride with a newly built bridge.

Head north and ride past a marsh area, cross 9 Mile and continue on through a tunnel-of-trees, in between residential neighborhoods and past more marsh until you reach a T in the trail at mile 1.1. Turn right (east). This runs between a wooded area on the right and the back of a long industrial building on the left. Cross McMunn Street and enter an open area that leads to McHattie Park on the right.

Once at Lafayette Street (also known as Pontiac Trail), there are a couple of options to connect to the beginning of the Huron Valley Trail a short way northeast. The most straightforward is to continue across Pontiac Trail and up Reynoldsweet. Cross Lake Street (10 Mile Road) and enter the pathway from there.

The other option, and the one mapped for our purposes, takes a left along Pontiac Trail until it reaches the downtown a few blocks north at Lake Street, then turns right onto Lake Street and goes east until reaching the entry to the official pathway. Either way works, but the ride into the heart of town offers a good sense of the town's interesting historical character. The commercial architecture is old and interesting, and the residences along Lake Street are well kept and historical as well. Keep in mind that mileage is calculated for the ride through downtown.

> ### Bike Shops
> **South Lyon Cycle:** 209 S. Lafayette St., South Lyon, MI 48178; (248) 437-0500; southlyoncycle.com
> **Town N Country Bikes:** 8160 Grand River Ave., Brighton, MI; (810) 227-4420; tncbikes.com

The entrance to the Huron Valley Rail Trail is marked by the large grain elevator on the north side of Lake Street, just beyond the still active CSX railroad tracks. Turn left, and you're on the trail. Lewis Hough, entrepreneur and creator of the Daisy BB gun company, was also the owner of this grain elevator in the late 1800s.

The pedestrian underpass that connects to Lyon Oaks County Park to the northeast

Though it passes out of a small commercial area and into neighborhoods on the outskirts of town, the ride north dives quickly into densely lined tree cover. As the trail arcs northeast, it passes along marshes teeming with birds, between subdivisions, and past small businesses, retaining its green, parklike atmosphere throughout. Be aware, however, that the road crossings can get busy at times with fast-moving traffic—in particular, Milford Road at mile 5.7 and Grand River Avenue at mile 6.2. The crossings all along the way are the reminders that this is a populous area. Otherwise, the trail is quite removed from all the busy activity.

The pathway splits at I-96 (mile 6.6), going west to Island Lake State Park and northeast to Lyon Oaks County Park.

To Island Lake State Park

The route to Island Lake parallels the highway or Grand River Avenue most of the way, with the buzz and hum of traffic along with the interesting juxtaposition of the pathway's unobstructed removal from that traffic (except, of course, for a few road crossings). You can feel smug and aloof as you ride along on a quiet pathway while those in their vehicles deal with all the pressures that busy roadway traffic presents.

After Milford Road (very busy because it's a highway interchange as well), the path goes through a fence and climbs a relatively steep grade as it skirts the edge of James F. Atchison Memorial Park. Mark this fence entry in your memory, as this one section of the trail routing is a bit confusing. You can't get far off if you miss it on the return, but it could be better marked.

Ride up the hill and look up and left across the open hill to see the sculptural cut-out of a man poised above. It's a piece by local sculptor John Sauve entitled *Mephisto,* a dramatic contrast on the bare hillside. The path rolls downhill for a short way until it takes a sharp left and climbs another steep grade, then evens out and drops back down to meet Grand River Avenue. Before crossing, it takes a sharp left and heads downhill alongside the avenue, passing a few subdivision entrances, until it reaches a busy interchange at mile 9.6. Take care crossing the series of signalized crossings. Once on the other side, the path enters into Island Lake State Park and meets up at a T, with the right leading to Kensington Metropark and the left heading farther into the Island Lake pathway network. There are picnic areas and restroom facilities within view and all along both routes.

To Lyon Oaks County Park

To continue northeast, pass under the recently constructed pedestrian underpass below I-96. The pathway passes into a tree-lined and partially wooded residential area. After Pontiac Trail (mile 7.0), the surroundings vary between commercial, residential, and vacant, untended open space. At Old Plank Road (mile 8.4) the path takes a sharp right (south), paralleling the roadway and crossing a series of driveways, then a small wood bridge as it climbs up to Pontiac Trail. Cross the signalized intersection and take a sharp left. Follow the path to the entrance to Lyon Oaks County Park at mile 9.4.

MILES AND DIRECTIONS

Huron Valley Trail

0.0 Leave the Volunteer Park parking area and roll down the connecting path to where it Ts into the main path. Turn left (north).

1.1 Turn right, heading east.

1.6 Turn left onto the walkway along Lafayette Street / Pontiac Trail. (There is the option to go straight and follow the path along Reynoldsweet, but that would mean missing charming and architecturally interesting downtown South Lyon.) The downside of going into town is crossing the numerous commercial curb cuts along Pontiac Trail.

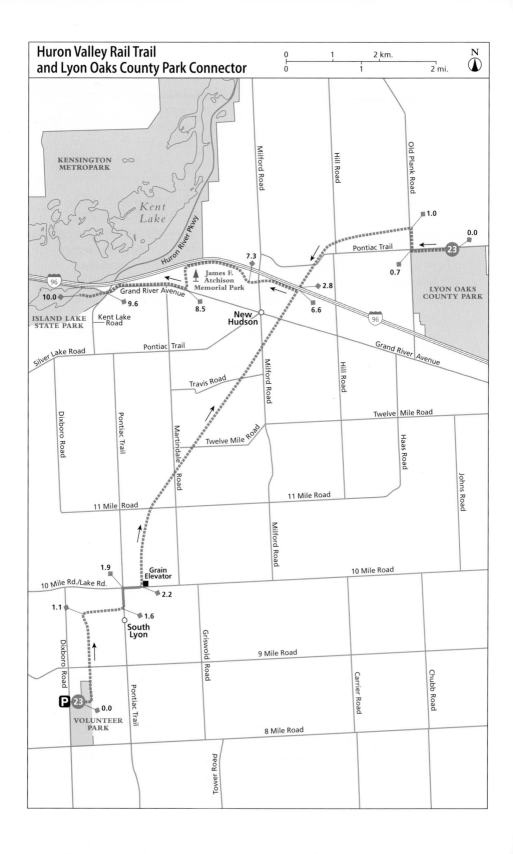

Huron Valley Rail Trail
and Lyon Oaks County Park Connector

0   1   2 km.

0   1   2 mi.

N

KENSINGTON
METROPARK

Kent
Lake

Milford Road

Hill Road

Old Plank Road

1.0

0.0

Pontiac Trail

0.7

23

Huron River Pkwy

7.3

96

James F.
Atchison
Memorial Park

2.8

LYON OAKS
COUNTY PARK

Grand River Avenue

8.5

6.6

ISLAND LAKE
STATE PARK

10.0

9.6

Kent Lake
Road

New
Hudson

96

Silver Lake Road

Pontiac Trail

Grand River Avenue

Dixboro Road

Pontiac Trail

Travis Road

Martindale Road

Milford Road

Twelve Mile Road

Hill Road

Haas Road

Johns Road

Twelve Mile Road

11 Mile Road

11 Mile Road

Milford Road

10 Mile Road

1.9

10 Mile Rd./Lake Rd.

Grain
Elevator

2.2

1.1

1.6

South
Lyon

Dixboro Road

Pontiac Trail

Griswold Road

9 Mile Road

Carrier Road

Chubb Road

P 23

0.0

VOLUNTEER
PARK

Tower Road

8 Mile Road

1.9 Turn right onto Lake Street / 10 Mile Road.

2.2 Immediately past the railroad tracks is the bike path. Turn left onto the path.

6.6 At the split in the path, going straight takes you to Lyon Oaks County Park; left takes you to Island Lake State Park. Turn left to get to Island Lake.

7.3 The path passes through a cyclone fence entrance onto a section of the path that also serves as a maintenance road for the adjoining park. Turn right, heading uphill, after passing through the fence.

8.5 Turn right, paralleling Grand River Avenue heading west.

9.6 Cross the signalized intersection at Kent Lake Road, then again over Grand River Avenue onto the path leading into Island Lake State Park.

10.0 Path intersects with the main path leading through Island Lake State Park as well as connecting to Kensington Metropark under the highway to the north.

Lyon Oaks Connector (beginning at Lyon Oaks)

0.0 Leave Lyon Oaks County Park and turn left (west) on the path.

0.7 Cross Pontiac Trail right, heading north.

1.0 Turn left, crossing Old Plank Road.

2.8 Go under the I-96 overpass and connect to the Huron Valley Trail.

RIDE INFORMATION

Local Events/Attractions

South Lyon is a sweet small town with numerous restored historic buildings in its downtown and surrounding neighborhoods. It's worth taking the time to wander through.

Restrooms

Start/Finish: Porta-johns at Volunteer Park; regular facilities at Island Lake State Park and at Lyon Oaks County Park.

I-275 Metro Trail

The I-275 Metro Trail is an interesting trek along a trail that, in concept, sounds the opposite of ideal. Who wants to ride along a major interstate highway? We ride to get away from traffic, not embrace it, right? But there's much more to this well-cared-for path than highway noise (though that is part of this experience). As you get used to the constant flow of the adjacent interstate, it eventually filters in and out of your ride awareness and other interesting things enter. The highway just becomes one part of a widely varied scene. And yes, it's a great place for a bike ride.

This, like so many other bike paths in the region, is one of those that keeps nudging its tendrils this way, then that, continuing to expand its reach into neigh-borhoods, along parklands, into the heart of commerce. There's even an active group known as Friends of the I-275 Metro Trail (i-275.michigantrails.org) that posts updates on any changes taking place along the trail (construction along the trail or at highway crossings, possible expansions, and so on). Any time you have trail groupies as adamant as these, you have a trail worth checking out.

The current north extent of the Metro Trail ends alongside a large inter-change at I-96, with plans for further expansion north over time, but for now it ends at Meadowbrook Road in an office complex area. At the south end, there are plans shown that extend the path to Willow Road with the intent of connecting it to the Metroparks in that area. As of this writing, the section below I-94 exists, but it's in such poor shape due to age that it's not recommended for use. Stay tuned for updates, as that may change over time.

Part of the trail jumps onto the Hines Drive bike path for a few miles. From 8 Mile down to Hines is a ride along an early section of the Metro Trail that hasn't been updated for a while. The pathway is narrower than that south of Hines Drive and a bit rough in spots due to age. It's still in reasonably good shape, though. South of Hines nearly all of the trail is new pavement. It's smooth, with plenty of space for passing.

The big surprise is the number of verdant marshes, the pleasant wooden bridges, the woodlands, occasional dramatic changes in elevation, and the chance to see wildlife in numerous places along the way. In all the hustle and bustle there's a sense of peacefulness as you pedal along. If there's a traffic tie-up on the highway, you can just keep pedaling and let that smile on your face grow wider.

Start: 8 Mile Road in the commuter parking area of the Meijer's parking lot

Length: 43 miles out and back

Approximate riding time: 2.5–4 hours

Best bike: Hybrid or road bike

Terrain and trail surface: Paved bike path. It can be rough in a few places where the asphalt needs to be repaved, but it's mostly in very good shape.

Traffic and hazards: Numerous signalized crossings on highly busy roads

Things to see: There's something joyous, perhaps drivers would call it smug, about taking a relaxing bike ride along an extremely busy highway. But there are also diversions that veer away from the highway into well-planted, tree-lined stretches, bridge crossings over marshlands and wildlife, and even a dramatic drop in the terrain that goes well below the highway. There's also a section that goes around a major landfill, now mostly covered and capped, though there are still large trucks and earthmovers high up on the hill moving about.

Maps: Friends of the I-275 Metro Trail: Route information is thorough, though it may be out-of-date (or optimistic) about completed sections; i-275.michigantrails.org; *DeLorme: Michigan Atlas & Gazetteer,* page 33

Getting there by car: From I-275 take exit 167 at 8 Mile Road and head west. Go 0.1 mile across Haggerty Road and turn left into the first entry drive into the Northridge Grove Shopping Center. There's a designated park-and-ride parking area at the north end of the lot. GPS: N42 26.258 W83 26.242

THE RIDE

Begin at 8 Mile Road in the large parking lot of the Northridge Grove Shopping Center, cross wide and busy Haggerty Road at the signalized crossing, then head south, parallel to I-275 along its western edge. From here to M-14 the path crosses three of the mile roads, 7, 6, and 5, in that order. 7 and 6 Mile are at signalized intersections; 5 Mile is an underpass. The surface crossings are busy, as this is a highly populated and active commercial and residential area, but they also have crossing islands and pedestrian signals. Note that there are small Metro Trail signs indicating where you are and how far it is to a select location.

Along with the ever-present highway on the left, the scenery is a mix of office parks, commercial buildings, large parking lots, open grassy areas, and residential subdivisions tucked up to the pathway edge. The path, though narrow by current standards, is still plenty wide for passing riders and pedestrians.

Up to 5 Mile the path has taken a steady, gentle descent. After going under 5 Mile, this changes to a steady ascent (mile 3.5) as the path arcs to the west, leaving the flank of I-275 and instead nestling alongside M-14. With the drama of a major highway interchange playing out to the left, the path climbs through a relatively narrow gap between the highway and an expansive residential area. At mile 5.3 the path descends once more at a rapid rate, passing under Northville Road, over Hines Drive, and dropping down a ramp at mile 5.8 to arrive alongside Hines Drive, which the path will share for the next 3 miles. Keep looping to the right until you cross below M-14, heading southeast along the Hines Drive Pathway.

At mile 6.4, with Wilcox Lake off to the left, the path crosses Northville Road, then crosses to the other side of Hines Drive. Hines Drive, another route in this book, is a scenic and highly popular park in the region. It's actually a series of linked parks that run alongside the Rouge River between Northville and Dearborn. On this route, you get two paths for the price of one.

Follow the path as it winds its way past a series of parks and signalized roadway crossings, until reuniting with I-275 at mile 8.7. Cross under the highway. Watch for the I-275 Metro Trail turn, as it takes a right (mile 8.9) while the Hines Drive Pathway continues straight. Turn right onto the Metro Trail (south) and begin the ascent out of the river valley on a winding tree-lined climb. I-275 is now on the right.

Cross Ann Arbor Trail on a slight jog in the path. The pathway has been recently upgraded for a good part of the ride from here south, with one or two short exceptions. It's wide and smooth. It passes alongside residential areas, transitioning to office parks and commercial districts here and there. There are a mix of surface crossings and pathway underpasses as well. The path also dips into small wooded areas as it takes momentary weaves away from the highway.

At mile 12.4, the pathway takes a bigger jog than usual in order to cross at Ford Road. It swings east to Lotz Road, crosses at the intersection, returns west to the interchange, and swings back south. There's a bike shop in the commercial area at the Lotz Road intersection.

There are large swaths of greenspace in this segment of the pathway. The recent landscape improvements have made for a nice parklike atmosphere. At mile 14.7 there's the opportunity to access the highway rest area if needed.

24

Between Palmer Road and Michigan Avenue, the path runs adjacent to a golf course and crosses a couple of recently constructed bridges. At mile 16.0 the Lower Rouge Trail connects to the Metro Trail. The Lower Rouge path runs west, under the highway and into a popular park/greenlink at the south edge of Canton. This path is mostly cinder and worth the detour if you have time. It goes to Canton Center Road, about 2.5 miles west. If you're spotting cars in order to do a one-way ride (i.e., you have two cars, each parked at opposite ends of your ride), there is a parking area in the Morton-Taylor park area, off Michigan Avenue on Morton-Taylor Road (N42 16.841 W83 28.126). There's even an easy-intermediate mountain bike trail in there if you'd like to mix up your ride.

The next section is one of the most unique along the Metro Trail. Past Michigan Avenue, the path descends to a wooden bridge that spans a heavily vegetated marsh, then returns to asphalt and rises steeply up and over a railroad, first going well below highway level and then directly adjacent to it, with traffic flying by on the other side of the guardrail separation. It's quite dramatic. Roll back down to Van Born Road. Directly to the southeast is a sizable landfill property. Cross the road and immediately turn right, going under I-275 once more. Once on the west side of the highway, turn left and head south once more.

Follow the path past a series of large warehouse businesses to Ecorse Road. Continue past more businesses to Tyler Road. Once past this, the path dives deep into a forest at mile 19.9. This is one of the pleasant surprises along this very urban and varied path. For a short way you feel like you're in a forest up north. Just as quickly you're back along the highway with, of all things, a sizable farm on the right. The trail takes a large arc to head west once again

Bike Shops

D & D Bicycles and Hockey: 121 N. Center St., Northville, MI 48167; (248) 347-1511; ddbicyclesandhockey.com

REI Northville: 17559 Haggerty Rd. (Haggerty and 6 Mile Rd.), Northville, MI 48168; (248) 347-2100

Sweet Bikes: 39904 Ford Rd., Canton, MI 48187; (248) 403-8049; www.sweetbikesonline.com

Town and Country Bikes and Boards: 148 N. Center, Northville, MI 48167; (248) 349-7140; townandcountrybikeandboards.com

Trails Edge Cyclery: 232 N. Main St., Plymouth, MI 48170; (734) 420-1200; trails-edge.com

Two Wheel Tango–Specialized Store: 6111 Canton Center Rd., Canton, MI 48187; (734) 335-7322; twowheeltango.com

I-275 Metro Trail biker

and join your third highway of the day, I-94. You're headed toward Chicago, but unfortunately, the path won't get you there. It basically ends at Hannan Road, mile 21.5.

There are plans to continue south, but the path beyond this point is in extremely poor condition for the most part. It was built many years ago and needs a major upgrade. Hannan and I-94 offer nothing in terms of amenities, so the path ends without fanfare.

MILES AND DIRECTIONS

0.0 Leave the parking area and cross the signalized intersection at Haggerty Road. Continue along the path paralleling 8 Mile Road until it curves south along I-275.

4.2 The path swings away from I-275 and heads west, paralleling M-14.

5.8 Turn right and descend the ramp to Hines Drive. Continue turning right in order to head below M-14 and south on Hines.

8.9 After passing under the I-275 overpass, turn right and head south up the hill.

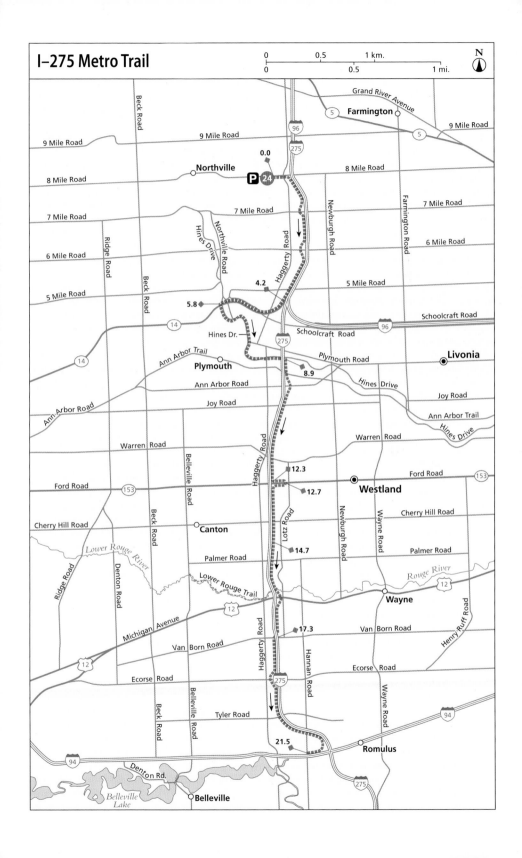

12.3 The path takes a long jog east due to the interchange.

12.7 Cross Ford Road right at the signalized intersection of Lotz and Ford Roads. Once across Ford, turn right again and the path goes west, then swings south along I-275.

14.7 This is a highway rest area accessible from the path.

17.3 Cross Van Born Road and immediately take a right on the other side of the road. Ride under the highway overpass, and a short way beyond take a left onto the bike path along the west side of the highway.

21.5 The improved path ends at Hannan Road. There is a right-of-way that continues south, but it is in poor condition. There are plans to improve this section all the way to Willow Metropark, but they haven't been implemented as of this writing.

43.0 Retrace pathway/return to trailhead.

RIDE INFORMATION

Local Events/Attractions

Since this is a highly populated area in metro Detroit there are restaurants and shops of all kinds, a major shopping mall in Novi, and an IKEA in Canton. The charming villages of Plymouth and Northville are nearby along this route.

The I-275 Metro Trail also connects directly—and even shares part of its pathway—with Hines Drive, one of the most popular linear park areas to bike in the state.

Near Michigan Avenue the Metro Trail also connects with the Lower Rouge Trail, a relatively short but pleasant cinder path ride through the woods along the Lower Rouge River.

Restrooms

Mile 6.5: Wilcox Lake
Mile 7.2: Gunsolly Mills
Mile 7.7: Plymouth Riverside Park
Mile 8.1: Haggerty West
Mile 14.7: I-275 Rest Area

25

Island Lake–Kensington–Milford

This ride passes through many jurisdictions: a state park, regional Metropark, township park, city park, and a pleasant village. That's a lot to experience in one ride. The parklands are some of the most popular in the region and for good reason. They offer many recreational opportunities within a beautiful green setting. Cycling is one great way to experience that, especially along these well-developed paths.

The connection to downtown Milford is an extra perk, as it's a pleasant place to take a break halfway through the ride. Except for the short stretch of sometimes busy roadway entering and leaving Milford, the ride is car-free the whole way. There are a number of well-marked crossings and the topography rolls up and down much of the way, but not to the point where it feels like a mountain stage at the Tour. And there are pleasant views nearly everywhere, whether it's into a woodland or out over a wide lake expanse. Some sections are out and back, but the return will offer a new perspective in the other direction.

Start: Park in the Riverbend parking area off Kent Lake Beach Road

Length: 28.4 miles

Approximate riding time: 2–4 hours

Best bike: Road or hybrid

Terrain and trail surface: Paved path and some roadways

Traffic and hazards: Some busy park and urban crossings. Active pedestrian areas and some mountain bike crossings in the parks. A stretch of road leading into downtown Milford has little shoulder space and it can get busy with traffic. Main Street in Milford is active, with traffic, parked cars, and pedestrian crossings.

Things to see: Wildlife, mature forests, wide-open fields, lakes, wetlands, areas of solitude and vibrant activity, rolling terrain, and an active and charming village

Maps: Kensington Metroparks: www.metroparks.com; Island Lake Recreation Area: www.michigandnr.com/parksandtrails/Details. aspx?type=SPRK&id=462; Huron-Clinton Metroparks Guide: free at all Metropark offices; an excellent map of the entire Southeast Michigan region; *DeLorme: Michigan Atlas & Gazetteer*, pages 40, 41

Getting there by car: From I-96 take exit 151 and head south on Kensington Road 0.5 mile to the Island Lake State Park entrance. Pass the entrance booth and take the first right onto Kent Lake Beach Road. Follow this 1.4 miles to the Riverbend parking area on the right. All State Parks and Recreation Areas require a daily or yearly Recreation Passport. All Huron-Clinton Metroparks require a daily or yearly pass. GPS: N42 30.284 W83 42.549

THE RIDE

Leave the Riverbend parking area and immediately head uphill on the bike path. Though the Huron River is not in view, the path basically parallels its course, though far above it. The first 0.5 mile is basically uphill. It then levels off. Watch for mountain bikers shooting out of the woods as they maneuver the trails that crisscross the bike path and dive back into the surrounding woods. Island Lake is a very popular park for all kinds of activities, but both the path and the mountain bike trail are especially so.

The path levels off for a while, still carving its way between a thick forest landscape, then parallels Kent Lake Beach Road for a short way before crossing the canoe access road. It drops through another stretch of woodland before emerging into a vast open field. Look for hawks in the updrafts overhead. Cross the paved road at mile 2.3, ride through a small tunnel under Kensington Road, and meander along rolling fields of sumac mounds and past small woodland thickets to another road crossing at the picnic grounds on Kent Lake at mile 3.1. This is the most active part of the park with kids and families crossing from the parking area to the popular beach. Ride with care and soak up the energy, then rise on a short climb up to the long plateau of grassy picnic areas with long views above the eastern edge of Kent Lake.

The pathway Ys at mile 4.2, with the right heading out to the Huron Valley Rail Trail and the left dropping below I-96 and into Kensington Metropark. Head to the left for a grand entrance into Kensington. Ride under I-96 and rise up to the Kensington loop pathway to mile 4.3. The view to the north is Kent Lake, one of the largest inland lakes in the region, created by damming the Huron River. The dramatic glacial landscape and forestland of Kensington has proven a popular success with opportunities for all kinds of activities, including birding, fishing, boating, picnicking, hiking, and cycling.

Kensington is the second largest Metropark in the system, only 100 acres smaller than the largest, Stony Creek. The Metropark system itself was devised in the 1930s to preserve parkland for recreational use in the metro area. It was originally intended to be connected with a parkway drive following the Huron and Clinton River corridors as a large ring around Detroit. The grand scheme proved too costly as land prices rose, but the basic concept still prevails. There are still plans to connect the parks with a bike path system, slowly expanding its network throughout the region.

Go right on the pathway that leads to a wood bridge, then on a winding paved path that passes picnic areas and through woodland transitions. There's even a water slide at Martindale Beach if you're so inclined. If not, ride to mile 7.7 where Huron River Parkway merges with Buno Road, and before the path begins its slow arc across the river and back around the lake.

Bike Shops

D & D Bicycles and Hockey: 9977 E. Grand River Ave., Brighton, MI 48116; (810) 227-5070; ddbicyclesandhockey.com
Hometown Bicycles: 10605 Grand River Rd., Brighton, MI 48116; (810) 225-2441; myhometownbicycles.wordpress.com
Town N Country Bikes: 8160 Grand River Ave., Brighton, MI 48116; (810) 227-4420; tncbikes.com
Trails Edge Cyclery: 525 N. Main St., Suite 180, Milford, MI 48381; (248) 714-9355; trails-edge.com

Take a right onto the extension path that heads northeast toward Milford.

Pass Windfall Bay on the left, and notice the nesting platform used by osprey. Watch for swallows, kingfishers, egrets, herons, and other wildfowl. At the right time of day you might even catch sight of a coyote, red fox, or muskrat. The rolling path leaves the official north car entrance to the park, but the park itself continues on for the cyclist where it passes through marshlands, along open fields, and under tall canopies of oak-hickory woodlands. As always, the Huron River is not far off, but it is out of sight along this section. At the Y in the path at mile 8.8 stay to the left.

Cross General Motors Road at mile 10.5. Turn right and follow General Motors Road (so named for the 4,000-acre GM Proving Ground 3.0 miles west, the original GM test facility built in 1924).

Follow alongside the road to the Hubbell Pond Park Trail on the left at mile 11.2. This passes over the Ford Dam (two car company names in one ride!) and wends its way between the Milford Trail, a popular twisting, 5-mile mountain bike trail in the surrounding woods. Watch for cyclists popping out of the woods to cross to other sections of the trail.

These are active multiuse paths.

At mile 12.6 the trail crosses Family Drive with the Milford YMCA on the left. Take a right onto Family Drive and pedal up to Commerce Street. Turn right onto the pathway adjoining Commerce. At the next street up, Peters Street, the path ends. Merge onto Commerce and ride this narrow shouldered section of roadway a few blocks up, under the railroad viaduct, and climb from there to Main Street at mile 13.3. This is the heart of Milford, with many places to shop and eat.

Return on the same route, but at the Buno Road/Huron River Parkway connection (mile 19.1), take a right to continue over the Huron River and loop around the west side of Kent Lake in Kensington Metropark. There's a spur to the right that will take you to the Farm Center. The park office is just beyond that. Ride a long downhill to a view across a marshy section of Kent Lake, then begin a stiff climb up to a large area of playfields. Cross the access road and follow the high ridgeline as it swings down and around to Maple Beach. From here the shaded path rolls up and down past mature canopy trees, crossing various lake area access roads, and pulling alongside, then away from the lake on the left. The Nature Center is at mile 22.8 across the park loop road.

The lake reappears in view with some wide panoramas at mile 23.3, where the path skirts the edge for the rest of the way within the Metropark. At mile 23.9 the path swings sharply left adjacent to I-96, then crosses a wooden bridge. At the end of the bridge is the return access at mile 24.1 that goes under the highway to Island Lake State Park. Take that right and drop down, then up a

long, relatively steep grade into Island Lake. Return along this same path to where you began in the Riverbend picnic area alongside the Huron River.

MILES AND DIRECTIONS

0.0 Leave the Riverbend parking area on the bike path headed north.

3.1 Cross Kent Lake Beach Road, ride around the edge of the parking lot, and climb the hill to the top of the ridge. Continue to the Y in the path.

4.2 The path to the right connects to the Huron Valley Trail, eventually leading to South Lyon. The path to the left crosses under I-96 and enters into Kensington Metropark. Take a left toward Kensington.

Island Lake–Kensington–Milford

4.3 Turn right onto the Kensington Metropark bike path. Follow along the eastside shoreline of Kent Lake past a series of picnic/activity areas.

7.7 Turn right onto the Milford Connector heading toward the village of Milford. Pass the entrance to Kensington Metropark.

8.8 At the Y, stay to the left on the pathway.

10.5 Cross General Motors Road and turn right onto the path.

11.2 Turn left onto the Hubbell Pond Park Trail.

12.6 Turn right at YMCA Drive.

12.9 Turn right onto the pathway adjoining Commerce Street and merge onto the Street a block up at Peters Road.

13.3 Turn right onto Main Street in downtown Milford. After checking out Milford, backtrack along the same route to the turnoff at Kensington Metropark.

19.1 Turn right, back onto the loop pathway around Kensington. Follow the path past the activity areas all the way back to the turnoff that returns under I-96.

24.1 Turn right onto the path connection that returns to Island Lake State Park. Go under the highway and reemerge on the path you rode out on. Backtrack along the same route through the State Park.

28.4 Arrive back at Riverbend parking area.

RIDE INFORMATION

Local Events/Attractions
See listing of Metropark events at metroparks.com and at State Parks and Recreation Areas at www.michigan.gov/dnr.

Restaurants
The Burger Joint: 312 N. Main St., Milford, MI 48381; (248) 685-9263
Gravity Bar & Grill: 340 N. Main St., Milford, MI 48381; (248) 684-4223
Le Rendez Vous: 239 N. Main St., Milford Township, MI 48381; (248) 714-6222

Restrooms
At most picnic areas in Island Lake State Park and Kensington Metropark

26

Lakelands Trail

Lakelands could almost be considered two trails in one. From Hamburg to Pinckney it's mostly paved, and when not, it's a smooth and pleasant ride on hard-packed dirt or cinder. This is the most popular section and it's a canopy-covered wooded lane with an occasional bridge over a marsh or river and a few openings for variety.

Cross M-36 just west of Pinckney, however, and the path becomes rough, loose, chopped-up cinder, dirt, and gravel. It's currently rather tough going mile after mile. That shouldn't deter you, as the countryside in this area is filled with scenic farms and pleasant woodlands and marshes, but it is good to be aware that this section is more challenging than your typical rail-trail. West of Gregory the path improves slightly and the rural character is peaceful and farmlands are majestic.

The entire route is basically flat, but if anybody asks, it actually climbs over 100 feet from Hamburg to Stockbridge. It takes 20 miles to do that, so you won't notice it.

Start: Park in the small parking lot on the east side of Hamburg Road at the south edge of downtown Hamburg

Length: Hamburg to Stockbridge (entire route): 20.3 miles one way; Hamburg to Pinckney (Pearl Street): 7.6 miles one way

Approximate riding time: 2–3 hours one way

Best bike: Cross or hybrid bike to Pinckney, adding the option of a mountain bike west of M-36 in Pinckney

Terrain and trail surface: Paved, cinder, hard-packed two-track dirt between Hamburg and Pinckney; loose, rough, chopped-up cinder/gravel west of M-36 on the west end of Pinckney to Gregory; hardpack and occasional loose cinder from Gregory to Stockbridge.

Traffic and hazards: Occasional driveways and a few major road crossings. Pedestrians share the pathway. Equestrian use is relatively heavy between Pinckney and Gregory.

Things to see: Woodlands, scenic farms, marshlands, the Huron River, bridge crossings, the small towns of Hamburg, Pinckney, Gregory, and Stockbridge. There are moments of total immersion in tunnels of trees, then openings out over broad farm fields.

Maps: *DeLorme: Michigan Atlas & Gazetteer,* pages 31, 32

Getting there by car: From US 23 take exit 53 and head west on 8 Mile Road. Follow the main road for 3.0 miles as it becomes Hall Road, Sheldon Road, and finally, Hamburg Road, now heading north. Turn right into the Lakelands Trail parking area. Park in the lot along the pathway directly to the south of the village of Hamburg on Hamburg Road. GPS: N42 26.854 W83 48.074

THE RIDE

Leave Hamburg and head west along the paved path through a dense tree cover. The trail opens into field and marshland in about 0.5 mile and reenters the forest after crossing Merrill Road. It comes to a long wooden bridge at mile 1.7 that crosses the Huron River. This is a great spot to see wildlife up or downriver.

A short way after this the trail emerges from the forest into a large open marsh area. There's a pedestrian bridge on the right at mile 2.0 that ventures into the marsh for those who want to explore that further. Once past Pettys Road, M-36 is visible on the right. The trail takes a jog over an active rail line at mile 2.4. For a short way, the trail parallels M-36 through a commercial area and past Zukey Lake Tavern, then back to a tree-lined pathway that soon straddles a marsh.

At this point you're on the outskirts of Pinckney, with houses becoming more prevalent. At mile 4.3 the trail ducks under M-36 through a small tunnel specially designed for the Lakelands Trail. From here through Pinckney the trail cuts between the backyards of Pinckney residential neighborhoods. After crossing Peaceful Valley Road. the pathway becomes a dirt road. At Pearl Street (mile 7.5) there's a semi-restored train

Bike Shops

D & D Bicycles and Hockey: 9977 E. Grand River Ave., Brighton, MI 48116; (810) 227-5070; ddbicyclesandhockey.com
Hometown Bicycles: 10605 Grand River Rd., Brighton, MI 48116; (810) 225-2441; myhometownbicycles.wordpress.com
Town N Country Bikes: 8160 Grand River Ave., Brighton, MI 48116; (810) 227-4420; tncbikes.com

Kids pedaling on the Lakelands Trail

depot, a small parking area, and public toilets. The path returns to cinder at this point.

After this, the path enters into a dense tree cover until coming to the M-36 road crossing. Once past the roadway (which is a busy highway, so take care when crossing) the trail surface gets much looser and harder to navigate. It's more of a horse trail than a bike path from here to Gregory, though the surroundings are less urban and quietly bucolic and worth the effort if you're up for it. From here to the next M-36 crossing at mile 12.4, it crosses a series of small streams and bridges, and passes through a mix of farm and marshland.

The village of Gregory appears at mile 15.0. There's a long series of buildings on the left just before Gregory Road that includes a party store/gas station and there's a grocery 0.5 block south, within view, so there are plenty of opportunities for replenishing supplies. There's a park on the west side of Gregory Road adjacent to the trail to rest and relax if needed.

Continue west into another heavily wooded section of the trail. The trail quality improves somewhat, and this is really one of the most beautiful segments of the ride. It immediately dives into an almost cathedral-like setting

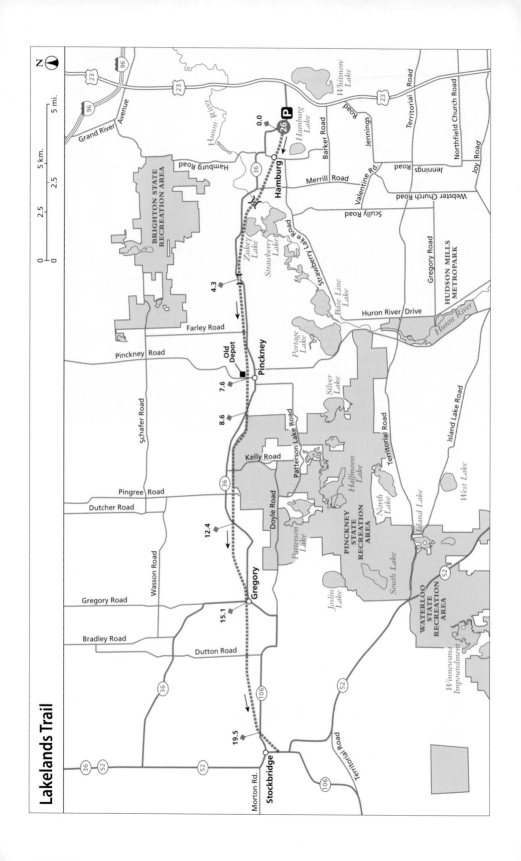

Lakelands Trail

N

5 mi.

5 km.

BRIGHTON STATE RECREATION AREA

Grand River Avenue

Huron River

Hamburg Road

Hamburg Lake

Whitmore Lake

Barker Road

Jennings Road

Territorial Road

Northfield Church Road

Joy Road

26 P

0.0

Hamburg

Merrill Road

Valentine Rd.

Jennings Road

Webster Church Road

Scully Road

Gregory Road

HUDSON MILLS METROPARK

Zukey Lake

Strawberry Lake

Strawberry Lake Road

Base Line Lake

Huron River Drive

Huron River

4.3

Farley Road

Pinckney Road

Pinckney

Old Depot

Portage Lake

7.6

8.6

Silver Lake

Schafer Road

Kelly Road

Patterson Lake Road

Halfmoon Lake

Territorial Road

Island Lake Road

West Lake

Pingree Road

Dutcher Road

36

Doyle Road

Patterson Lake

PINCKNEY STATE RECREATION AREA

North Lake

Island Lake

Wasson Road

12.4

South Lake

52

WATERLOO STATE RECREATION AREA

Gregory Road

Gregory

15.1

Joslin Lake

Bradley Road

Dutton Road

Winnewana Impoundment

36

52

106

106

52

Territorial Road

52

19.5

Morton Rd.

Stockbridge

36

52

52

106

with tall trees and embankments rising up along the path. The trail from this point to the outskirts of Stockbridge is a continual line of trees along a combination of dense forest, marshland, and vast, actively tended field crops interspersed along the way.

The trail slips in behind the back of Stockbridge and ends in a parking area on M-52 just south of downtown. There are plans for it to continue on down to the city of Jackson, but for now this is the end of the line.

MILES AND DIRECTIONS

0.0 Cross Hamburg Road from the parking lot heading west.

2.4 There's a jog in the path here that crosses an actively used railroad track. Cross with care.

4.3 Go through the tunnel underneath M-36 and continue on into Pinckney.

7.6 There's a porta-potty here at the old depot just past Pearl Street.

8.6 Cross M-36 with care. Traffic moves fast and is heavy at times. Beyond this point, the trail is heavily used by equestrians, and it's quite chewed up and often difficult to ride a bike through. The surface is both rough and loose, sometimes relentlessly so.

12.4 Cross back over M-36, again with care.

15.1 Cross M-36/Main Street in the village of Gregory. There's a small park on the left if you want to take a break. There's also a grocery and a party store nearby for snacks.

19.5 Cross Morton Road, a main route out of town, so watch for traffic.

20.3 The path ends in a parking lot along M-52 just to the south of downtown Stockbridge.

RIDE INFORMATION

Restaurants
Zukey Lake Tavern: 5011 Girard Dr., Pinckney, MI 48169; (810) 231-1441

Restrooms (in season)
Mile 7.6: Pearl Street at the old depot, Pinckney
Mile 15.1: In the Gregory city park on the west side of M-36 adjacent to the trail

Lower Huron–Willow–Oakwoods Metroparks

Three Metroparks, one ride. If you haven't discovered the regional Metropark system yet, you're in for a treat. This line of three parks in particular is a major asset to cyclists. The pathway runs diagonally, following the course of the Huron River, from near Belleville to the north almost to Flat Rock to the south. It cuts under I-275 and connects to what is currently an old and unimproved section of the I-275 Metro Trail, though there are plans in the works to put this back into riding condition.

What's best is that this is a beautiful bike path. It winds and weaves its way through fields and forests, and the views over the river are often breathtaking.

Start: Park in the North Fishing Site parking lot in the Lower Huron Metropark

Length: 23.6 miles round-trip

Approximate riding time: 2–3 hours

Best bike: Hybrid, road bike

Terrain and trail surface: Asphalt bike path in good condition throughout

Traffic and hazards: The path is used by cyclists, pedestrians, dog walkers, and Rollerbladers. It can get busy on warm weekends. There are numerous roadway crossings, mostly drive entrances to park areas, but also some busy roads.

Things to see: Three well-maintained Metroparks on a pathway that generally follows along or near the Huron River. There are marsh areas, oak-hickory forests, fields, and views along the river.

Maps: Huron Clinton Metroparks: www.metroparks.com; *DeLorme: Michigan Atlas & Gazetteer*, page 33

Getting there by car: From I-94 at exit 192, head south on Haggerty Road. In 0.6 mile Haggerty crosses Huron River Drive and becomes South Metro Parkway, the entrance to Lower Huron Metropark. Continue 1.1 miles to the North Fishing Site parking area on the right. A daily or yearly Metropark pass is required for entry into the Metropark. GPS: N42 11.962 W83 25.561

THE RIDE

Pedal forth along the path heading southwest from the North Fishing Site parking area in the Lower Huron Metropark. The river is right beside you. Take note of how well cared for the park is. This has been a consistent experience of mine since moving to the area nearly 30 years ago. There's a lot of pride in these Metroparks.

The path basically parallels the roadway through Lower Huron. Traffic speeds on the road are low enough, and the path gently eases near and away from it, that its presence is minimally felt. Overall, the entire path is flat to gently rolling, with barely 50 feet of elevation change, at most, the whole route. Variety on this ride comes through the way the path weaves in and out of small groups of trees, nips along the edge of the river, then away to another type of landscape, or crosses the river on a nicely crafted wood-and-steel bridge. The theme is water, wildlife, trees, and fields, a nice combination in a busy, built-up part of the world.

One of those bridges comes early on, at mile 0.9, just past the Walnut Grove campground. Following this, there are a series of entry drive crossings along open activity areas, with the Park Office down the road to the right at mile 2.0.

The path then dives into a long, tree-lined section that occasionally opens into short clearings, then dives back into the trees. It crosses the park road at mile 3.5, then crosses Waltz Road and exits Lower Huron Metropark in a 3.2-mile transition area, known generically as the Hike-Bike Trail Connector, heading to Willow Metropark. (You might be able to plant a flag and declare it your own country. Inbetweenia?) It actually just feels and looks like a part of the Metropark system, which it is.

After riding through an expansive open area, the path swings left to avoid dumping riders into the river and to climb a short rise to reach Huron River Drive, where it takes a sharp right across a set of railroad tracks (mile 4.3). The railroad tracks have an intricate zigzag crossing as a precaution, as this is still active with train traffic. After crossing, there's a small, well-kept cemetery on the right with a description of early settlement in the area.

The path follows alongside the river until it reaches the pathway underpass at I-275. There is a connection to the I-275 Metro Trail here, but currently this segment of the Metro Trail is old and in need of upgrading. (There is a separate description of the current I-275 Metro Trail in Ride 24.) There are plans to improve the Metro Trail and thus add a more extensive pathway network.

Go under the interstate and immediately cross a bridge over the Huron River into Willow Metropark. This segment of the trail is quite a lush and beautiful natural area. It soon crosses a wooden boardwalk over a marsh area, then climbs to a perch that overlooks the river. Though just beyond the interstate, it feels pleasantly removed, quiet, and natural in character.

The path winds through a forest and pops out on a mown open area, arriving at a T in the pathway at mile 6.7. Straight ahead is the bike rental building. Unless you've been pretending to pedal up to this point, you're good, but it's nice to know where these places are.

Turn left (you'll come from the other segment of path on the return trip). This part of the path keeps hugging the river off to the left. There's a mid-loop connector at mile 7.9 that crosses to a concession stand in the Activity Center. Go right if food cravings dominate. Go straight to continue the ride.

There's a pathway crossroads at mile 8.5. Stay left to continue to Oakwoods Metropark, as the right turn will loop you back into Willow. Cross Willow Road and enter Oakwoods. The path first follows a hedgerow, then takes a jog left into the midst of a long open field area. This is also, as of this writing, the least maintained part of these three Metroparks. Not that it's in poor shape, but the path could use some freshening up. Otherwise, it's the most open of the three parks, where you can envision the farmlands that once covered this area. The river is out of sight on the other side of the park to the northwest.

Bike Shops

Rentals at the **Boat & Bike Rental Center** in Willow Metropark (GPS: N42 07.873 W83 22.410)

At mile 11.3 or so, there's a reconstructed native plant prairie across the roadway to the north. The pathway comes to a large parking area. Stay to the right and you'll ride from the open landscape into a dense stand of trees, finally arriving at the farthest extent of the route, the Nature Center. Continue around to the back of the Nature Center to an observation deck that looks out over the Huron River.

Once this panorama is absorbed, along with a stop in the Nature Center to pick up some information about the natural areas you've been riding through, head back up the pathway the way you came. It's all the same except for the loop in Willow Metropark, where, just after crossing Willow Road, you'll return to the pathway crossroads. Stay to the left. This will take you through a rather densely wooded section of Willow, in contrast to the riverine segment on the way down. The access point to the Activity Center concession stand is at mile 16.4, to the right. Otherwise, continue to the pathway crossroads near the bike rental building at mile 17.0 and stay to the left. This puts you on the return path to Lower Huron Metropark.

MILES AND DIRECTIONS

0.0   Leave the parking area and head south on the paved multiuse path.

3.5   Cross the main road through the park, the Metropolitan Parkway.

3.7   Cross Waltz Road.

Steel pedestrian bridge over the Huron River

4.3 Cross the railroad tracks.

5.6 Cross under I-275 into Willow Metropark.

6.8 Turn left onto the pathway and follow along the river.

8.5 Stay to the left and cross over Willow Road into Oakwoods Metropark.

11.8 Arrive at Oakwoods Nature Center. For a great view of the Huron River walk your bike behind the Nature Center to the viewing platform.

Return Route Variation through Willow Metropark

0.0 Leave Oakwoods Nature Center on the same pathway, ride back through Oakwoods, and cross Willow Road.

3.3 Turn left and follow the path through the woods on the west side of Willow Metropark.

5.2 Turn left and return to Lower Huron Metropark on the same path you came in on.

RIDE INFORMATION

Local Events/Attractions
Visit the Metroparks website for current listings; www.metroparks.com

Restaurant
Activity Center concessions in Willow Metropark

Restrooms
These are plentifully placed all along the path route.

Macomb-Orchard Trail

To ride the Macomb-Orchard Trail is an adventure. It's a long day out if you ride the entire route out and back. But it's also a study in transitions from the relatively open, suburban pathway south of Romeo to the series of tree tunnels north of that, spreading into open farm country with wide-ranging farm fields all around as it arcs through Armada on down to the active and charming town of Richmond.

The Macomb-Orchard Trail is really just an extension of the Clinton River Trail. In fact, the ride begins on what is officially the Clinton River Trail in Rochester due to the easily accessible parking area. Once across Dequindre Road, the Macomb-Orchard Trail begins. It's also connected to the Stony Creek Metropark Trail at Shelby Road and 25 Mile.

The corridor was once an active railway known as the Michigan Air Line Railway. It went through a phase of ownership by Canadian National Railway, but over time the trains were not a lucrative form of transport on this route and it went into disuse. The rail lines that once carried the resources to play a primary role in the early settlement of the region were no longer viable. But the corridor, and others like it, have been a boon for recreational opportunities. It's only been a short time, since the turn of this century, that a dedicated group formed to turn the abandoned railway into a rail-trail.

Start: Begin in the public parking area off 2nd Street/Letica Drive in Rochester. There's a fix-it station with a tire pump alongside the trail at this location for any minor repairs necessary.

Length: 26 miles one way

Approximate riding time: 2–4 hours

Best bike: Road or hybrid

Terrain and trail surface: Paved or cinder path

Traffic and hazards: Road crossings, some busy

Things to see: Wetlands, wildfowl, tunnel-of-tree sections, forests, expansive farm fields, small towns

Maps: Friends of the Macomb-Orchard Trail: www.orchardtrail.org; *DeLorme: Michigan Atlas & Gazetteer,* pages 42, 43

Getting there by car: From M-59 take exit 46 and head north on Rochester Road for 3.4 miles. Turn right onto 2nd Street and follow this for 0.6 mile to the Clinton River Trail public parking area on the right. GPS: N42 40.801 W83 07.339

THE RIDE

Leave the parking lot heading east on the well-packed cinder path. Note that at the 0.4 mile mark there's a trail that goes to the right off the path. This is a connection over the Clinton River to the Bloomer Park mountain bike trail. Also in Bloomer Park is the only velodrome in the region. So, if you're interested in adding a few trails to your ride, or a couple laps around the velodrome, this is your opportunity. Or perhaps another day.

Pass the large pond on the left (keep an eye out for herons and egrets) and arrive at the official beginning of the Macomb-Orchard Trail across Dequindre Road. I met a woman one day alongside the pond as I was taking photos. She wasn't sure where she was. I soon determined that she'd ridden out of Stony Creek Metropark on the connecting path. It was a beautiful day and she was having the time of her life, thrilled that there was so much to explore.

The Clinton River heads south, but the path heads north and east through a heavily populated suburban area. Still, the path itself is lined with a good greenbelt of trees, shrubs, and wildflowers. Cross 24 Mile Road (this begins a series of mile road crossings). At 25 Mile Road there's a double crossing of the signalized intersection, across 25 Mile and Shelby Road. This is also where Macomb-Orchard connects to Stony Creek Metropark, north up Shelby Road. There's another double crossing at 26 Mile and Mound Roads.

Approaching West Road there's a series of rough-hewn yet picturesque old buildings on the left that house the Washington Elevator fertilizer company. Across West Road is a parking area, benches, information kiosk, and restroom. Note, there are information kiosks strategically placed all along the route to keep you apprised of your whereabouts.

At mile 5.6 the path follows alongside Van Dyke Road, then begins to pull away from it after crossing Van Dyke and 29 Mile Roads at mile 7.1. The path begins to open up at this point, beginning the transition to farm fields as it breaks slowly away from the more developed suburban areas.

Past 31 Mile it begins to enter the realm of Romeo. Thirty-two Mile, going west from the path, will take you into the heart of downtown, with a view of a well-preserved village with buildings dating back before the Civil War. The Victorian residential areas surrounding downtown are also worth a detour.

The road arcs right, over M-53, on a large pedestrian overpass. It drops down the other side for a change of character, slipping through the first tunnel-of-trees. It then crosses a small bridge over a stream, and the path opens up once more for a short stretch. The ride now is primarily through countryside and farmland, as it reaches Powell Road. Just beyond is a good bridge over a branch of the Clinton River, a nice place to pause and watch the water pass beneath and scan the area for wildlife. At mile 14.4 is the second tunnel-of-trees section.

Bike Shops

Hamilton Bicycles & Outfitters: 69329 Main St., Richmond, MI 48062; (586) 727-5140; hamiltonbikes.com

KLM Bike & Fitness: 2680 Rochester Rd., Rochester Hills, MI 48307; (248) 299-0456; klmfitness.com

Main Street Bicycles: 5987 26 Mile Rd., Washington, MI 48094; (586) 677-7755; mainstreetbicycles.com

RBS Rochester Bike Shop: 426 S. Main St., Rochester, MI 48307; (248) 652-6376; rochesterbikeshop.com

Stoney Creek Bike: 58235 Van Dyke Rd., Washington, MI 48094; (586) 781-4451; stoneycreekbike.com

The path crosses Romeo Plank Road, passes a small parking area, then crosses 33 Mile Road and dives back into the trees. You're basically riding along one extremely long hedgerow, as fields, hedgerows, and farmsteads are the character of the surrounding area filtering through your views from the trail. At mile 16.4 there's a large bridge crossing over Coon Creek that offers another good opportunity for a break and possible views of wildlife.

Though the trail has passed through some beautiful tunnel-of-tree sections, none compare with that at mile 17.2 just west of Armada Ridge Road. Most of the trees are red maples and they're beautiful and unique, most dramatic in the fall, but their form alone, en masse, is amazing any time of year.

At mile 19.0, the path reaches the small village of Armada and begins its arc from heading northeast to turning southeast. The village was the home of sportscaster Dick Enberg during his high school years. If anyone reading this is a bike rider (long shot, I know), Enberg was the first radio announcer of the Little 500, the Indiana bicycle race that gained fame through the film *Breaking Away*.

The ride from this point to Richmond is along a continuing esplanade of trees passing through a mix of dense forests, over bridge-covered streams,

Rollerblader on the Macomb-Orchard Trail

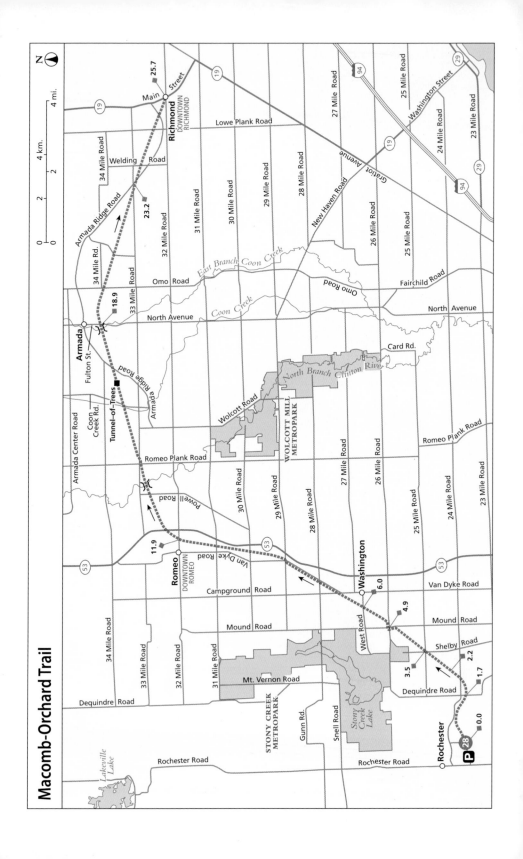

Macomb-Orchard Trail

and across open farm fields viewed through the lines of tree trunks all along the way. Considering that the ride began in a heavily populated suburban area, the change is quite stunning.

Only as you near Richmond do you notice the fields replaced by back-yards that look through nicely kept historic residential areas. The path ends near Main Street at a small plaza with a covered gazebo and a restroom. Ride into town for a short detour into Michigan small-town history, as Richmond, like Romeo, shows pride in its past with a nicely restored downtown and pleasant surrounding neighborhoods. Check out the clock at the corner of Main and Park Streets. It's been in this spot since 1924.

MILES AND DIRECTIONS

0.0 Head east onto the Clinton River Trail.

1.7 Cross Dequindre Road and begin on the Macomb-Orchard Trail.

2.2 Restroom.

3.5 Access to Stony Creek Metropark.

4.9 Cross 26 Mile Road, then Mound Road and a short way ahead swing left onto the path.

6.0 Restroom, parking, and information kiosk.

11.9 Downtown Romeo, left.

18.9 Downtown Armada, left.

23.2 Restroom.

26.0 Restroom. Downtown Richmond, left on Main.

RIDE INFORMATION

Local Events/Attractions
Romeo Peach Festival over Labor Day weekend
City of Richmond's Good Old Day Festival, the weekend after Labor Day

Restrooms
Mile 2.2: Beyond Dequindre Road, nearing 24 Mile Road
Mile 6.0: West Road
Mile 23.2: Armada Ridge Road
Mile 25.7: Richmond

Paint Creek Trail

Paint Creek Trail is one of those many bike paths that Oakland County is so good at supporting. Like most of the trails, it's actually part of a connected system that could have you riding for weeks. It directly connects to the Clinton River Trail to the south (which, in turn, connects to the Macomb-Orchard Trail to the northeast and the West Bloomfield Trail to the southwest). Paint Creek Trail is also not far from the Polly Ann Trail to the north. But wait, there are more. They may not all connect yet, but there's a move afoot (awheel?) to keep connecting these trails until you'll be able to wander the state trail by trail. That's a bike outing.

If you only have an hour or two to take a ride, the Paint Creek Trail is a great choice. Its crushed limestone surface is firm and the 8-foot width is good for riding two abreast and/or passing hikers or other riders. It's also a flat ride and great for kids and families.

There are two bike fix-it stations located along the trail. One is in Rochester Municipal Park and the other is at Gallagher Road in the Paint Creek Cider Mill (mile 3.8). This includes a tire pump and basic repair tools.

There are numerous parking areas all along the way with restroom facilities at some of them. Note also that there are a couple of ways that the path mileage is marked. The diamond-shaped signs with the D before the number indicate the mileage from the center of Detroit to that point. There are other rectangular mile markers as well at each gate, road crossing, and bridge that measure the distance from Rochester.

Horses are allowed on the trail north of Dutton to Lake Orion, a 7-mile stretch.

Start: Rochester Municipal Complex, on Pine Street off West University Drive

Length: 8.9 miles one way

Approximate riding time: 1 hour one way

Best bike: Road bike, hybrid

Terrain and trail surface: Cinder trail

Traffic and hazards: Periodic road crossings. Some can be busy.

Things to see: Marshes, forests, cider mill, streams, painted rock area

Maps: Paint Creek Trail: www.paintcreektrail.org (with links and maps to other trails in the area); www.destinationoakland.com/parksandtrails/trailsoakroutes/pages/default.aspx; *DeLorme: Michigan Atlas & Gazetteer,* page 42

Getting there by car: From M-59 take exit 46 and head north on Rochester Road for 3.6 miles. Turn left onto University Drive and go 0.1 mile to Pine Street. Turn right onto Pine and follow it back into the Rochester Municipal Complex parking lot. GPS: N42 41.034 W83 08.200

THE RIDE

From the Rochester Municipal Complex parking lot, cross the bridge over Paint Creek and take a right onto the path adjacent to the playground. Paint Creek Trail is straight ahead. At the T take a left (a right will take you to the Clinton River Trail in about 0.8 mile).

This route, connecting Rochester to Lake Orion and passing through an area of reasonably high population, feels removed from the urban activity with its lush, parklike character all along the way. There's obvious pride in supporting this trail by the attention made toward maintaining it.

Along the way you'll find numerous small bridges as the Paint Creek zigzags its way back and forth across the path. The path can be very active on weekends, but there are still opportunities to see deer, heron, egret, and other wildlife, particularly in and around the marsh areas.

The 16-acre Dinosaur Hill Nature Preserve is at mile 0.8 on the right. It's land that was set aside by the community for education, and it's a family-friendly place to get in tune with the outdoors. It's a bonus to be integrated with the pathway.

At mile 3.8 there's the Paint Creek Cider Mill, where you can fill your tires (at the fix-it station) or fill your stomach. It offers food as well as cider. Across Gallagher

Bike Shops

KLM Bike & Fitness: 2680 Rochester Rd., Rochester Hills, MI 48307; (248) 299-0456; klmfitness.com
Paint Creek Bicycles: 27 E. Flint St., Lake Orion, MI 48362; (248) 693-9620; paintcreekbicycles.com
Rochester Bike Shop: 426 Main St., Rochester, MI 48307; (248) 652-6376; www.rochesterbikeshop.com

Cyclists out on a cool day along the Paint Creek Trail

Road is a sculpture titled *On Prairie*, in the form of a bur oak leaf with grasses, recognizing the native plants in the region.

At mile 4.6 you'll pass under Gunn Road through a stout and scenic railroad trestle, a reminder of the original purpose of this old rail corridor.

A good way to get the pulse rate up is to put an Archery Club warning sign along the path. That happens just after you cross Adams Road at mile 6.1. Keep moving and you'll be rewarded with a quiet, vernal section of the trail a short way ahead with the creek flowing right alongside you.

For a literal interpretation of painting along the creek, there's a graffiti display on a short walk down a side path to the left at mile 7.6. It's quite a dramatic and colorful display in this natural setting.

The trail ends, rather unceremoniously, along a commercial strip a few blocks south of downtown Lake Orion.

MILES AND DIRECTIONS

0.0 Leave the Municipal Complex parking lot, cross the bridge over Paint Creek, stay right past the play area. Turn left onto the Paint Creek Trail.

3.8 Paint Creek Cider Mill with a bike fix-it station.

7.5 Connection to Bald Mountain South mountain bike trail.

8.9 Trail ends at the southern edge of the village of Lake Orion.

Best Bike Rides Detroit and Ann Arbor

RIDE INFORMATION

Restaurants
Chomp: 200 S. Main St., Rochester, MI 48307; (248) 608-1054
Downtown Cafe: 606 N. Main St., Rochester, MI 48307; (248) 652-6680
Lipuma's Coney Island: 621 N. Main St., Rochester, MI 48307; (248) 652-9862

Restrooms
Start/Finish: Rochester Municipal Park and Rochester Police Department
Mile 1.1: Tienken Road parking lot/trailhead
Mile 3.8: Paint Creek Cider Mill Building, Gallagher and Orion Roads
Mile 7.5: Clarkston/Kern Roads in Orion Township

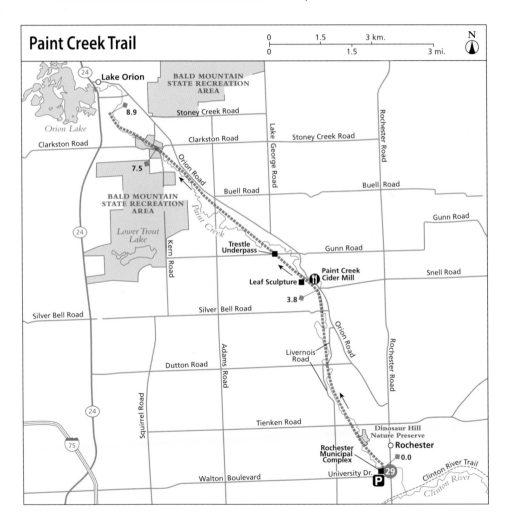

Paint Creek Trail

Polly Ann Trail

The rail line that is now the Polly Ann Trail was beset with either misfortune or mismanagement throughout its existence, but we can't complain. It's now a very enjoyable and varied rail-trail that weaves its way through the woods, neighborhoods, and fields of Oakland County, past numerous marshes and lakes, the quaint town of Oxford, and the small village of Leonard, and dips its toe into Lapeer County.

Built in the railroad frenzy of the 1880s, it carved a route from Pontiac to Caseville on the shores of Saginaw Bay. This ride focuses on part of that route, staying mostly within the bounds of Oakland County, from Civic Center Park in Orion Township to the small town of Leonard near the county border, then a few miles farther. The trail does continue well beyond that point, but 1.5 miles past Leonard is the Lapeer County line and the trail turns to dirt from there on. For the adventurous it's well worth the ride for a while, but it gets shaggier the farther you go, eventually coming to eroded ditches, bridges in disrepair, and untended pathway. If we're fortunate, one day the bike path may connect along its entire route, but for now this is a nice ride, offering a taste of wild adventure without the aggravation.

In Oakland County the path is well taken care of and either paved or cinder, with only a short stretch of dirt single-track in Lapeer County. At 18.4 miles one-way or double that out and back, it will make for a grand day out.

And where does the name Polly Ann come from? It was once called the Pontiac, Oxford & Northern railway, or PO&N, coined as Polly Ann (with some linguistic sleight-of-tongue).

Start: Begin in Civic Center Park off Joslyn Road

Length: 18.4 miles one way, 36.8 miles round-trip

Approximate riding time: 1.5–2 hours one way; 3–4 hours round-trip

Best bike: Road, hybrid, or cyclocross

Terrain and trail surface: Paved, hard-packed cinder, and a short section of dirt

Traffic and hazards: Numerous road crossings, some busy

Things to see: Rural greenery, marshes, small lakes, tunnels of trees, small towns

Maps: Polly Ann Trail: www.pollyanntrailway.org; *DeLorme: Michigan Atlas & Gazetteer,* pages 41, 42

Getting there by car: From I-75 take exit 83 (northbound) or 83A (southbound) and head north on Joslyn Road for 2.9 miles to Civic Center Park on the right. GPS: N42 44.560 W83 16.907

THE RIDE

In a general sense, the path is relatively open and exposed to the sun south of Oxford, and it begins to fill in with arched canopies of trees as you make your way north. There are exceptions here and there, but keep in mind that there's more shade in the northern sections of this ride.

Ride behind the Orion Township Building as you leave Civic Center Park and take a right onto Greenshield Road. Within 0.1 mile is the entrance to the Polly Ann Trail. Turn left (north). Check the marsh on your left for wildlife. An egret or heron and perhaps a chorus of croaking frogs are definite possibilities here.

You'll pass through a short section of wooded pathway, but nearing Clarkston Road the housing developments begin. There's still plenty of greenery, though. Cross the bridge at Square Lake, worth stopping at momentarily to absorb the view. After this, the path takes a jog around a golf course. This is one of the only awkward detours on the entire route. Depending on your comfort level, either take the pathway or Joslyn Road to the right and follow Joslyn Road at the next left. Hop on the narrow, wooded pathway at the next left on Indianwood Road and ride it for 0.3 mile to the crossing to the right.

Bike Shops

Main Street Bicycles: 5987 26 Mile Rd., Washington, MI 48094; (586) 677-7755; mainstreetbicycles.com
Paint Creek Bicycles: 27 E. Flint St., Lake Orion, MI 48362; (248) 693-9620; paintcreekbicycles.com
Stoney Creek Bike: 58235 Van Dyke Rd., Washington, MI 48094; (586) 781-4451; stoneycreekbike.com

Riding along a flower-lined section of the Polly Ann Trail

A short way farther you'll pass under a stout railroad trestle and back out into the open. From here to Oxford the path passes among a mix of forest-edged ponds, marshes, and residential areas. At Burdick Street there's the option to take a 0.4-mile detour into downtown Oxford.

Though its commercial district is only 2 blocks long, and the main street is rather wide, downtown, with its charming, well-tended brick buildings, retains much of its character from a century ago. There are also numerous places to grab a bite to eat.

Back on the trail, after passing Burdick Street, the path comes to Pleasant Street, where it rises up significantly on a large pedestrian overpass. It also offers good views of downtown Oxford at the top.

Up to this point, the path has been asphalt pavement, but after exiting off the bridge, the path turns to cinder. From here the route passes through the northern outskirts of Oxford, some residential, some vacant untended land, and a peninsula that divides two lakes. After leaving this area, however, it takes a small swing to the left, then the right, and dives into a long stretch of forested pathway. The rural character of the pathway now comes to the fore, with tunnels-of-trees and verdant marshlands. The cinder track becomes grass-laden down the median in places, with a canopied shade much more predominant. The cinder is hard-packed and well maintained, so the riding is still very pleasant.

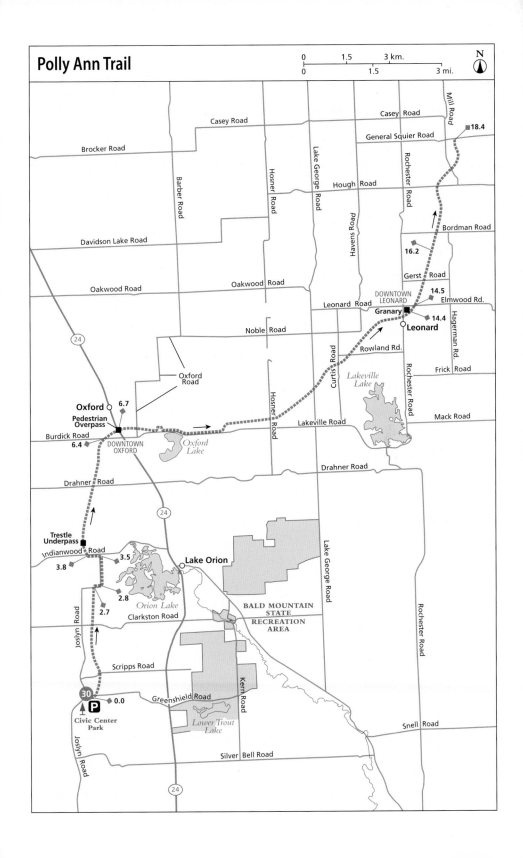

Polly Ann Trail

0   1.5   3 km.

0   1.5   3 mi.

N

Casey Road

Brocker Road

Casey Road

General Squier Road

18.4

Barber Road

Hosner Road

Lake George Road

Hough Road

Rochester Road

Mill Road

Davidson Lake Road

Bordman Road

16.2

Oakwood Road

Oakwood Road

Havens Road

Gerst Road

14.5

DOWNTOWN
LEONARD

Leonard Road

Granary

Elmwood Rd.

14.4

Leonard

Hagerman Rd.

24

Noble Road

Rowland Rd.

Frick Road

Oxford
Road

Curtis Road

Lakeville
Lake

Oxford ○ 6.7

Hosner Road

Rochester Road

Pedestrian
Overpass

Burdick Road
6.4

DOWNTOWN
OXFORD

Oxford
Lake

Lakeville Road

Mack Road

Drahner Road

Drahner Road

24

Trestle
Underpass

Indianwood Road   3.5

3.8

2.8

Joslyn Road

2.7

Lake Orion

Orion Lake

Clarkston Road

BALD MOUNTAIN
STATE
RECREATION
AREA

Lake George Road

Rochester Road

Scripps Road

Kern Road

30

P

0.0

Greenshield Road

Civic Center
Park

Lower Trout
Lake

Snell Road

Joslyn Road

Silver Bell Road

24

You can't miss Leonard with its historic old granary alongside the path at Elmwood Avenue. Leonard's downtown is a couple of blocks to the left with small markets for refreshment.

The trail passes beyond Leonard, 1.7 miles to the Lapeer County line at Bordman Road, where it transitions from cinder path to dirt single-track. The path continues for a couple more miles through some beautiful dense woodland to General Squier Road, where it rises steeply up to meet the road. This is the end of the designated route and perhaps an odd place to finish up, but there is something peaceful and beautiful about this spot, as well as the quiet path cutting through the forest that led here. It's such a unique experience that it's worth the addendum.

MILES AND DIRECTIONS

0.0 Leave north end of parking lot and turn right onto Greenshield Road, then left onto the Polly Ann Trail.

2.7 Turn right onto the path alongside Joslyn Road.

2.8 Turn left onto the continuation of Joslyn Road on the adjacent path.

3.5 Turn left onto the narrow section of path adjacent to Indianwood Road.

3.8 Turn right and cross Indianwood Road to the pathway.

6.4 Downtown Oxford is 0.4 mile to the right.

6.7 Restrooms. Beginning of pedestrian ramp over Washington Street.

14.4 Leonard Polly Ann Trail parking area. Restrooms.

14.5 Downtown Leonard 0.2 mile to the left.

16.2 Lapeer County Line. Path becomes dirt single-track.

18.4 Route ends at General Squire Road. The rail trail continues north, in varying and minimal levels of maintenance.

36.8 Retrace pathway/return to trailhead.

RIDE INFORMATION

Restrooms
Start/Finish: Civic Center Park
Mile 6.7: Pleasant Street in Oxford at the base of the pedestrian overpass
Mile 14.4: Trail parking lot in Leonard

Stony Creek Pathway

This is a short bike path, but as it's in the largest of all Metroparks in the system, and as it circles a majestic man-made lake and it's highly popular for good reason, it makes sense to include it among the other, much longer, bike paths in the area. Perhaps just as important is its close tie to the Macomb-Orchard Trail that passes just south of Stony Creek. It offers an option for those riding that rail-trail to spin up the hill into the park and enjoy a different riding experience.

Though the Trolley Trail is basically a two-track dirt road and the bike path is paved, they're both accessible on a hybrid bike, often the bike of choice for riding on bike paths. The Trolley Trail is a small loop that connects to the access path. It's not marked out in this section, but I mention it for those who want to venture farther afield. It's a hybrid pathway in itself, with an odd mix of a hilly, wooded, and twisting two-track, transitioning to straight line roads along open fields, some of which pass through unkempt park service and maintenance areas. The wooded areas are quite nice and there's even one rather steep hill.

Start: Park in the Baypoint Beach lot.

Length: Loop path 6.0 miles; connection from Macomb-Orchard Trail: 2.0 miles

Approximate riding time: 0.5 hour

Best bike: Road, hybrid

Terrain and trail surface: Gently rolling to flat paved path

Traffic and hazards: Occasional access road crossings to various activity areas

Things to see: Tree-lined pathway, open fields, expansive views over a man-made lake with wildfowl, glimpses of other wildlife, and all kinds of other recreation activities besides biking

Maps: Huron-Clinton Metroparks website for Stony Creek:
www.metroparks.com/metroparks/parks/index_all.aspx?ID=11&r=0;
DeLorme: Michigan Atlas & Gazetteer, pages 94 and 42

Getting there by car: From M-59 take exit 48 and head north on
Dequindre Road 3.2 miles to Avon Road. Turn right onto Avon, which
shortly resumes as Dequindre again. Take this 2.7 miles to Mt. Vernon
Road and turn right. Follow this for 1.5 miles as Mt. Vernon becomes 26
Mile Road. Follow this to the exit right into the Metropark and follow the
signs 4.0 miles to the Baypoint Beach parking area. Metropark entrance
fee by the day or year. GPS: N42 44.002 W83 05.266

THE RIDE

Baypoint Beach is on the far side of the lake from the entrance, but it's a good
place to start as there's a nice picnic and beach area for pre- or post-ride activities, and there's also a bike rental service on the weekends. There are bike rentals at Eastwood Beach, another activity area in the park, throughout the week.

Like all of the Metroparks in the system, Stony Creek is very well maintained. The fields are often mowed (unless they're intended as native landscape areas), structures like bridges are in good shape, and the path is
smooth (or, if not, it soon will be, as crews are out and about constantly).
There's also plenty of signage letting you know where you are in the bigger
scheme of things.

Also like most Metroparks, there's a lot going on in a relatively small natural area. On the path alone will be Rollerbladers, walkers, runners, and other
cyclists. On the ring road, besides auto traffic, there are usually fast-moving
cyclists on their road bikes. The lake is ringed with anglers and often dotted
with boaters of all kinds as well as kite-boarders. There's a disc golf course on
the east side, a regular golf course on the west side, a popular mountain bike
trail, a BMX challenge course, and a series of hiking/nature trails that head
north from the ring road. Add to that the picnickers, beachgoers, bird-watchers,
and sunbathers and there's a lot going on simultaneously. This is activity central in the area. That also makes it a great place to share in and watch what
people do for recreation.

Leave the parking lot and at Park Road take a left onto the bike path. This
is a two-way path, so future rides can be in the opposite direction for a different perspective. The first stretch is through an open area with groves of trees
at the margins of the open fields. It reaches a greater sense of enclosure at the
bridge crossing at mile 0.8.

The path is used for all kinds of activities.

The path views open once again after crossing the access road to Winter Cove, with views down to the lake on the left. The path adjoins the ring road at mile 1.5 for a short stretch, then separates until mile 2.0, where it crosses a bridge over the creek the park is named after. This section has great views out over the lake and the opportunity to often watch sailboats and kite-boarders ply their crafts. Nearer shore the marsh is often populated with flocks of large birds such as swans and ducks.

Round the bend at the bottom of the lake and you'll find a line of stored boats. Eastwood Beach at mile 2.9 is another beach area worth checking out; this is where you can rent a bike if you're just pretending to be on one up to this point. There are picnic areas at all the access points if you're out for a day of exploring the various park locales for different lakeside vantage points.

The path leading to the park office, and also out of the park, goes to the right, crossing Park Road, at mile 3.1. Stay to the left to continue the loop ride. On the entire ride, Park Road is often in view, but there are many points where the path ducks and dips away into large groves of trees, often maple, oak, or hickory or associated varieties. Though the topography is pretty gentle along the entire path, the highest point is reached at mile 3.9. From here the path opens up with long views over the fields to the left until it reaches the dam crossing. The views from the causeway looking south give a sense of the extent of the panorama. It's also another great place for bird-watching.

From there, the views of the lake are replaced by a large woodland as the path arches back to the Baypoint parking area.

Bike Shops

KLM Bike & Fitness: 2680 Rochester Rd., Rochester Hills, MI 48307; (248) 299-0456; klmfitness.com
Main Street Bicycles: 5987 26 Mile Rd., Washington, MI 48094; (586) 677-7755; mainstreetbicycles.com
RBS Rochester Bike Shop: 426 S. Main St., Rochester, MI 48307; (248) 652-6376; rochesterbikeshop.com
Stoney Creek Bike: 58235 Van Dyke Rd., Washington, MI 48094; (586) 781-4451; stoneycreekbike.com
Bike Rentals
Metropark Bike Rentals: Memorial Day through Labor Day
Eastpoint Beach: Daily single-speed bike rentals
Baypoint Beach: Weekend-only single-speed bike rentals

Connection from the Macomb-Orchard Trail

For those veering from the Macomb-Orchard Trail, there's a spur north at Shelby Road that quickly arrives at 25 Mile Road. Cross 25 Mile and begin a long, steady ascent toward Stony Creek past first a residential area, then into the park, past the office and onto an overpass that crosses over 26 Mile Road.

For those interested in a dirt two-track diversion, the Trolley Trail access point is at mile 1.3. If not, continue up to the Park Road crossing and onto the 6.0-mile bike path loop.

MILES AND DIRECTIONS

This is a relatively short and straightforward loop around the lake. Keep in mind that this is a wide two-way path, so either direction is an option.

0.0 Leave Baypoint Beach parking area and turn left.

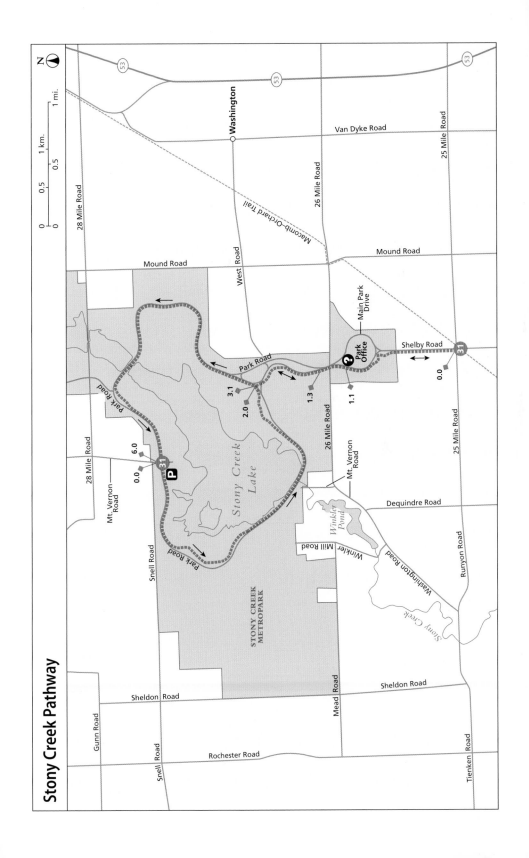

Stony Creek Pathway

3.1 Option to go right to access the Trolley Trails, the main office, or to exit the park. Go straight to continue along the lake loop.

6.0 Return to Baypoint Beach access road.

Connection from Macomb-Orchard Trail at 25 Mile Road

0.0 From Macomb-Orchard Trail head north across the signalized intersection at 25 Mile Road.

1.1 Access to the park's main office is on the right.

1.3 Trolley Trail access is on the left.

2.0 Connect to the multiuse loop path.

RIDE INFORMATION

Local Events/Attractions
The Metroparks have events throughout the year. See www.metroparks.com for up-to-date information.

Restaurants
Downtown Cafe: 606 N. Main St., Rochester, MI 48307; (248) 652-6680

Restrooms
In picnic/activity areas throughout the park

MOUNTAIN BIKE TRAILS

Quick, answer this: where in Michigan can you mountain bike all day on at least ten different trails all within an hour or so of each other? (If you can do all ten in one day you're one tough pedaler by the way.) Of course, it's a loaded question, but would urban Southeast Michigan be the first area to come to mind? If you're already riding a lot of the trails in the area, then probably so, but if not, your brain's probably still wandering up north somewhere. Maybe even in the Upper Peninsula. Bring your thoughts back down to this corner of the state.

Now, look at a map that graphically indicates green recreation areas across the region. The Huron-Clinton Metropark map tends to show this well. Notice an interesting diagonal line running northeast to southwest from north and central Oakland County down through Livingston County and into northwest Washtenaw County. Those green recreation areas are there for a reason. The main reason is that the land was too hilly and marshy to be used as agricultural land or for other kinds of development, so large parcels were set aside as natural area.

When the mountain bike craze hit the country in the '80s and '90s a lot of people recognized the wealth of opportunity in that belt of green. Mountain bike trails sprouted all over, and they're still growing.

Oakland County alone, the historic recreation release for urban Detroiters since the late 19th century, has all kinds of places to mountain bike. Even with—and maybe stubbornly because of—the massive growth this area has been consumed by in the past 40 years or so, the dedication to maintaining its park areas is impressive. There are many excellent mountain bike areas in the county: Pontiac Lake, Highland, Holdridge, Bald Mountain, Stony Creek, Holly, Proud Lake, Milford, Addison Oaks, Bloomer Park. All of these are well worth dropping a tire on and pedaling through. Five of those just mentioned are explored in detail in this book. All of those mentioned have something unique to offer.

There are other mountain bike areas worth exploring as well, particularly Island Lake State Park and Brighton Recreation Area (Murray Lake and Torn Shirt) in Livingston County, smaller parks like Maybury State Park and Lakeshore Park in northwest Wayne County, and the largest of them all, the Potawatomi, or just Poto to the locals, in western Washtenaw County. The Poto has a little bit of everything, including an intimidating reputation. It is challenging, but it also goes through a beautiful swath of the countryside that's worth building the skills to ride through.

There are so many options, and these trails aren't so far from one another that they're inaccessible. If you want a highly technical ride, then

Highland, Holdridge's Gruber's Grinder, or Torn Shirt are great choices. Something faster? Then Pontiac Lake, Maybury, Island Lake, Murray Lake, or the Poto (though this includes some hilly technical sections as well) will get your heart pumping.

No matter what your ability, beginner to advanced, there's a trail out there for you not too far off. What's more, the Michigan Mountain Bike Association (MMBA) has a great website (mmba.org) with a relatively up-to-date Trail Guide page with info and maps on all of the mountain bike trails in Southeast Michigan and throughout the state.

Additional bike paths worth exploring in the region

Lakeshore (previously known as Novi Tree Farm), Novi; 8.1 miles; GPS: N42 30.632 W83 29.173
At the southern end of Walled Lake, this beginner- to intermediate-level trail system is a good, gentle introductory ride for those still developing their skills, though it flows so well and there are enough small challenges that it's quite exhilarating at speed. Even better, there's a dedicated group who build and maintain all kinds of skills obstacles (log rails, large wood piles, steps, jumps, a pump track, and much more to test your courage). Finally, these are beautiful woods to ride through and you cross the mighty Rouge River, which at this point is a small trickle of a stream.

Milford Trail, Milford; 5.2 miles; GPS: N42 35.327 W83 36.543
Right out downtown Milford's back door, this is a very fun hilly trail that alternates between flowingly fast and trickily technical, and fits a lot into a small space.

Proud Lake Recreation Area, Milford; GPS: N42 34.202 W83 33.578
I hesitate to give a specific distance because this is a trail system still in development. There are markers, but they can be confusing at times. It's very easy to get disoriented in this park, but that's also part of its charm. Imagine a bike trail before bike trails were much of a thing and you'll understand Proud Lake. Also be aware that these same trails are used by equestrians, so be prepared to share the trail. State of Michigan Recreational Passport required for entry.

Bloomer Park, Rochester Hills. N42 40.518 W83 06.806. 8 miles+-
This is a mix of riverside rail-trail and wicked technical sections with a free-for-all sense to it directionally. Someone called it a mountain bike playground and that's an apt description. Very easy mixed with very challenging technical areas that morph with the whims of the trail caretakers. Fun, freestyle place to ride. Entrance fee.

Addison Oaks County Park, Leonard. N42 48.331 W83 10.133. 7 miles
Well-maintained, fast, hilly trail. Not overly technical and nicely flowing. Beautiful glacial terrain. Daily fees for residents and non-county residents.

Rolling Hills County Park, Ypsilanti. N42 10.625 W83 39.069. 5 miles
This is a well-tended, growing trail system in this popular county park. It's a relatively flat to lightly rolling trail with a lot of technical twists and turns and a new mound section. Great place for beginners to learn mountain biking skills. Daily entrance fee.

Hewens Creek, Ypsilanti. N42 10.362 W83 37.789. 4.5 miles
This trail winds through an ancient flat lakebed through open tree-filled forestland, dense shrub-covered areas, and wide-open fields. It's a great place to observe wildlife. It's a relatively easy ride, which lulls you into complacency, but there are some roots and rocks here and there to keep an eye out for. Also, the trail is still in its infancy without many markers. It's easy to get disoriented. It's near Rolling Hills and can be quickly accessed via a connecting dirt road.

Ann Arbor Local Loop, including Olson Park, Ann Arbor. N42 19.057 W83 43.866
This is an unmarked trail system that flows around the periphery of Ann Arbor through numerous parks and woodlands with connecting trails and dirt roads. It includes Bluff Park, Barton Park, Leslie Park, and Olson Park, to name a few. I mention it not as a specific trail, but as a vision of what urban areas can do to create linear park connections for recreational use. If you want to discover it to the fullest, the key is to find someone who knows the trail network and ride along behind them. Olson Park has a designated, relatively easy, tightly twisting trail that's a good place to start your journey.

Morton-Taylor Trails, Canton. N42 16.818 W83 27.972. Various small loops
This is a series of small loop trails along the Lower Rouge River. There are optional obstacles on many of the loops. Generally pretty flat, but twisting, trail system.

Bald Mountain has two mountain bike trails in close proximity, though not really connected. This north trail is the more challenging of the two. It's longer, with hillier terrain, narrower trails, and more obstacles. It has a nice smooth flow and it's not overly technical, nor are the hills overly long in comparison to some other trails in the region. It's a great ride for the intermediate biker, yet it can still offer a good day out for the advanced rider as well. Parts of this trail can be muddy after rains and in the spring season.

Best of all, this is a beautiful trail to ride. The varied terrain, numerous ponds and water crossings, and the lush oak-hickory forest make for a nice place to spend some time.

Start: Park in the lot at Harmon and Predmore Roads. This is a State Recreation Area parking lot and requires a daily or yearly Recreation Passport.

Length: 6.9 miles

Approximate riding time: 1–2 hours

Best bike: Mountain bike

Terrain and trail surface: Narrow, smooth-flowing single-track over gently rolling trails for the most part with some steep hills here and there to get you breathing hard. This is a great place to improve mountain biking skills without getting over your head. There are some challenging hills and many roots to negotiate, but they're not overwhelming.

Traffic and hazards: Exposed roots, mud, some stones. An occasional road crossing.

Things to see: Woodlands, rolling topography, marshes, and wildlife

Maps: Michigan DNR–Bald Mountain North Unit; *DeLorme: Michigan Atlas & Gazetteer*, page 42

Getting there by car: From I-75 head east at exit 81, then swing around the exit ramp and head north (right) on Lapeer Road. Follow Lapeer for 2.1 miles to Silverbell Road. Turn right onto Silverbell and go 2.4 miles to Adams Road. Turn left onto Adams and go 3.6 miles to Stoney Creek Road. Turn right on Stoney Creek for a short 0.1-mile jog to Harmon Road. Turn left onto Harmon and take it 0.5 mile to the Bald Mountain parking lot on the left at the intersection with Predmore Road. GPS: N42 46.974 W83 11.817

THE RIDE

This is a directional trail with numbered trail markers (note: these are not mileage markers). There are actually three distinct loops as designated on the trail signage: a white, blue, and orange loop, plus there's a green trail that connects the orange to the white loop. The ride outlined here will include all of the blue and orange loop, and most of the white loop. The other sections are on the trail sign maps, and you can check these out in the future.

Head south from the parking lot on the white loop, down the hill to the marsh filled with cattails. Climb from there to the first trail marker, #2. This is where the green trail connects from the orange loop off to the left. Continue through the woods to marker #3 (mile 0.5), where the blue loop begins. The white loop connection is the trail straight ahead, but you'll take a left here onto the blue loop. Now the hilly fun begins. There are some teaser hills to begin with, but at mile 0.9 is the first real test of your climbing acumen. The hill is not overly long, 0.25 mile in total, but the first third of it has quite a pitch that will get the heart pumping nicely. It's one of the steeper sections of the entire trail. Enjoy.

From there the trail undulates over the top of the ridge, then back down to the marshy shores of Carpenter Lake and a wood boardwalk crossing at the bottom. This of course means more ups, then more downs with some exposed roots to spice things up, until you reach a T in the trail at marker #5. This is where the blue loop ends and the white loop resumes. Turn left and meander through the woods to mile 2.4, where there is a Y in the trail. The segment to the left leads off to a

Bike Shops

Main Street Bicycles: 5987 26 Mile Rd., Washington, MI 48094; (586) 677-7755; mainstreetbicycles.com

Paint Creek Bicycles: 27 E. Flint St., Lake Orion, MI 48362; (248) 693-9620; paintcreekbicycles.com

Stoney Creek Bike: 58235 Van Dyke Rd., Washington, MI 48094; (586) 781-4451; stoneycreekbike.com

Prince Lake along the Bald Mountain North trail

residential neighborhood. Don't go there. Nobody's cooking lunch for you. Curve to the right and continue on the white loop.

Ride your heart out over hills and down into valleys on this smooth section of trail, with nice curving arced turns and downhills lending momentum to the uphills. Marker #6 is at mile 3.2, where the trail crosses Harmon Road. (The white loop takes a right turn and returns to the parking lot.) Cross the road and connect onto the orange loop at marker #7. Turn left (north).

The trail weaves in and out of the woods, then swings left and comes to a sharp right-hand downhill with a view across Harmon Road over Shoe Lake. Continue descending to a scenic wooden bridge that crosses the west branch of Stony Creek, a great spot for a short break with some nice views in either direction. The trail ascends from the creek to a high point that then drops dramatically down an embankment filled with exposed roots. Take care descending, particularly if the roots are wet from rain.

The drop is fast and fun if you like the challenge. It sweeps you down to an exposed section of trail that nips the southern shore of Prince Lake (mile 4.2). Continue on into the forest and over a relatively easygoing section of the trail. The longest climb of the day comes at mile 4.8, where it rises about 70 feet in 0.25 mile. You're rewarded with a long descent of nearly 0.5 mile. At the bottom is another Stony Creek crossing over a wooden bridge, then a gently rolling ride on the trail alongside Graham Lake to the right. An outhouse is tucked about 30 feet into the woods to the left, at mile 6.1.

Best Bike Rides Detroit and Ann Arbor

Bald Mountain North

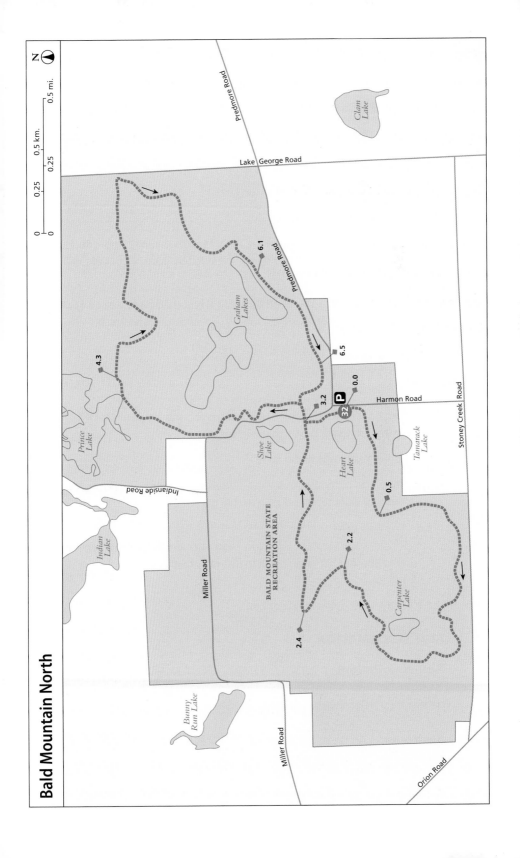

There's a road crossing at mile 6.4, and at marker #15 the trail splits with the option to take the green connector back to the white loop (left) or stay on the orange loop. Keep going toward marker #7 on the orange loop. Once there, turn left and keep in mind that this is a two-way connection back across Harmon Road to marker #6 and the white loop. Turn left at marker #6 (mile 6.8) and within 0.1 mile you'll climb out of the woods to the parking lot where you began your adventure.

MILES AND DIRECTIONS

0.0   Start in the dirt parking area at the intersection of Predmore and Harmon Roads. Head south and immediately downhill out of the parking lot.

0.5   At trail marker #3 there's an option to take a shortcut to marker #5 or continue on to marker #4 to the left. Go left toward marker #4.

2.2   This is a T in the trail at marker #5. Turn left.

2.4   There's a somewhat confusing Y in the trail at this point. Keep to the right.

3.2   The trail crosses Harmon Road. Just beyond this is trail marker #7 with a Y in the trail. Stay to the left and head north.

4.3   At marker #9 stay to the right.

6.1   There's an outhouse somewhat hidden in the woods to the left. FYI, this is one of the few public toilets in the area.

6.5   The trail splits at marker #15. Stay to the right, head back to marker #7, take a left crossing Harmon Road once more, then immediately take another left on the trail that shortly climbs back to the parking lot.

6.9   Arrive back at the starting point.

RIDE INFORMATION

Accommodations
There are two rustic cabins available: (800) 447-2757; www.michigandnr.com/parksandtrails/Details.aspx?id=435&type=SPRK

Restrooms
Mile 6.1: Outhouse in the woods near the trail

Highland Recreation Area

"If I do all four loops of Highland, that's it for me for the rest of the day," one guy said to me in the parking lot at another mountain bike trailhead in the region. *"I have to go home and lie down."* That says it. It's not just the physical challenge of the trail, it's the need to concentrate. A moment's lapse and you may discover you're on another adventure altogether. I did that one day and found myself flipping over a log and doing a beautifully acrobatic series of backward somersaults down a steep slope. This may say more about my clumsiness than the trail's challenges, but after repeated rides, I've found that unless I'm focused, the wheels end up in places I'd rather they weren't.

This may scare some off, but my guess is that it will spur many on to accept the challenge. This is single-track mountain biking at its technical best. Where many mountain bike areas are lauded for their smoothness and speed, Highland addresses all those skills that require prowess and technical ability. Speed takes a backseat to handling ability.

All that said, it flows beautifully. The switchbacks, roots, rocks, log piles, spiky slopes, tight trees, and never-ending turns are there, but not at the expense of the ability to enjoy the line of the trail under your wheels. It's brilliant.

The nice part about the loop system is that you can select the loops you're up for on a given day and leave the others for another ride. This is not a novice ride, but it's a great challenge for someone who wants to improve their technical riding skills.

Start: Parking lot along Livingston Road between Waterbury and Duck Lake Roads

Length: All loops, 13.6 miles; A Loop, 3.3 miles; B Loop, 4.9 miles; C Loop, 2.1 miles; D Loop, 3.3 miles

Approximate riding time: 2–3 hours

Best bike: Mountain bike

Terrain and trail surface: Narrow dirt single-track. Relentlessly undulating trail filled with roots and rocks. Challenging even at its easiest.

Traffic and hazards: Hikers and crossings for horseback riders; rocks, roots, off-camber turns, steep short ascents and descents, trees close in on the trail

Things to see: Woods. This is a dense forest trail nearly everywhere. There are occasional views of ponds and low marsh areas.

Skill level: Intermediate to advanced. This is not the place to begin someone's experience on a mountain bike. Get some good skills on the bike, then come here to take them up a few notches.

Maps: Michigan DNR–Highland Recreation Area: www.michigandnr. com/parksandtrails/details.aspx?id=455&type=SPRK; *DeLorme: Michigan Atlas & Gazetteer,* page 41

Getting there by car: From US 23 at exit 67, head east on M-59 8.6 miles to Waterbury Road. Turn right onto Waterbury and go 1.0 mile to Livingston Road. Turn left onto Livingston and go 0.2 mile to the trailhead parking area on the left. GPS: N42 38.367 W83 34.638

THE RIDE

The trail is divided into four loops, A, B, C, and D. There are those who will tell you that A and B are the easiest and C and D are very tough. My sense is that part of this perception is due to the fact that by the time you've completed parts of A and B, you're already a bit worn down and C and D just seem particularly menacing.

Then again, the C and D Loops are a bit tighter with perhaps a few more challenges than A and B, but it's only a matter of a slight degree. It's not like C and D are eviscerating, they're just a good challenge.

Highland is a long, rather narrow, highly undulating property filled with rolling hills and marshland kettles. The loops take as much advantage of the land available as they possibly can. The woods are so dense that it's easy to think you're deep into a forest far from anyone else, but in fact the trails switch back and around so much that you're often close to the trail going the other way, or to another loop. Don't be surprised if you hear other bikers (talking or cursing, depending on their experience). Horse trails also cross through and hikers are welcome as well, so there are often others nearby, though, again, the forest cover doesn't always make that obvious.

Leaving the parking lot and heading out on the A Loop, you'll drop down a rooted trail to a small wood bridge, then rise out and follow the markers to the left at mile 0.2. The trail will undulate from here with a series of twists and turns. This is the character of the ride. There are no misleadingly easy sections early on. You'll know at this point what the experience will be.

At mile 0.6 there's a steep, crafted stone ramp uphill with a turn at the top. It's the kind of attention to detail that makes this trail so enjoyable. At mile 1.5 there's a hilltop landing where you can take a short break and get your bearings. These kinds of landings are interspersed throughout, and they offer nice spots for a snack, or a place to let your friends catch up before you lose them again on the next series of hilly challenges.

B Loop begins at mile 2.2. There's a crossover to the continuation of A Loop, or you can venture farther on into the trail system with B Loop. A, B, and C basically follow one after another from north to south and back. D Loop is a side loop off the return section of A. In other words, if you choose to continue on B, you're getting farther from the trailhead. Assess your skill/energy level at this point and either go deeper or begin the loop back. If you want to push on, but you're wondering whether it's a wise decision to get too deep, be assured that there's another cut-over, this time to the return section of B, at mile 3.9. The trail ahead offers some great scenery and at least one landing area, so keep that in mind as well.

After this, at about mile 4.0, there's a rough-and-tumble plummet down a twisty, rooted section of the trail. It's one of the thrill rides of Highland. After more winding trail, there's a bench with a view over a lowland area. Farther on, at mile 5.6, C Loop begins. This is the smallest loop, but it's also one of the tightest parts of the trail. Turning skills, especially those on uphill switchbacks, are honed here. Not that they don't happen elsewhere on the ride, but they're a steady diet in C. Somewhere in

Bike Shops

Cycletherapy: 3545 Elizabeth Lake Rd., Waterford, MI 48328; (248) 681-8600; ctbicycles.com

D & D Bicycles and Hockey: 9977 E. Grand River Ave., Brighton, MI 48116; (810) 227-5070; 7330 Highland Rd., Waterford, MI 48327; (248) 461-6550; ddbicyclesandhockey.com

Hometown Bicycles: 10605 Grand River Rd., Brighton, MI 48116; (810) 225-2441; myhometownbicycles.wordpress.com

Kinetic Systems Bicycles: 60 S. Main St., Clarkston, MI 48346; (248) 625-7000; kineticsystemsbicycles.com

Town N Country Bikes: 8160 Grand River Ave., Brighton, MI 48116; (810) 227-4420; tncbikes.com

Trails Edge Cyclery: 525 N. Main St., Suite 180, Milford, MI 48381; (248) 714-9355; trails-edge.com

Highland single-track

here there's also a log pile on a sharp left turn. You can opt out, but it's a true test of skill if you can handle it.

Emerge from C (see if you can ride out between the rocks) and continue the loop back on B. Slip between the V Tree at mile 8.1 and work your way to the turnoff for D Loop at mile 9.3. If you've had enough, then continue on A. If you're a glutton for more enjoyment, then turn left onto the D Loop trail connection. As you begin D Loop, you may notice that neither the C nor D Loop trails are as packed down as A and B. The single-track is narrower. So, if you have gotten this far, you'll realize you're one of the true adventurers willing to

Best Bike Rides Detroit and Ann Arbor

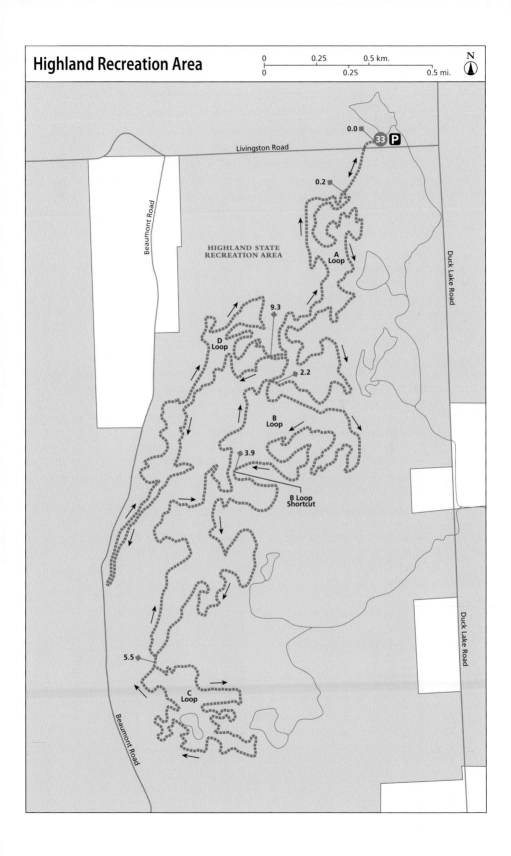

Highland Recreation Area

0   0.25   0.5 km.
0   0.25   0.5 mi.

N

Livingston Road

Beaumont Road

Duck Lake Road

HIGHLAND STATE
RECREATION AREA

0.0

33 P

0.2

A
Loop

9.3

D
Loop

2.2

B
Loop

3.9

B Loop
Shortcut

5.5

C
Loop

Beaumont Road

Duck Lake Road

go that extra few miles. D has some special challenges, such as a gnarly, rock-strewn uphill climb and a drop or two that will up the thrill factor. The twisty switchbacks continue, but by this time you welcome them (keep telling yourself that) because your skills have improved immensely from a couple hours back when you were just a lowly bike wrestler. You've earned your stripes.

At mile 12.6 you're back to the start of D Loop. Take a left on the connection to A and once there make the hard uphill left for your last blast on the trail. Sections of this final mile or so have a few places where you can finally open up and feel the bugs in your teeth. Before you know it, you're crossing that small wooden bridge and climbing through the roots to where you started. Congratulations! You've done Highland. Now you can go home and lie down.

MILES AND DIRECTIONS

0.0   Leave parking lot, cross the road, and enter onto the trail.

0.2   This is the beginning of A Loop. Stay to the left.

2.2   B Loop begins, along with a crossover, right, to continue on the A Loop.

3.9   B Loop crossover shortcut to the right.

5.5   C Loop begins, or return on B Loop to the right.

7.7   B Loop continues to the left. End of C Loop.

8.7   B Loop crossover to the right. Possible to redo the last part of B Loop.

9.2   B Loop crossover to the right. Possible to redo all of B Loop.

9.3   D Loop begins to the left.

12.5 End of D Loop. A Loop continues to the left.

13.6 End of A Loop. Return to parking area to the left.

RIDE INFORMATION

Restrooms
Start/Finish: Outhouse at parking lot

Pontiac Lake

Of all the trails in the region, this is possibly the one most people have tried and the one most know about. In an informal survey of riders I met on other trails, Pontiac Lake consistently came up as one that falls into their top three list.

I think there are a few good reasons. First, it's centrally located in an area of high population. Second, it's challenging without being overwhelmingly hard. Third, it's fast. It flows in a way that you can build a head of steam and keep powering most of the way. Fourth, it's hilly without being leg crushing, though there's at least one hill that's long and probably a tough ascent for many. Fifth, it's nice landscape to ride through. It's mostly woodland, the topography changes up the views on every turn, and the occasional marshes add a colorful accent and the chance to spot some wildlife. Sixth, it's short enough to get in a quick ride if time is a constraint, yet challenging enough that one loop is a good workout. If not, two loops will do the job for sure.

That popularity comes at a modest cost. It can get busy on the weekends, and the trail takes a beating from heavy use. There's a lot of exposed gravel and a few rutted areas. This doesn't detract from the ride, but be aware that the turns can sometimes be skittish due to the exposed gravel.

This is a fast and flowing trail that's not overly technical. There are a few relatively tight single-track sections, but for the most part this trail lends itself to those who like to accelerate. Like all mountain bike trails, this trail takes concentration, but nowhere near that of nearby Highland. Most of the hills are clear of obstacles, so it's just a matter of how strong you can climb.

Start: Parking lot off North Williams Lake Road between Gale Road and M-59 (Highland Road)

Length: 9.7 miles

Approximate riding time: 1–2 hours

Best bike: Mountain bike

Terrain and trail surface: Fast flowing wide single-track, rolling hills, loose gravel to hard-packed dirt, a few rocks and roots

Traffic and hazards: A couple of paved road crossings, hikers, and horse trail crossings. It's easy to lose traction on gravel surfaces, rutted downhills, and sharp gravelly turns at the bottom of fast downhills. Speed may be your biggest hazard. It's easy to overcook on some parts of the trail.

Things to see: View over Pontiac Lake, woods with kettle ponds and marsh areas, wildlife, and a radio-controlled airplane field

Skill level: Intermediate to advanced. Smooth flow with some tough hills and gravel.

Maps: Michigan DNR–Pontiac Lake Recreation Area: www.michigandnr .com/parksandtrails/Details.aspx?id=225&type=SPTR; *DeLorme: Michigan Atlas & Gazetteer,* page 41

Getting there by car: From I-75 take exit 93 and head south on Dixie Highway (US 24) 1.5 miles to White Lake Road. Turn right onto White Lake Road and continue onto Nelson Road 2.5 miles to Maceday Lake Road and turn left. Follow Maceday for 1.0 mile to Williams Lake Road and turn right. Take Williams Lake 1.0 mile to the State Park entry road and turn right into the park. Follow the road back to the parking area. Requires a daily or yearly State Recreation Passport for entry. GPS: N42 40.272 W83 26.759

THE RIDE

Leave the lot and ride north out through an open field with a view of Pontiac Lake off to the left. Cross Gale Road at mile 0.2 and ride up the wide two-way tree-lined path to Marker #2 at mile 0.4. There are numbered markers periodically placed along the trail (not related to mileage) for identifying location. These are on wood poles that also include a map and arrows indicating direction to the next marker.

Turn left at Marker #2. The one-way trail begins here in a clockwise direction. Ride through an open area that begins to skirt in and out of the trees for a mile or so along some easygoing trail. Pontiac Lake Trail is kind in that way. It lets you get your legs warmed up and settled into the rhythm for a good opening stretch.

Between the trees in Pontiac Lake

The first climb of the day isn't overly demanding, and there's a nice view at mile 1.0 over the treetops to Pontiac Lake to the south. The trail then twists and turns until it comes to a rooted drop with trees close in on both sides.

At mile 1.7 the trail pitches up more dramatically. This is the base of the most challenging hill on the trail, so now that you've dedicated yourself to the ascent, dig into those pedals and go for it. The biggest challenge may not be the pitch itself, but the loose gravel in spots where you want grip, and the sharp turns that test your balancing skills. By mile 1.9 you'll have reached the peak of your Everest. There's a short descent, then another dig to a peak at mile 2.3 and after that a lot of downhill momentum for a while.

The trail briefly skirts the edge of an open field at mile 3.2, surprising for its break into the sunlight, since the trail has been immersed in a large oak-hickory forest for a long stretch. This is short-lived, however, as the trail submerges back into the woods and begins a climb once more, only this time more gradual.

At mile 3.8 it crosses Maceday Road. The trail takes on a flowing rise and fall, carving its way over and around the glacial topography until mile 4.7, when it once again emerges into the light of day as it reaches White Lake Road on the left and a large open field on the right used for radio-controlled aircraft. It crosses the "airport" entrance drive at Marker #7 and goes down a long forested descent, where it begins to even out on rolling trail at mile 5.3. The trail soon begins to rise once more, slips tightly between a pair of trees, then drops to a small wooden bridge crossing a marsh at mile 5.8.

The trail ascends again after this, riding the crest of a ridge, then arriving at the first spot where a decision has to be made: take the easy option or the hard (mile 6.1). The hard option to the left is a true test of descending skills. This is for skilled riders only. Take the banked series of turns on a plummeting drop to a stretch along the edge of a lake, then a long climb up the side of a hill on a narrow single-track. The easy option crosses over to the continuation of the trail after the hard parts are complete, missing the drama entirely.

Bike Shops

Cycletherapy: 3545 Elizabeth Lake Rd., Waterford, MI 48328; (248) 681-8600; ctbicycles.com
D & D Bicycles and Hockey: 7330 Highland Rd., Waterford, MI 48327; (248) 461-6550
Kinetic Systems Bicycles: 60 S. Main St., Clarkston, MI 48346; (248) 625-7000; kineticsystemsbicycles.com

The trail then descends to Marker #9, where it ventures through more thick forest, coming to another easy/hard at mile 7.8. This hard option, though, is only moderately more difficult than the easy. Cross back over Maceday Road

Pontiac Lake

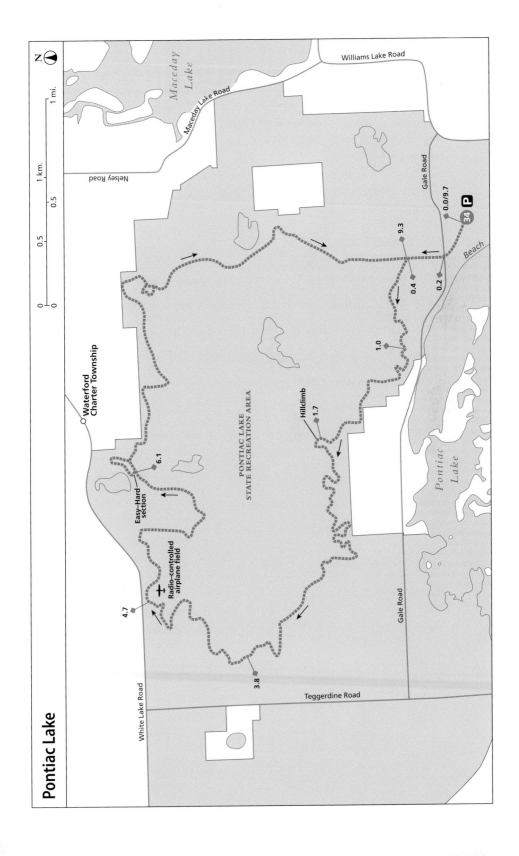

at Marker #11 and ride over a series of rolling forestland, descending finally to the base of the last hill at mile 9.0. Climb the final ascent on a twisting trail, roll over the top and back down a twisting descent to a wider trail lined with an esplanade of trees. Pass Marker #2 at mile 9.3 and you're back on the two-way trail you came in on. Either jump back on for another loop, or make your way back to the parking lot.

There is a large, maintained beach on Pontiac Lake, as well as spacious restroom changing facilities. It's a good spot to wash off the trail dust before heading home.

MILES AND DIRECTIONS

0.0 Leave the parking lot heading north through the field.

0.2 Cross Gale Road. This section of the trail is two-way at this point.

0.4 Turn left at Trail Marker #2 onto the one-way trail.

1.0 The view south is out over Pontiac Lake.

1.7 The steepest climb of the day comes early on.

3.8 Cross Maceday Road.

4.7 White Lake Road is on the left; the radio-controlled aircraft field is on the right.

6.1 The easy-hard option with the banked turn drop.

9.3 Merge with return two-way trail.

9.7 Return to parking lot.

RIDE INFORMATION

Accommodations
There are camping facilities in the Pontiac Lake Recreation Area: www .michigandnr.com/parksandtrails/details.aspx?id=485&type=SPRK

Restrooms
Start/Finish: At the trailhead

Holdridge

Holdridge is a labor of love by a few intrepid mountain bikers (Kirk Costello, Ed Kohlman, Randy Estes, Paul Gruber, and Rick Jerrell, along with other family members and volunteers; thanks to Tony Klein for the information) who decided to develop a trail system on some public land that the state representatives offered access to. Sometime around 1991, a group of riders set forth to build some single-track on a rough tract of land used for hunting, horse trails, and two-track access to ponds. They put together the three loops and built the parking area and pit toilets all as volunteer labor. Over 20 years later this is still an actively used and maintained mountain bike area and one of the largest (and most challenging) in the region.

I mention all of this because much of the work that's done to create and maintain the mountain bike trails in the region is performed by dedicated volunteer labor. This is one good example.

Holdridge is really three different mountain bike trails in one. The North Loop is short and easy, the West Loop is moderately challenging with a slightly more challenging technical section, and the East Loop, often known as Gruber's Grinder, is a highly technical and longer trail for the advanced cyclist. There's something for everyone here.

Start: Trailhead parking area.

Length: North Loop, 1.8 miles; West Loop (with a separate technical spur and lake spur), 5.3 miles as marked; East Loop, 12.0 miles

Approximate riding time: North Loop, 20–30 minutes; West Loop, 30–60 minutes; East Loop, 1.5–3 hours

Best bike: Mountain bike

Terrain and trail surface: Mostly single-track, with some wider trail sections in the North Loop. This is primarily a rough, hilly area, with the toughest sections of trail on the East Loop. The North Loop is relatively flat.

Traffic and hazards: None, except for hilly and steep switchbacks on the East Loop

Skill level: North Loop, beginner; West Loop, intermediate to advanced; East Loop, advanced intermediate to advanced

Things to see: Dense forest, glacial moraine, marshland, wildlife, including various wildfowl, as well as a very vocal frog population in season

Maps: Michigan DNR–Holly-Holdridge Mountain Bike Trail: www.michigandnr.com/parksandtrails/details.aspx?id=278&type=SPTR; *DeLorme: Michigan Atlas & Gazetteer,* page 41

Getting there by car: From I-75 at exit 101, take Grange Hall Road west 0.4 mile and turn right onto Hess Road. Follow Hess Road 1.4 miles back to the trailhead parking area on the left. State of Michigan daily or yearly Recreation Passport required. GPS: N42 49.867 W83 35.164

THE RIDE

North Loop (easy)

The North and East Loops leave the parking lot on the same easygoing, densely wooded trail that rings a large marsh area off to the left. At 0.4 mile in, the East branches to the right and the North arcs to the left. This North Loop is great for beginning riders learning to develop their skills. Except for a root or two, this is a smooth, packed, and flat trail. There's a bench at mile 1.4 to take a break and look out onto Holdridge Lake. There's a small bridge at mile 1.6.

West Loop (moderate, with built challenges in the tech spur)

The West Loop may be the most popular, as it offers challenges, but they're not out of the realm of the rider with intermediate biking skill. And the terrain is rolling and beautiful, with some great views over marsh areas alive with frogs, birds, and other wildlife. There are also many ways to approach this loop. The route here is one interpretation that shows a good balance of what it has to offer.

Leaving the parking lot, this trail gets the blood pumping right off as it heads downhill on a trail that winds through the forest. In less than 0.5 mile, it comes to the edge of a kettle pond. Depending on the time of year, it may

Woodplank bridge on the Holdridge West Loop

be croaking its heart out with a frog chorus. More ponds await in succession ahead, as does the dense forest and enough roots and stones on the trail to keep you attentive. This is a Southeast Michigan theme.

This trail has a faster flow than the East Loop, but it still demands respect. The single-track is narrow, constantly pitching up and down, back and forth, and though trees aren't right up to the trail's edge, they aren't far off. The oak-hickory forest is quite open though, with views through the trees unimpeded for the most part by the lack of shrubs.

There are occasional obstacles placed along the path, a low log to jump for instance, but in general the introduced challenges are options. For those who like rock ramps, log ramps, log piles, log rails, and the like, these are in abundance. Some are showing signs of wear, but others are in good shape.

At mile 2.8 there's a choice to make. To the right is a downhill plummet over a rather eroded and rooted descent that is the biggest challenge in the entire trail system. I chose in routing this to go around the knoll and come back to the base of the climb, then scale it on foot, just so it's on record. You can approach it (or avoid it) in the way you feel most comfortable. There's enough erosion that it may require a reroute eventually in any event. Be aware that mileage from here on includes this detour.

At mile 3.1 is the official Tech Loop. There's usually the option to avoid the major challenges, but even if you don't do them, they're fun to look at: drops, log pairs, extra-long log rails, and a rock rail. It's all impressive. There was a shortcut to avoid it altogether, but why, when you can see what some riders do to defy gravity?

Leave the Tech Loop and cross a small bridge heading toward the Lake Loop. Like the Tech Loop, the Lake Loop can be avoided altogether. It has an entirely different character than the rest of the overall West Loop. It's a tight single-track trail, heavily vegetated with shrubbery, that sometimes rolls over long sections of wood slats. It's close to the lake in many places and potentially muddy in the early wet season and after heavy rains. It's also a beautiful section of the trail and a nice change of pace.

The trail rises high up and away from the lake, then drops rapidly down to a bridge alongside an even larger lake, followed by one last climb to the parking lot. Return another day and take this loop with an entirely different variation of the route for another experience altogether.

East Loop (expert and highly technical) also known as Gruber's Grinder

The East Loop is the least used of the three main trails. This directional trail is marked with a numbering system, but the numbers don't correlate to mileage. The nice thing is that the trail is less worn and sometimes feels as if you're breaking untried ground. The downside is that, at least early on, the trail sometimes disappears and it takes a bit of searching to find the right course.

For those who like to feel they're in the backcountry on a highly twisting single-track trail, this is made for you. Once the trail breaks from the North Loop, the topography changes in earnest and the adventure begins. What makes the East Loop so fun is the constant technical skills called into play. The trail doesn't just twist and turn, it does so while climbing or dropping. This is one of those forest landscapes that has small hillocks, ridges, holes, and steep hills all tossed around like a mixed salad. Throw in some roots and rocks and you're out for a day of advanced bike handling.

It's almost comical, then, when the sound of highway traffic starts to enter your focused consciousness. Sometimes it's there in the first mile, depending on wind direction, but it definitely appears at the 1.5-mile mark when the cars themselves come into view. And these aren't just vehicles on a rural highway. These are flashing by on I-75 quite close to the trail. I-75, the highway that goes from northern Michigan to Florida. It just seems so out of place here, but it also lends an interesting otherworldly juxtaposition between these verdant woods and that commercial national highway. In some ways it makes those tires biting into the dirt all the more rewarding.

At nearly 2.0 miles in, the trail swings away from the highway and the woods once again dominate. Soon, the trail has you so focused that the road is a distant memory. There might be a tree down that you have to negotiate, the hills and twists are putting you to the test and then . . . the highway returns. But who cares because the trail is going up and you're breathing harder. Eventually it peaks at a spot (mile 3.7) where the trail once again goes inward and downward.

Log piles start to become a part of the experience, the climbs get a bit steeper, and hopefully the rhythm in your riding has come into play. At trail marker #7 (mile 5.7) there's a cutoff two-track to the right that will knock about 2.0 miles off the ride. Otherwise continue on to a series of rock piles and ponds in the Meadows Loop at the southern end of the trail. If you've had enough trail riding and you decide to cut back to Hess Road, there is a connection west at the Thorndog Cutoff at mile 7.6 (after doing the Meadows Loop).

At this point the hills aren't as long, though the trail continues its tight single-track ways on smaller,

Bike Shops

Cyclefit & Snow Sports: 1006 N. Leroy St., Fenton, MI 48430; (810) 750-2348; cycle-fit.net
Kinetic Systems Bicycles: 60 S. Main St., Clarkston, MI 48346; (248) 625-7000; kineticsystemsbicycles.com

sharply pitched ups and downs. There are a series of beautiful ponds along with a couple of bridges. There's one more good, punchy hill at mile 11.1, and after that it's a rolling up-and-down return to the parking area.

Though they are both unique experiences, Holdridge East Loop has similarities to the Highland mountain bike trail to the southwest, near Milford. The technical level of focus and concentration are very alike in each. Neither is a hard-charging hammerfest. These are scrimshaw trails, finely detailed and meant to elicit respect for skill over speed.

MILES AND DIRECTIONS

Disclaimer: There are many options on these trails, particularly the West and East Loops. This can cause confusion when indicating mileage, since there are numerous ways to vary each ride. I give coordinates, along with my own mileage, at key points to clarify locations. In other words, your mileage may be different, but the coordinates will be close to the same. Be aware that there is sometimes more than one name for a given area.

North Loop

0.0 Leave the parking lot headed north.

0.4 The trail splits, with the North Loop going left and the East Loop going right. Take the left. (GPS: N42 50.040 W83 35.095)

1.4 Bench.

1.8 Return to parking area trailhead.

West Loop

0.0 Leave southeast side of the parking lot on a descent.

2.8 Fork in trail. Top of hill climb. (GPS: N42 49.814 W83 35.829)

2.9 Choice to loop back to hill climb or continue ahead on the trail. (GPS: N42 49.857 W83 35.791)

3.1 Beginning of Technical Loop. (GPS: N42 49.918 W83 35.766)

3.8 End of Technical Loop. (GPS: N42 49.977 W83 35.803)

4.0 Beginning of the lake area. (GPS: N42 49.932 W83 35.574)

5.1 Rejoin main trail. (GPS: N42 49.839 W83 35.333)

5.3 Return to trailhead parking area. (GPS: N42 49.867 W83 35.164)

Holdridge

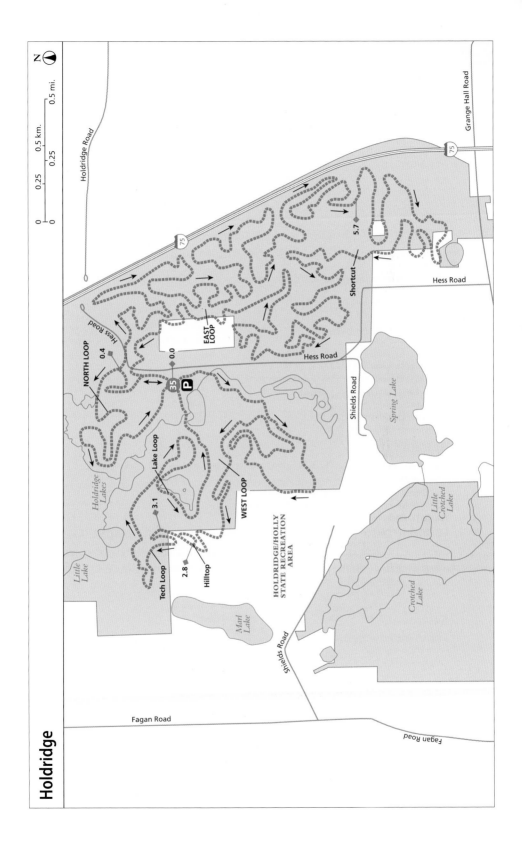

East Loop

0.0 Leave the parking area headed north.

0.4 The trail splits, with the North Loop going left and the East Loop going right. Take the right. (GPS: N42 50.040 W83 35.095)

1.4 The trail comes up alongside, and follows parallel to I-75 at this point.

5.7 At Trail Marker #7 there's a crossover shortcut. (GPS: N42 49.297 W83 34.383)

7.6 This is known as the Thorndog Cutoff where there's access to nearby Hess Road to the west. (GPS: N42 49.304 W83 34.632)

7.9 The beginning of the Orchard Loop. (GPS: N42 49.517 W83 34.615)

11.7 Dirt road crossing.

12.0 Return to trailhead

RIDE INFORMATION

Local Events/Attractions
Michigan Renaissance Festival: August–September; www.michrenfest.com

Restaurants
The French Laundry: 125 Shiawassee at Adelaide, Fenton, MI 48430; (810) 629-8852; www.lunchandbeyond.com

Accommodations
Michigan Department of Natural Resources, Holly Recreation Area: There's a 144-site campground in the Holly Rec Area at McGinnis Lake, plus a few available cabins; www.michigandnr.com/parksandtrails/details.aspx?id =459&type=SPRK

Restrooms
Start/Finish: At the trailhead

Island Lake Mountain Bike Trail

Island Lake is a state park directly across I-96 from Kensington Metropark to the north. They're connected by a below-the-highway bike path, but while Kensington is a beautiful park, it doesn't have a mountain bike trail. Island Lake does, and it's one of the most popular in the region. It's actually composed of two loops, the Blue and the Yellow (which is probably a play on the maize and blue colors of the U of M Wolverines just down the road in Ann Arbor. If not, let's just say it is).

The Blue and Yellow trails are two loops adjacent to and crossing one another within the park. The Blue Loop is somewhat less arduous than the Yellow Loop, though it's also a third longer at 8.9 miles compared to the Yellow Loop's 5.4 miles. Both loops cross or follow the Huron River at various points, meandering through a rich hardwood forest in some areas, and along open meadows in others. These single-track trails are some of the most graceful in the region, appropriate for beginner and expert alike.

Be aware, this trail can get crazy busy on summer weekends and sometimes even during weeknights in peak season. The range of riders and rider abilities varies widely. Take this into account if speed is your life's goal and patience is not. This popularity is due in part to the relative ease of these trails compared to some others in the region. The Blue Loop is beginner friendly with only a few root-strewn hills that could be considered a challenge. The Yellow Loop is marginally more challenging but still a good ride for someone wanting to up their skills to the intermediate level.

But that's not the only reason it's popular. It's also a beautiful place to ride. It winds through the Huron River valley, and the designers of the trail exploited the scenic opportunities at every turn. As in all of Southeast Michigan, it's not the majestic landscape statement that's made, it's the accumulation of beautiful small things, one after another. It's the marsh filled with marsh marigolds followed by a meander alongside the river, then a scented stand of pine with needles carpeting the trail, a weaving path through the maturing oaks and hickories, and a view out over a vast open field with a large gnarled white oak center stage. Island Lake has this over and over. Add to that a park well-maintained by its stewards and you have a nice day out.

Start: Mountain Bike Trailhead parking lot

Length: Blue, 8.9 miles; Yellow, 5.4 miles; total, 14.2 miles

Approximate riding time: 1–3 hours

Best bike: Mountain bike

Terrain and trail surface: Single-track nearly the entire length, with a few short jogs on paved road crossings. Like much of this region in Southeast Michigan, the terrain rolls up and down, though this is one of the most gentle of all the trails. The hills are short and, except for a couple of exceptions on the Yellow Loop, not very steep.

Traffic and hazards: Numerous bike path crossings, road crossings, and a very short section near the trailhead where the two trails meet and riders go in opposite directions

Skill level: Beginner to intermediate. Advanced riders will have fun here also.

Things to see: The forest—mostly hardwoods with a few distinct stands of conifer—the river and stream crossings, the hillside views of ponds and the river, the wide-open meadows, and the gently rolling topography make the well-designed trail a joy to meander along. It's really the variety of experiences in one trail that makes this stand out. Island Lake State Park also boasts the only hot-air balloon park in the system. These normally go up in the early morning or evening.

Maps: Island Lake Recreation Area: www.michigandnr.com/parks andtrails/Details.aspx?type=SPRK&id=462; *DeLorme: Michigan Atlas & Gazetteer,* page 40

Getting there by car: From I-96 at exit 151 take Kensington Road 0.5 mile south and turn left into the entrance at Island Lake State Park. Go 0.3 mile and turn right onto Kent Lake Beach Road. Take this 1.2 miles to the mountain bike trailhead access road. Follow the road back to the parking area. Daily or yearly Recreation Passport entry fee, as in all Michigan State Parks. GPS: N42 30.502 W83 42.505

THE RIDE

This is *the* mountain bike trail in the region that attracts beginners, occasional bikers, and those who want to experience the joy of riding single-track without the fear of getting in over their heads. Not that the more advanced avoid the trail. On the contrary, this offers enough length and just enough challenge to also draw the expert looking for a good day out without the find-your-edge obstacles found elsewhere.

It's not a flat trail by any means, but there are plenty of sections where the rises and the descents are gentle enough not to intimidate the recreational cyclist. This is the kind of trail you'd bring your young kids to, as well as your cycling grandparents. Plenty of both are found on their bikes here. The trail is well-marked, with a couple of exceptions, with distance markers every 0.5 mile or so.

Blue Loop

If you want to take it easy for your first few miles, the Blue Loop is a great warm-up (or a good ride just on its own). From the expansive parking area, the trail immediately dives into a tight forest with many twists and turns. In about 0.5 mile the trail crosses the paved State Park Road, turns right, dips under a railroad trestle, then takes a left off the pavement and back onto a gravelly climb. Beware the unmarked turn from trail to pavement. If you go under the trestle, then see the path on your left, you're on the right path.

After a short climb along the railroad tracks, the trail drops back into the woods, where you'll stay for over a mile. Nearing the 2.0-mile mark, it opens up on a large sandy expanse with wide-open views in all directions. Spring Mill Pond comes into view, with a long parking area and a beach area. The trail takes a few spurs here that can take you off track, so stay on the trail on the right that parallels the parking area in order to avoid getting lost or waylaid. This is one of the most open parts of the trail and also one of the sandiest.

Bike Shops

D & D Bicycles and Hockey: 9977 E. Grand River Ave., Brighton, MI 48116; (810) 227-5070; ddbicyclesandhockey.com
Hometown Bicycles: 10605 Grand River Rd., Brighton, MI; (810) 225-2441; myhometownbicycles.wordpress.com
Town N Country Bikes: 8160 Grand River Ave., Brighton, MI; (810) 227-4420; tncbikes.com

From here, the ride weaves in and around the hardwood forest and rolls up and down for quite a few miles. The designers did a great job of keeping the sweep of the turns flowing, yet unpredictable enough to put a fast rider

On the single-track at Island Lake

on their guard. Ride slowly and enjoy the surroundings without fear of too many obstacles. Ride fast and the trail offers some pleasant thrills. Though the climbs aren't long or leg ripping, there are a few in this area that will test the beginner and those still working to build fitness.

The trail crosses State Park Road a couple of times in this area. The second time, at mile 4.3, it goes along the road for a short way and it's important to turn right from trail to pavement, cross the bridge over the river, and look for the trail entrance ahead on the left. Dive back into the woods on another short climb and enjoy the forest. This eventually leads to one more road crossing, then at about 5.8 miles it takes a left onto State Park Road, crosses a railroad

Best Bike Rides Detroit and Ann Arbor

track, and takes a sharp right onto the trail nestled between the tracks and Island Lake with houses on the left. After this, the trail dips and rises through some very fun twists in the surrounding forest.

At mile 8.1 it connects with the Yellow Loop. Your choice is to swing onto the Yellow Loop or return on the last 0.8 mile to the trailhead parking lot. If you do decide to go to the trailhead, it becomes a two-way trail. The descent to the river is wide, though gravelly. Watch for riders climbing the steep incline. A short way past the river the trail takes a sharp left onto single-track. This section has dense vegetation on the curves, so take extra caution for oncoming riders here. Fortunately, the Blue Loop takes another left and the two-way ends. This climbs past a bike path and into a beautiful twisting section of pines, with needles carpeting the ground and the heady smell of conifer. One rider I came across called out, "This is my favorite part of the trail." It's another one of those nice variations that finishes up the ride as it spills, surprisingly, out into the open parking lot where you began your ride.

Yellow Loop

Now for the Yellow Loop, shorter but slightly more challenging. It's still tame by the standards of other trails in the region, but the climbs are steeper and longer than those on the Blue Loop and the obstacles require more technical savvy.

Leave the parking lot and wander along a single-track, but watch for oncoming bikers finishing the Blue Loop at mile 0.3. Cross the bridge over the Huron River and climb a sandy uphill. This is still a two-way section of the trail. After mile 0.5 you'll swing onto the one-way continuation of the Yellow Loop and begin paralleling the Huron River. You'll ride a rolling trail with great views down onto the water and into the woods beyond.

The trail descends to a marsh, then onto a long bridge crossing Woodruff Creek at mile 1.3. Once over the bridge the trail carves along the base of a drumlin, then takes a curve that begins to climb. This becomes one of the longer and more challenging climbs of the whole trail system, with a steep left-side slope. The trail reaches the top, takes a short descent, then climbs once more through the woods, eventually descending to a right turn onto a bridge over the Huron and alongside Kensington Road.

Beyond the bridge is a sharp right that returns downriver, eventually opening up to a wide prairie view on the left before making a final plunge into the forest on a continuation of the twisty rolling trail. Like the Blue Loop, the trailhead emerges when you're just starting to think you've got this trail stuff figured out.

Whether you've tackled them both or just one, the loops at Island Lake are fun for riders of all ages and levels. Even those who think they're beyond it

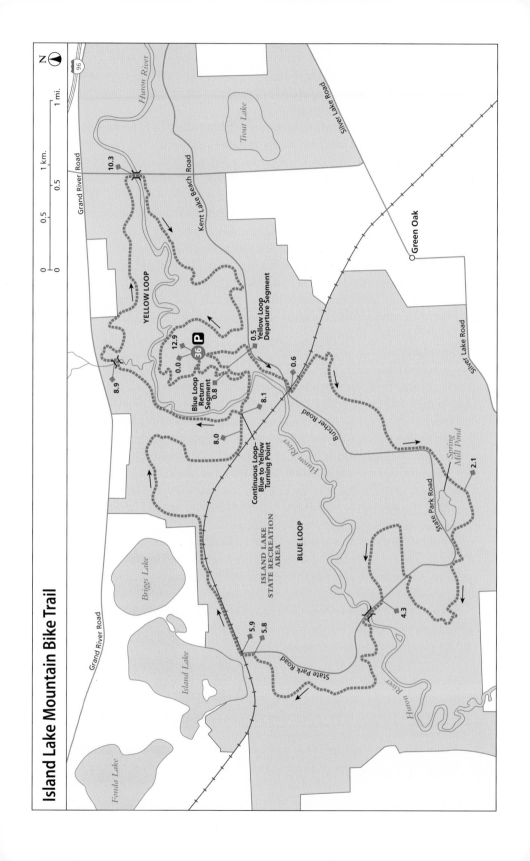

Island Lake Mountain Bike Trail

YELLOW LOOP

Huron River

Trout Lake

Silver Lake Road

Grand River Road

10.3

Kent Lake Beach Road

0.5
Yellow Loop
Departure Segment

12.9

0.0

36 P

0.8

0.6

8.9

Blue Loop
Return Segment

8.1

8.0

Continuous Loop—
Blue to Yellow
Turning Point

Butcher Road

Huron River

Silver Lake Road

Spring
Mill Pond

2.1

State Park Road

ISLAND LAKE
STATE RECREATION
AREA

BLUE LOOP

4.3

Briggs Lake

5.9

5.8

State Park Road

Huron River

Island Lake

Fonda Lake

Grand River Road

96

Green Oak

N

0   0.5   1 km.
0   0.5   1 mi.

in terms of skill still find themselves returning over and over because it's such a well-designed trail and such a great place to ride.

MILES AND DIRECTIONS

0.0 Leave the parking lot on the Blue Loop first.

0.6 Exit the trail and stay to the right, merging with Kent Lake Road westbound. Cross underneath the railroad bridge and immediately take a left back onto the trail.

2.1 Hug close to the parking area as you pass by Spring Mill Pond. There are trails wandering all over the place in this wide-open area, and it's not hard to get off track.

4.3 Turn right, merging onto State Park Road. Cross the bridge over the Huron River and turn left back onto the trail.

5.8 Turn left, merging onto State Park Road.

5.9 Cross the railroad tracks and immediately turn right back onto the trail that parallels the tracks.

8.1 Stay left at Y in the trail to continue on and transition to the Yellow Loop. If you want to get back to the parking lot, go right. The parking lot is 0.8 mile ahead.

8.9 Cross the wooden bridge at Woodruff Creek and head uphill.

10.3 Cross over the Huron River and take the trail right to parallel the river for a short way. From here the trail weaves back to the trailhead parking lot.

12.9 Arrive back at trailhead.

RIDE INFORMATION

Restrooms
Start/finish: At the trailhead, as well as picnic areas along the route

Maybury State Park

Consumption. That's what it was called back in the early part of the 20th century when the land was developed as a tuberculosis quarantine area. It was hoped the natural setting would help those with the disease recover. The center was closed in 1969 as TB became less common, and by 1975 it became a state park. By the late '80s part of the park was used for mountain biking, and by the mid-'90s an organized group took over maintenance and upkeep of the trails.

Maybury is a relatively short mountain bike trail by standards of other mountain bike areas in the region, but there's a lot to experience in this small area. At 5.4 miles from trailhead to trailhead, it's long enough to get immersed in, yet short enough not to capitalize on a day. It's good for beginners, but it has enough challenges to make mid-level and advanced riders keep on their guard and hone their riding skills. This is a twisting single-track with a smooth-enough flow to get a good roll going. The topography has many ups and downs, but even on the steepest climbs the rise is relatively moderate.

At the western edge of Wayne County, it's in a high population area, yet it dives deep into a beautiful forest that takes you far from the madding crowd. This is a nice place to introduce someone new to mountain biking, a place to bring kids after they've got a few fundamentals under their pedals, or a spot to get in a quick lunchtime ride.

Start: The paved path begins in the southeast corner of the parking lot and leads 0.6 mile to the trailhead

Length: 6.5 miles

Approximate riding time: 0.5–1.5 hours

Best bike: Mountain bike

Terrain and trail surface: Rolling dirt single-track with roots and sometimes loose gravel surface. Log piles, rock gardens, tight trail sections with bypasses for those who prefer to avoid obstacles. There's a well-marked paved 0.6-mile path from the parking area to the trailhead.

Traffic and hazards: There are pathway crossings with pedestrians and cyclists to watch for

Skill level: Beginner to intermediate. There are some technical sections near the beginning that will test the limits of a beginning rider, but the trail settles into a more gently flowing ride after that.

Things to see: Dense forest, marsh areas, wildlife

Maps: Michigan DNR–Maybury State Park: www.michigandnr. com/parksandtrails/details.aspx?id=469&type=SPRK; Motor City Mountain Bike Association: site.mcmba.org/index.php/our-trails/ mayburystatepark; *DeLorme: Michigan Atlas & Gazetteer,* page 33

Getting there by car: From I-96 at exit 160 go south 3.9 miles on Beck Road and take a right onto 8 Mile Road. Follow 8 Mile 1.1 miles to the entrance to Maybury State Park on the left. Take the entry drive to the T in the road, turn left, and continue to the large parking area. A Michigan State Park "Passport" or a day pass is required. GPS: N42 25.862 W83 32.112

THE RIDE

Ride from the parking lot through a small patch of woods, then left onto the paved path. Follow the signs to the trailhead at mile 0.6. There's a large information kiosk with event postings and trail information at the trailhead. This is also the exit from the trail, so when heading out, make sure to take the trail to the left.

The single-track wastes no time in indoctrinating you to the challenge of uphill, twisting trail conditions. The first section of Maybury is some of its most technical, with many roots to contend with along with the tight single-track. If you're a bit over your head at this point, realize that it does lighten up after a mile or so. Also be aware that you're never far from a place to exit the trail. The paved bike trail is often in view during parts of the ride.

There are introduced obstacles along the way that you can opt out

Bike Shops

D & D Bicycles and Hockey: 121 N. Center St., Northville, MI 48167; (248) 347-1511; ddbicyclesandhockey.com
REI Northville: 17559 Haggerty Rd. (Haggerty and 6 Mile Rd.), Northville, MI 48168; (248) 347-2100
Town and Country Bikes and Boards: 148 N. Center St., Northville, MI 48167; (248) 349-7140; townand countrybikeandboards.com
Trails Edge Cyclery: 232 N. Main St., Plymouth, MI 48170; (734) 420-1200; trails-edge.com

Pedaling through the forest

of or partake in. There's always the choice. Some of the most distinct obstacles appear at mile 1.2, where there's a rock garden to test your skills; at mile 2.6, where there's a log pile; and at mile 4.7, with more rocks. This is an actively maintained trail, so don't be surprised if more obstacles appear or if they change from time to time. There are also benches and information signs strategically placed along the trail where you can take a break, munch an energy bar, and chat about what you just experienced. Mile markers are placed every 0.5 mile.

There's a section called B Loop at mile 4.7 that's basically a Y in the trail that either reconnects you to a section of trail you passed over previously (right) or continues to the trailhead (left). If you loved that last section of trail you were on, you could be there all day, over and over.

Basically, you'll be immersed in forest the entire time, winding this way and that, making the area seem more expansive than it is. Civilization is never far off, but if all you see is trees and trail, then it seems pleasantly far far away in your imagination. That's the magic of Maybury.

Then, finally but perhaps too soon, the trail rises up, and at mile 5.9 you're back at the trailhead. Now it's decision time. One more loop? Or back to the car on the paved path you came in on?

MILES AND DIRECTIONS

0.0 Head south out of the parking lot through the woods, then take a left onto the paved bike path. Follow the signs to the trailhead.

0.6 At the trailhead take the left-side trail (this is a directional trail). The flow of the trail is straightforward for quite a while.

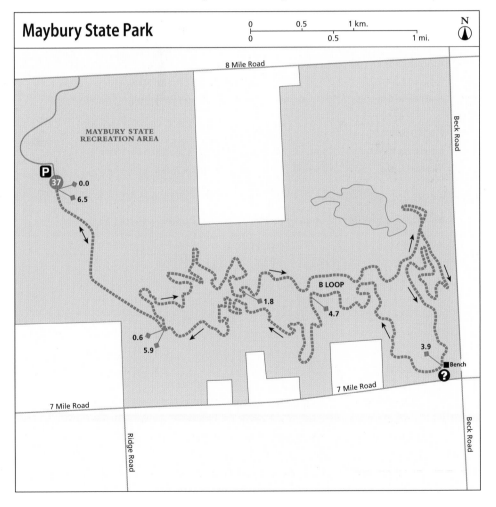

1.8 Bench and trail map.

3.9 This is the far southeast corner of the state park with benches and an information board.

4.7 B Loop begins.

5.9 Trailhead. Turn right onto paved path to return to parking area.

6.5 Back at parking area.

RIDE INFORMATION

Local Events/Attractions
There's a working farm open to visitors on the park property.
Northville is nearby and the historic neighborhoods are a great place to ride through for a post–mountain bike ride cool-down.
In nearby **Novi** there's another relatively short, well-maintained, intermediate mountain bike trail, the Lakeshore Trail in Lakeshore Park, 601 S. Lake Dr. (GPS: N42 30.632 W83 29.173), if you're interested in fitting another ride in. It also has numerous obstacles that are optional on a moderately rolling 8-mile loop.

Restaurants
Edwards Cafe: 115 E. Main St., Northville, MI 48167; (248) 344-1550
Tuscan Cafe: 150 N. Center St., Northville, MI 48167; (248) 305-8629

Restrooms
Mile 0.0: Alongside the main parking lot. There is water available as well.

38

Murray Lake–Torn Shirt

Murray Lake is less challenging than Torn Shirt, but that's not to say Murray Lake doesn't have its challenging hills, off-camber sections, roots, a few built obstacles, and tight single-track. It's intermediate in terms of mountain bike skill level overall. The topography rolls almost continually up and down, with some gentle, long climbs and a few short and steep ascents. Still, it's not something that would put a moderately skilled rider out of his or her depth.

What's more, the trail rolls through beautiful woodlands that are the antidote for an actively developing area in the region. It's not too far from I-96 and US 23, so access to the trail is good, but that's also led to rapid growth as the connections both east-west and north-south are excellent.

Murray Lake has had a bit of a face-lift recently, with some rerouting and trail expansion at the north end, along with the addition of a new wooden bridge crossing into the "Lost Loop" and some trail addition called the "Found Loop." (You need a program to keep the names straight.) This is a trail to savor and more is better. Be aware that some of the posted trail maps and online maps are of the old trail without the added sections.

Torn Shirt is more gnarly and twisted a single-track with some truly challenging (some would say evil) though short climbs. Part of the challenge is the root-laden trail, the loose gravel and sometimes rocks, and the sharp switchbacks on both up and down steep sections of the trail. The shirt wasn't torn on an easygoing amble through the forest. This demands technical skill, even at slow speeds. If you come back with just a torn shirt, consider yourself fortunate.

If you are up to the challenge, Torn Shirt is a real treat. It's tough, but it's also beautiful, with a lot of variety because of the ever-changing terrain.

Start: Trailhead parking lot at Brighton Recreation Area off Bishop Lake Road.

Length: Murray Lake Trail, 10 miles; Torn Shirt Trail, 5.1 miles

Approximate riding time: Murray Lake Trail, 1–2 hours; Torn Shirt Trail: 1–2 hours

Best bike: Mountain bike

Terrain and trail surface: Single-track sand and clay. Hilly throughout. Steeper, tighter sections are on the Torn Shirt Trail.

Traffic and hazards: Some dirt road crossings on the Murray Lake Trail, though traffic is light

Skill level: Murray Lake: advanced beginner to intermediate, though advanced riders will like the flow; Torn Shirt: advanced intermediate to advanced, for the stout-hearted

Things to see: Oak-hickory forest, marshland, small inland lakes, wildlife

Maps: State of Michigan DNR–Pinckney Recreation Area: www.michigandnr.com/parksandtrails/details.aspx?id=438&type=SPRK; *DeLorme: Michigan Atlas & Gazetteer,* page 40

Getting there by car: From US 23 at exit 58, take Lee Road west to the roundabout that exits onto Whitmore Lake Road headed south. Follow Whitmore Lake for 0.4 mile to Maltby Road and turn right. Go 2.2 miles to Hamburg Road and turn left. Go 0.2 mile and turn right onto Bauer Road. Follow Bauer for 0.6 mile to Bishop Lake Road and turn left. Follow Bishop Lake for 1.2 miles to the state park entrance on the left. Take the first right past the entry station to the parking lot trailhead. The trail leaves from the west side parking area heading south. State Recreation Passport required for entry. GPS: N42 30.048 W83 50.091

THE RIDE

Murray Lake Trail

Leave the parking lot on the designated trail, which begins as the trailhead for the Bishop Lake Hiking trail, and Torn Shirt and Murray Lake mountain bike trails. It's two-way for a short phase. The hiking trail splits to the right at about 200 feet in. Stay to the left and cross Bishop Lake Complex Road, then jump back onto the trail and continue to the trail split at mile 0.1. Torn Shirt is to the right, Murray Lake to the left. Go left. It drops through the woods and crosses the return section of trail at mile 0.2. It then crosses Bishop Lake Road. Bishop Lake, though dirt, has fast-moving traffic, so cross with care. At mile 0.3, the trails cross the return portion for the last time. Stay to the right.

The trail now unleashes itself on some sandy rolling terrain. There's a dramatic dip at mile 0.6 that drops and rises back to a short but biting climb. It

In the right conditions the trails are good to ride year-round.

feels all the more difficult because it's so early in the ride and the leg muscles are still trying to loosen up. This will get them well on their way. The climbs won't be as steep for quite a while, but there are few places from here on out that could be considered flat. Flats do exist, but they're soon followed by the opposite of flat.

This isn't considered a technical trail, but with all the tight twists and turns it does require focus. The turns have a smooth flow for the most part. Just don't get overly complacent because every now and then there's a tight switchback just when you get the momentum going.

At the top of the climb on mile 1.8, there's a shortcut (trail marker #4) that will connect to the final section of the trail. This isn't a bad place to reassess if you feel that the trail is more than you'd imagined it would be. Or if you realize you're supposed to be at the dentist office in 10 minutes. It's a quick jaunt back to the trailhead from here. If all is well, head down the hill and continue on through the woods.

Pedal on to mile 2.7, passing two small bridges in succession, then swinging right at marker #5 onto a newly developed stretch of the trail and crossing

Log over the trail

a dirt access road at mile 2.8. There will be a large new wood bridge crossing a small stream at a Y in the trail just beyond the road. Again, if it's time to head back, this is a spot that cuts about 3.0 miles off the trail if you turn left at the Y and take the return trail.

Continuing on, cross the bridge, after which is trail marker #6. Stay to the right and head into what is known as the Lost Loop. At mile 3.2 there's an aromatic section of pine trees with a nice bed of needles to roll over. The trail on the Lost Loop basically wraps back and forth along a ridge line. There are some old mile markers on the trail that are now inaccurate due to the added trail. They may be removed by the time this is printed, but if not, that's why your GPS and the trail's mile markers are now off.

The trail coordinators have added an extra mile in the back here and for good reason. Though it's hard to say one section is more beautiful than another, this section certainly qualifies as one of the finest in the park. There are some good lake views, some low marsh areas, and some all-around excellent single-track.

By this time you'll have noticed that there's been a lot of topographic relief. It doesn't go much beyond 75 vertical feet since the trailhead, but it's so constant that you might be feeling its effects. After crossing back over the bridge, take the Y to the right and cross back over the access road. The trail arcs right and begins a steady climb up through the trees. It eventually reaches a log rail along a winding descent at mile 6.7. It soon comes to the marshy edges of Murray Lake and weaves along this for a short way before working its way back inland.

At mile 8.0 there's another shortcut onto the return trail. Otherwise, take the trail east to a large 180 at marker #4 (the first shortcut in the series). Swing back west, paralleling the trail you were just on to a marker indicating a choice of Easy or Hard. The Hard choice goes to the right and is very short but also very challenging, the most challenging section on the whole ride so far. If you can ride the whole thing, you get bonus points. The Easy section is just that.

After passing Hard/Easy, the trail rolls along and eventually drops to the margin of Reed Lake. That's the sign that the Murray Lake Ride is almost over. Follow the signs back across Bishop Lake Road, then Bishop Lake Complex Road back to the trailhead.

Torn Shirt

Depart the trailhead in the same spot, cross Camp Road and at the Y in the trail (mile 0.1) go right, or to be more accurate go straight. Torn Shirt has a well-deserved reputation as a tough trail, though it's a bit deceiving for the early part of the ride. It's not overly challenging, and it rides through some beautiful marshland. Sure, it twists and turns more sharply than Murray Lake, but the rises and falls aren't that much different. Then the hills get a bit more edgy and a few roots show their rooty bodies, and something starts to change.

Soon turns are aggressively placed on those biting little climbs and drops. At a little under the first mile it

Bike Shops

D & D Bicycles and Hockey: 9977 E. Grand River Ave., Brighton, MI 48116; (810) 227-5070; ddbicyclesandhockey.com
Hometown Bicycles: 10605 Grand River Rd., Brighton, MI 48116; (810) 225.2441; myhometownbicycles.wordpress.com
Town N Country Bikes: 8160 Grand River Rd., Brighton, MI 48116; (810) 227-4420; tncbikes.com

Murray Lake–Torn Shirt

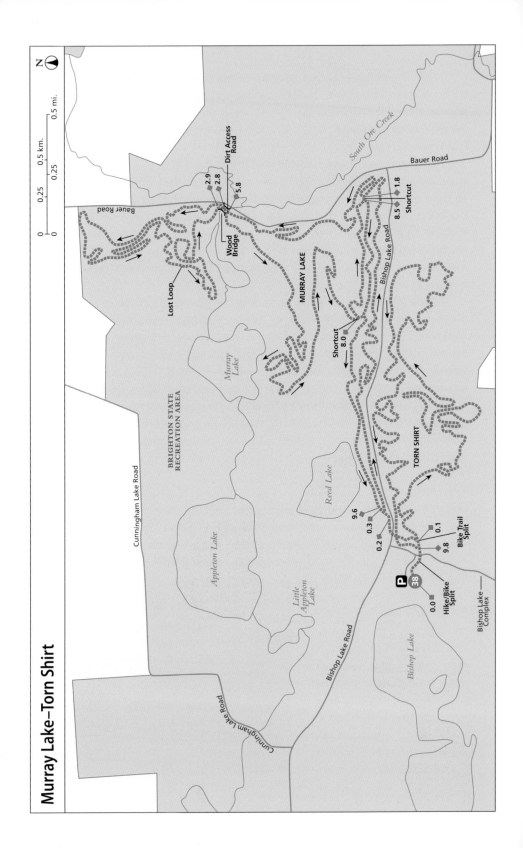

becomes evident that you're not on your grandmother's mountain bike trail (unless your grandma is a wild daredevil). After another section that lulls you once again into complacency, the true nature of the trail is revealed. At about mile 1.2 all goes steeply up, rutted with gravel and roots.

From there it's a roll over what seems like the top, then a short descent and another upward trajectory with more rocks and roots to plague you. Soon it's a long drop to a fecund marsh on the left, a switchback at the bottom, and then the climb of the day, an average grade of 10 percent with a few sections much steeper, and with—say it with me—roots and tight turns! This is single-track heaven for those who know bike handling technique.

Of course, the descent is the next exciting adventure, dropping rapidly. Continue on with a series of spiky sections and rooted drops. At around mile 3.2 the trail swings back in the direction of the trailhead and parallels Bishop Lake Road. If fatigue is setting in and you want to find relief in a dirt road return, watch for some of the small emergency exit trails to the right that will get you onto the road. If you do take one of these, once you get to the road, take a left and head west back to home base.

Or stay on the trail and resume the challenge that is Torn Shirt. The largest hills are behind you, but there are still plenty of roots, and the trail still puts you and your bike to the test. At mile 3.9 is a refreshing pine grove, and at mile 4.0 is the large marsh that you passed between a couple of large hills earlier in the ride. Rock and roll back to the connection with the Murray Lake Trail and follow the signs back to the trailhead. A pat on the back for taking on this short but very technical trail.

MILES AND DIRECTIONS

0.0 Leave the Bishop Lake parking area on the trail. A short way up, the trail splits. The right trail is for hiking only. The left trail is the biking trail. Take the left trail and cross Bishop Lake Complex Road (complex name!).

0.1 Trail splits again. Right is the Torn Shirt Trail, left is Murray Lake Trail. The following is the description of the Murray Lake Trail. Torn Shirt is intricate, filigreed, relatively short, and straightforward.

Murray Lake Trail

0.2 Cross Bishop Lake Road to the trail on the other side.

0.3 The trail splits once more. The exit from Murray Lake Trail is on the left. The entrance is on the right. Go right.

1.8 There's a shortcut crossover to the end of the Murray Lake Trail at this point. Stay to the right.

2.8 This is another shortcut crossover point where you can return before completing the entire route. To continue, cross the dirt road and go over the bridge. To turn back, take a left onto the road and find the return trail on the left.

2.9 Keep right at the fork in the trail.

5.8 Cross the bridge once more (two-way) and keep to the right-side trail.

5.9 Outhouse next to the trail.

8.0 Fork in trail with shortcut crossover option.

8.5 Crossover option to redo an earlier part of the trail.

9.6 Cross Bishop Lake Road.

9.8 Return to two-way section of trail. Cross Bishop Lake Complex Road and follow the trail back to the parking area.

10.0 Arrive back at trailhead.

RIDE INFORMATION

Accommodations
There are campground sites and rustic cabins in the recreation area. Call (800) 447-2757 for more information.

Local Events/Attractions
The town of **Brighton** is nearby with numerous shopping and food options.

Restaurants
Brighton Bar & Grill: 400 W. Main St., Brighton, MI 48116; (810) 229-4115; www.brightonbarandgrill.com
Two Brothers Coffee: 423 W. Main St., Brighton, MI 48116; (810) 588-4087; www.twobrotherscoffee.com
The Wooden Spoon: 675 W. Grand River, Brighton, MI 48116; (810) 588-4386; woodenspoonmarket.com

Restrooms
Start/Finish: At trailhead parking area
Mile 5.9: Along the trail

Potawatomi Trail

There are three trails in one in this recreation area, the infamous and long Poto Trail, the mid-length Crooked Lake Trail, and the shortest Silver Lake Trail. None, not even the Silver Lake Trail, could be considered beginner's trails. There are just too many hills and roots to make that claim. Silver Lake is more an intermediate trail, and the Poto and Crooked Lake are advanced intermediate- to expert-level trails.

The Poto, as it is known, is the largest and longest of all the mountain bike trails in Southeast Michigan. It's somewhat legendary, since it was once rated by many as one of the better trails in the country. Perhaps due to the increased popularity of the sport, and the improvement and growth of other trails, it's no longer on countrywide top ten lists, but it's still a daunting, challenging, and fun trail. At 17.5 miles for the longest loop, it also offers a good, hearty day out, especially due to the constantly rolling terrain. It's not for the faint of heart by any means. Even intermediate-level riders will be tested to their limits at times. Enter with caution and be ready to take one of the shorter options if it proves to be more difficult than expected. You won't be the first.

The Poto has been compared to Pontiac Lake mountain bike trail, only twice as long. There are similarities, mainly in terms of the fast flow of the trails, the oak-hickory forest, the hilly terrain, and a place to swim when you're done. But, really, they're very different in character. As good as Pontiac Lake is, the Poto, because of its greater size, has more time to unfold in constantly different ways with bridge crossings, boardwalks, varied climbs and descents, lake and marsh views, and overall variation in surface types. Neither trail, though, is overly technical in ways that Highland or Holdridge's Gruber's Grinder are. There are occasional technical options on the Poto—the roots can be daunting in places, a few of the climbs are relatively long, there are some soft sand sections—but the Poto flows in a way that allows riders to pedal hard and fast in most cases, even while tackling a technical section. It's almost rhythmic in its ability to accommodate for speed, yet constantly pitch the bike either up or down a hill. Sometimes momentum carries you up and over, other times it's up to those legs to keep cranking…and cranking.

Perhaps because it's both challenging and fast, it's an extremely popular mountain bike trail. On weekends it can get very busy. It's not just busy with bikers either. The trail is open to and used by hikers and runners as well. It's not unusual to come across a troop of Boy Scouts or pack-laden campers hoofing along. The trail was established and laid out by the Boy Scouts in 1964. It's gone through some re-routing here and there to lessen erosion and to accommodate the various user groups, but this is a multiuse trail. Please be courteous to all other users.

There's a nice beach area with a concession stand, restrooms, and outdoor showers at the west end of the parking lot overlooking Silver Lake. Bikes are not allowed to ride in this area. There are also water fountains, in season, for filling bottles.

Start: Parking lot off Silver Hill Road in Silver Lake State Park parking lot. There are two very large parking lots, one just up the hill from the other.

Length: Poto Trail, 17.5 miles (full), 13.4 miles (with midway shortcut); Crooked Lake Trail, 5.1 miles (with shortcut), 7.8 miles (extended); Silver Lake Trail, 2.4 miles (with shortcut)

Approximate riding time: Poto Trail, 2–3 hours; Crooked Lake Trail, 1–2 hours; Silver Lake Trail, 0.5 hour

Best bike: Mountain bike

Terrain and trail surface: Fast flowing varying-width single-track, rolling hills, loose gravel to hard-packed dirt, a few rocks and many, many roots. You'll need skill levels of intermediate to advanced on all trails.

Traffic and hazards: A couple of paved road crossings, a few dirt road crossings, hikers and runners are common, and hunters are out and visible during the fall hunting season. It's probably a good idea for you to be visible as well. Gravel surface in places makes it easy to lose traction, with rutted downhills, and sharp gravelly turns at the bottom of fast downhills. Speed may be your biggest hazard.

It's easy to overcook on some parts of the trail. Roots are common on the uphill climbs and downhill ascents. Steep sections. Wooden bridges and boardwalks can be dangerously slippery when wet.

Things to see: Views over Pickerel Lake, Dead Lake, and Gosling Lake, kettle ponds and marsh areas, lush woods, ravines and drumlins, along with wildflowers and wildlife, including deer and sandhill cranes. This is a lake area, and there are a couple of post-ride lakes that are ideal for cooling off after a long ride. Silver Lake is at the trailhead. Pickerel Lake, a quiet lake, is off Hankerd Road on a dirt access road.

Maps: MMBA: mmba.org/trail-guide/#18; State of Michigan DNR–Silver Lake State Park: www.michigandnr.com/parksandtrails/Details .aspx?id=484&type=SPRK; *DeLorme: Michigan Atlas & Gazetteer,* page 32

Getting there by car: From US 23 at exit 49, take North Territorial Road west 10.4 miles to Dexter Townhall Road and turn right. Take Dexter Townhall 1.1 miles to the state park entrance and turn left. Follow the entry road 0.7 mile back to the parking area. State of Michigan Recreation Passport or day pass required for entry. GPS: N42 24.895 W83 57.877

THE RIDE

Poto Trail–17.5 miles

There used to be a wicked log-filled, steep climb at the start of the Poto. Dreaded by some, proof of prowess by others, it was often the most humbling part of the ride with stiff, cold muscles. It's gone. There's still a climb, but it's been adjusted to create a much more gently manageable beginning.

Leave the parking lot and climb the short two-way single-track to Silver Hill Road and continue on to the forest trail. Look to the right and you'll see remnants of the old route. Be happy and pedal on. The trail weaves its way up and down, back and forth in a way that allows for you to get a good rhythm going without taxing the legs too much. At mile 0.5 that flow is arrested by a 1,000-foot stretch of roots in an uneven arrangement.

Immediately past this the trail splits with a less challenging shortcut going straight and a longer, hillier section to the left (the shortcut is 1.1 miles, the longer segment is 3.3 miles). Turn left onto the longer segment. After a short grade upward, the trail takes a long downhill run to a narrow passage around a barrier at the 1.0-mile mark. Keep arcing to the right onto a continuation of the trail as it begins a pair of short but steep climbs, to roll out on a more gentle series of hills. The next few miles are a repeat of this, with sweeping, relatively fast rolling trail, a few sharp pitched but short ascents and descents, and some brief rock-strewn sections to keep you on your guard.

At the trail crossing point at Marker #4 (mile 3.8), there's the choice to go down and across a bridge over a part of the lake, or a left that rises up on a ridge along the south rim of the lake. Take the left. The trail to the right is the reconnection of the shortcut from Marker #5 passed at the 0.5-mile mark of the ride. The views over Pickerel Lake are beautiful through the trees. It's a small, quiet, spring-fed lake, with no structures anywhere along its shore. There's a turn off the main trail at mile 4.1 that takes you to the beach area.

Continue up the trail on the left to a sandy drop where the access road meets Hankerd Road (mile 4.4). Cross Hankerd. Traffic moves fast here, so cross carefully. Drop down to a boardwalk through a colorful marsh area on both sides, then climb out and up a long, mostly gentle uphill that gets increasingly dramatic topographically. There's a fast, twisty downhill chute that leads along the margins of Dead Lake, then up above it to a bench with a great view down the slope and out over the water.

Climb farther and soon experience the first root-laden downhill. There are many ways to approach the descent: either jump off the root ledges or carve around them, it's up to you. The trail takes a hard left and drops to a small bridge, then rolls through more roots to one of the toughest hill climbs of the route. It would be moderately challenging if it weren't for some ledge-like roots that need to be negotiated on the steep uphill turns. That raises the level from moderate to difficult. I call the hill the Root of All Evil. If you make it over the top without dabbing a foot, you're a pro.

Sweep through a series of turns and hills to a sandy downhill and a sharp right turn at mile 6.5. Left is currently a hiker-only trail, and straight is a steep wall of a hill that's long since been rerouted to avoid more erosion. Take the sandy right and sashay through a series of turns to a series of drops one after another that I've labeled the Leaps of Faith. At the bottom is an outhouse and past that the Blind Lake campground and Blind Lake itself. Turn a sharp left on the short but biting uphill at mile 6.7. At the top is a two-track road. Follow it west to mile 6.9, where there's a single-track spur to the right. Take this to Crescent Drive, a dirt road. Cross Crescent and begin ascending a sandy uphill. Depending on the time of year, this can be relatively hard-packed or very loose and loamy. It's a relatively long ascent and it gets gnarled with roots as you near the top, a nice combination of legs burning from the effort and a test of technical skill. At the lip of the hill is a connection to the left that leads to the nearby Boy Scout camp. Keep going straight to reap the reward of that climb, nearly 0.5 mile of level trail, a rarity on this ride.

The descent, beginning at mile 7.5, is steep, twisting, and (what else?) rooted. Enjoy. It levels off on a sandy run-out that comes to a T in the trail. Take a left. This leads to a tall wood bridge spanning a narrows between Half-moon Lake and Lake Watson. It's a good place for a short break and some great views over the water on each side. Drop back down the other side and immediately up a short, steep, rooty climb leading to some rolling terrain and down to a boardwalk over a marsh (before the boardwalk was built, this was a quagmire in the wet season with hub-deep mud and a base of slippery roots). Praise the boardwalk builders among us.

Roll among the trees and wildflowers to Max Drive. Cross Max with gusto, as there's an angry steep ascent on the other side, much of it covered in erosion

Bridge view over one of the many scenic lakes in the area

control webbing. Follow that to a sharp right-hander and up another tricky ascent, this time with large jutting roots angled across the trail. Once over that, it's through the woods to the sandiest climb of the day. There are some tricks and lines better than others, but to each his own. At the top of the climb is the halfway point of this route, at mile 8.8, with a welcoming bench for a snack break. It's also the split for what's known as the Shortcut. It takes the entire back Gosling Lake Section off the route and is a great option for those who know their limitations or for those just limited on time. It's a 1.0-mile shortcut down the trail, past the yurt, up a two-track, across a left-right jog on Glenbrook Road, back onto two-track, and over to the return section of the Poto.

Continue on the main trail, which follows some gentler but sometimes rooted single-track to Patterson Lake Road. Like Hankerd, traffic moves fast here, so cross with care. There's a dirt parking area on the other side and the trail continues on behind that. This section of the trail, all the way back out and around to a re-crossing of Patterson Lake Road, is known as the Gosling Lake Loop. During the early spring season and wet times of year, riding this is not recommended as there are many springs (even on the upper portions of some of the hills) and low, muddy areas along the trail. Otherwise it's a fun, quiet section of very hilly trail. There's a well-placed bench at mile 9.7 with a view of Gosling Lake to the east. A rest might be just the thing. Shortly beyond this is a wickedly steep section of the ascent. The trail passes Doyle Road at mile 10.4, then rises to a line along fenced University of Michigan nature study area land and back down a long sandy chute (beware of the sandy right-hand turn at the bottom) and through some winding trail to Doyle once more. Cross over to enter a section of numerous boardwalks and small bridge crossings. This, too, was once a sloppy mess before the angels of wood-spanning did their handiwork.

This section of trail has some great up- and downhill sweeping and even chicane-like single-track. The trail reemerges at the Gosling Lake parking area onto a two-track dirt access road. Take the access road to Patterson Lake Road (Hell is 1.0 mile east, in case you were wondering). Cross Patterson Lake Road and dive back into the woods for a series of long uphill and downhill rolls. There's even another section of short drops, one after another.

At mile 13.5, the trail meets that of the halfway Shortcut. When wet, this section of trail can be greasy for a short way. It then reaches a long, narrow wood bridge over a marsh, goes back into the woods, and over another long, narrow wood bridge, then onto one of the most steadily rolling sections of trail on the route. It's a series of repeated ups and downs, dotted with occasional sharp twists and short, leg-biting rooted climbs. Get your mojo going and it's a great time. Cross a small wood bridge at mile 14.6 and dig in for another hard, short uphill. The beat goes on until Marker #9 at mile 14.9, where there's also a well-placed bench for those who want a short respite after that series of sawtooth rollers.

Turn left and follow the trail on a still-rolling, but much gentler trajectory for the next 0.5 mile to where it drops to a bridge over a small, scenic stream. Follow the stream until the trail begins to rise once more. At this point, hope that you've left enough reserve for the longest climb of the day. It rises up, first bitingly over some large roots, then to a sharp left-hand turn and nearly straight up a heart-pumping, leg-searing hill that's not overly steep but, not to be under-stressed, long. Some call this Alpe D'Huez, perhaps overstating the case by an Hors category or two, but it can feel that way after putting out all that effort over the previous 15-plus miles. Walking is not uncommon.

Bike Shops

Aberdeen Bike & Outdoors: 1101 S. Main St., Chelsea, MI 48118; (734) 475-8203
Dexter Bike and Sport: 3173 Baker Rd., Dexter, MI 48130; (734) 426-5900; www.dexterbikeandsport.com

Over the top, another trail joins in on the left. Stay right and drop down, then up one last pitch to another bench at the day's high point and what once was a great view south over Crooked Lake, but is now impeded by a dense thicket of trees and shrubs. (Just to get your bearings, this is directly above the Crooked Lake campground.) Descend a long, gravelly, curving downhill. Watch for hikers, as this is near enough for groups to hike from the Silver Lake parking area where you began this journey. At mile 16.1, the trail crosses the access road to Crooked Lake and continues along a fast, sandy descent through the woods. Cross Silver Hill Road at mile 16.4 and climb to the last rock- and root-strewn section of glacially carved hills where Silver Lake will come into view if you're not so concentrated on keeping the bike upright that longer views are not a priority. Watch for the boardwalk along this section, as it comes up on a somewhat blind curve and can prove perilous if wet or if approached at too high a rate of speed and you overshoot it, ending up in the marsh.

At mile 16.9, the trail comes to a T. Left is for hikers only. Turn right, through the roots one last and joyous time, and climb to Silver Hill Road. Turn left and follow this to where you entered the trail (mile 17.2). Turn left, watch for oncoming bikers, as this is now two-way, and roll into the open alongside the parking area.

Crooked Lake Trail–5.1 miles (with shortcut) or 7.8 miles (extended)

The Crooked Lake Trail is a great option if you want a short ride, or if you want to add to the longer one. From the trailhead, ride to Trail Marker #4, as noted in the Poto ride above (with or without the shortcut at Marker #5), and instead of going left at #4 to Hankerd Road, go north across the bridge at Pickerel Lake. The views from this bridge are excellent, with a mix of marshland close in and a broad vista over the lake with the surrounding hills in the longer view. The trail climbs, then descends to a small bridge farther on, then rolls up and down to a T in the trail at Marker #3. Turn left and follow the hilly, rooted, and rocky trail until it descends to a bridge over a stream separating Crooked Lake from Pickerel Lake. Then, climb a steep ascent until it levels off on a sometimes sandy section of trail. The views over Pickerel Lake are quite stunning from here.

Follow this to where it crosses the dirt Glenbrook Road. The sand can get quite deep on this descent, but after crossing a small bridge, it returns to hard-pack trail, then arrives at Marker #9, where it rejoins the Poto Trail. See Poto description above for more details to get back from here.

Silver Lake Trail–2.4 miles (with shortcut)

This is the shortest trail option in the trail system, and it's no compromise in terms of beauty. From the trailhead, make your way to the Marker #4 trail crossing via the shortcut at Marker #5. On the shortcut, note the ruins of a house, fireplace still intact, at mile 0.8. Though there are some extensive root areas on this shortcut, the hills are very gentle. Once at #4, take the trail segment right (heading north) across the bridge over the marshy east end of Pickerel Lake. Follow this to the T in the trail at Marker #3 and take a right. The trail slowly climbs and falls around a series of glacial kettles and drumlins with extensive views down long slopes, into dry bowls or marshes. This trail also has one of the steepest hills in the system, often requiring a dismount and a push to the top. The views are worth slowing down for. Once over the top, descend to Silver Hill Road at mile 2.0. Turn right and ride the dirt road to mile 2.3, where you'll turn left on the two-way access trail that returns to the parking lot trailhead.

MILES AND DIRECTIONS

Poto Trail

0.0 Climb out of the parking lot up the short climb and cross Silver Hill Road to start the trail ride.

0.6 The trail offers two options at Trail Marker #5: straight ahead or left. Straight ahead is a shortcut. Go left.

1.0 There's a very short section of pavement here then a sharp right turn back onto the trail and up a series of short, spiky climbs.

3.8 Trails converge at Trail Marker #4. Stay to the left and climb along the ridge above Pickerel Lake.

4.1 Stay to the left at the Y in the trail.

4.4 Emerge from a sandy section of the trail onto the Pickerel Lake access road (watch for cars). Cross Hankerd Road and descend to a boardwalk.

6.5 Take a right at the bottom of a sandy downhill where trails converge.

6.7 There's an outhouse here at the edge of the Blind Lake Campground. Take an uphill left on the unmarked turn just up the trail a short way (otherwise you'll end up on the shore of Blind Lake). Once over the hill stay left on the two-track road.

6.9 Turn right onto the single-track. The two-track continues straight. Cross Crescent Drive (watch for cars) and begin climbing the hill.

7.6 Turn left onto the trail.

7.8 Atop the tall wooden bridge on the canal between Watson and Halfmoon Lakes.

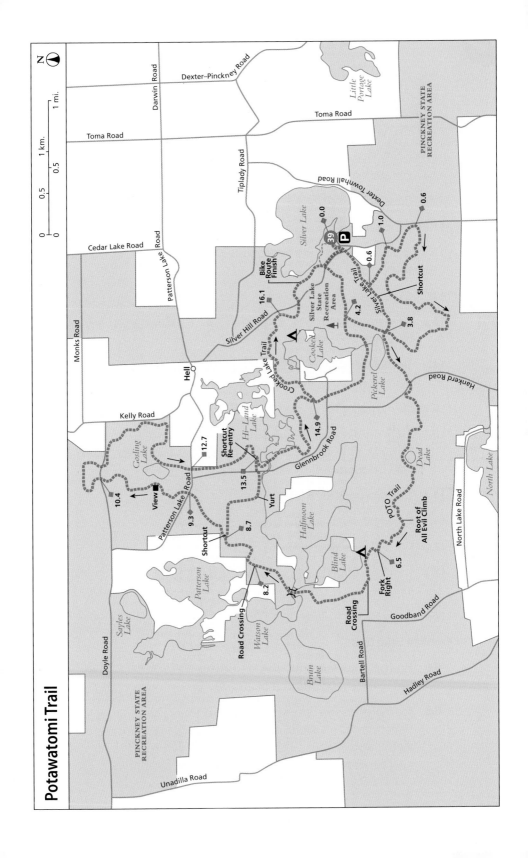

Potawatomi Trail

Dexter–Pinckney Road

Darwin Road

Toma Road

Toma Road

Little Portage Lake

Tiplady Road

Patterson Lake Road

Cedar Lake Road

Monks Road

PINCKNEY STATE RECREATION AREA

Dexter Townhall Road

PINCKNEY STATE RECREATION AREA

Silver Lake

Silver Lake Trail

0.0

0.6

1.0

0.6

Shortcut

4.2

3.8

Cooked Lake

Crooked Lake

Silver Lake State Recreation Area

Bike Route Finish

16.1

Silver Hill Road

Hell

Kelly Road

12.7

Shortcut Re-entry

Hi-Land Lake

14.9

Glennbrook Road

Pickerel Lake

Hankerd Road

Gosling Lake

10.4

View

9.3

Shortcut

8.7

Yurt

13.5

Patterson Lake Road

Patterson Lake

Sayles Lake

Doyle Road

Watson Lake

Road Crossing

8.2

Hallmoon Lake

Blind Lake

Road Crossing

POTO Trail

Dead Lake

Root of All Evil Climb

6.5

Fork Right

North Lake Road

North Lake

Bruin Lake

Bartell Road

Goodband Road

Hadley Road

Unadilla Road

PINCKNEY STATE RECREATION AREA

N

0   0.5   1 km.

0   0.5   1 mi.

39

P

8.2 Cross Max Drive and dig in for the steep uphill climb.

8.7 The unofficial halfway point of the Poto Trail. There's a bench available to rest your weary bones. There's also a shortcut to the right that passes by the yurt and removes about 4.8 miles from the overall route.

9.3 Cross Patterson Lake Road (fast-moving traffic—cross with caution).

10.4 Cross Doyle Road (dirt).

11.0 Cross back over Doyle Road.

12.4 Emerge from the trail into the Gosling Lake parking area and follow the two-track out to Patterson Lake Road.

12.7 Cross Patterson Lake Road.

13.5 Cross the dirt road. (This is where the shortcut from the yurt merges back onto the main trail.)

14.9 Turn left at Trail Marker #9. (This is where the Crooked Lake Trail re-merges with the Poto Trail.)

15.7 Stay to the right.

16.1 Cross the dirt road. It's somewhat of a blind crossing that comes up quick, so watch for cars. This is the access road to the Crooked Lake Campground.

16.4 Cross Silver Hill Road (dirt).

16.9 Turn right. The trail to the left is for hikers only.

17.0 Turn left onto Silver Hill Road.

17.2 Turn left onto the two-way trail back down to the trailhead parking area.

17.5 Arrive back at trailhead.

Crooked Lake Trail

0.0 As on all these trail rides, leave the parking lot, climb the hill, and cross over Silver Hill Road onto the trail.

0.6 The trail offers two options at Trail Marker #5: straight ahead or left. Straight ahead is a shortcut. Go left, though if you want to take the shorter route it will cut a 3.3-mile loop out of your ride. The shortcut is a 0.5-mile connection to Trail Marker #4.

1.0 There's a very short section of pavement here then a sharp right turn back onto the trail and up a series of short, spiky climbs.

3.8 Trails converge at Trail Marker #4. Go straight north across the wooden bridge over the marshy end of Pickerel Lake.

4.2 Turn left at Trail Marker #3.

5.3 Cross Glenbrook Road (dirt).

5.4 Crooked Lake Trail merges once more with the full Poto Trail at Trail Marker #9.

6.2 Stay right.

6.6 Cross Crooked Lake Campground access road (dirt). Watch for cars.

6.9 Cross Silver Hill Road.

7.4 Turn right. The trail to the left is for hikers only.

7.5 Turn left onto Silver Hill Road.

7.7 Turn left onto the two-way trail back down to the trailhead parking area.

7.8 Arrive back at the trailhead.

Silver Lake Trail

0.0 Leave the parking lot, climb the hill, and cross over Silver Hill Road onto the trail.

0.6 The trail offers two options at Trail Marker #5: straight ahead or left. Straight ahead is a shortcut. Take the shortcut, though if you want to take the longer route it will add a challenging 3.3-mile loop to your ride.

1.1 Trails converge at Trail Marker #4. Turn right (north) across the wooden bridge over the marshy end of Pickerel Lake.

1.5 Turn right at Trail Marker #3.

1.8 This is a very steep, long climb, probably the steepest in the whole Poto Trail system.

2.1 Turn right onto Silver Hill Road.

2.3 Turn left onto the two-way trail and ride down to the trailhead parking area.

2.4 Arrive back at the trailhead.

RIDE INFORMATION

Accommodations

There are two tenting campgrounds in the park, one at Crooked Lake, which cars can access, and the other at Blind Lake that's hike-in only. There's also a yurt along the bike trail shortcut and a cabin available. See Pinckney State Recreation Area website for details: www.michigandnr.com/parksandtrails/Details.aspx?id=484&type=SPRK

Local Events/Attractions

The following events are somewhat informal, but they are posted seasonally on the Michigan Mountain Biking Association website (mmba.org) shortly before they are held.

Abominable Snowman Ride: Held each December, preferably in snow.

Single-speed World Championships: Tongue-in-cheek-titled event held periodically during the year that highlights single-speed mountain biking.

Triple Trail Challenge: An event held on these trails each September that opens some trails normally off-limits to bikers.

Restaurants

Back to the Roots: 115 S. Main St., Chelsea, MI 48118; (734) 475-2700

Common Grill: 112 S. Main St., Chelsea, MI 48118; (734) 475-0470

Dam Site Inn: Just to say you ate in Hell at least once in your life. Pub food; 4045 Patterson Lake Rd., Hell, MI 48169; (734) 878-9300

Zou-Zou's (cafe): 101 N. Main St., Chelsea, MI 48118; (734) 433-4226

Restrooms

Start/Finish: trailhead

Mile 6.7: Blind Lake Campground

Stony Creek Mountain Bike Trail

This is a very popular mountain bike trail, partly due to location in a highly popu-lated area and partly to the wide-ranging variety of challenges it offers as well as the beauty of the terrain. It caters to riders of all levels, depending on the sections of the trail traversed. These sections are labeled on the park trail map (available online and at the office) with color designations: green for easy, blue for interme-diate, and black for most difficult.

The easy sections are basically two-track roadways that cover mostly flat to gently rolling terrain. The intermediate sections are similar in character to the easy, with perhaps a few steeper slopes. The black sections range from twisting and flat single-track to twisting with steep drops and climbs. These tend still to be moderate in difficulty, but they would put novice riders onto challenges that might go beyond their comfort zone.

The multiple personalities of this trail are both its strength and its weakness. The easy parts might not fascinate those looking for technical adventure, and the difficult sections might be more than someone wants when looking for an easygoing day on the trail. The entire system itself is relatively short when compared to other trail systems in the area, and when broken into difficulty levels, they're shorter still.

Add to the above that the trail numbering system can be confusing to those who haven't spent a good chunk of time getting acquainted with it. After #8, the consecutive arrangement gets muddled and from there on it becomes a free-for-all. In talks with regular trail users, I got the sense that eventually they just figure out their own lines and shape their ride to their own specific interests. To someone new to the system, it can be daunting, both in trying to stay oriented and in keep-ing to the designated one-way flow. This is a one-way directional trail system for the most part, with a few exceptions.

All that said, this should not deter anyone from riding Stony Creek. It truly is one of the finest areas to ride in the region. The woods and the topography alone are worth riding through. There were many sections where I had to stop and soak it in, thankful for the opportunity to be in such a beautiful place. And the afore-mentioned variety of experiences in this glacial moraine made it often seem like many separate, enjoyable rides in one. For a small area, it packs a lot in.

The area of the park where the mountain bike trail is situated was part of a family hunting estate once owned by the Sheldons of Detroit. Ruins of the home can be found near the adjoining golf course. The fact that the park is known as "Stony" Creek comes from the glacial aspect of a moraine, which leaves large and varied stone deposits as the glacier advances and recedes. The trail itself, however, isn't overly stony, but like many trails in the region there are loose gravelly sections in the areas worn by use.

Start: West Branch picnic area parking lot

Length: 11.2 miles

Approximate riding time: 1–2 hours

Best bike: Mountain bike; cyclocross or hybrid on the green trails

Terrain and trail surface: Varies from lightly rolling two-track to hilly single-track. It's maintained by the Clinton River Mountain Bike Association (CRAMBA) at www.cramba.org, where there's more information posted about this trail and other trails in the area.

Traffic and hazards: This is a self-enclosed trail system. There's no traffic. Occasional technical challenges that would test the skills of novice riders.

Things to see: Lush forested area, hilltop views, glacially shaped terrain, marsh areas, old fields

Maps: Huron-Clinton Metroparks website for Stony Creek: www. metroparks.com/metroparks/parks/index_all.aspx?ID=11&r=0; *DeLorme: Michigan Atlas & Gazetteer,* page 42

Getting there by car: From M-59 take exit 48 and head north on Dequindre Road 3.2 miles to Avon Road. Turn right onto Avon, which shortly resumes as Dequindre again. Take this 2.7 miles to Mt. Vernon Road and turn right. Follow this for 1.5 miles as Mt. Vernon becomes 26 Mile Road. Follow this to the exit right into the Metropark and follow the signs 3.7 miles to the West Branch Picnic Area. GPS: N42 43.814 W83 06.394

THE RIDE

This ride is one that I shaped in order to experience as varied a route as possible. Though there is a trail numbering system, and it needs to be followed in some form in order to stay on the one-way flow, there are probably as many different approaches to riding this as there are riders. Once you get used to the terrain, you can make your own route.

Depart from the West Branch picnic area along a wide two-track trail leading into a tall deciduous forest. Markers #1, #2, and #3 come quickly, within the first 0.5 mile, with a Y in the trail at #2. Stay to the right, continuing on to #3. At mile 0.5, the trail emerges from the woods into an open area of old field, with a mix of shrubs, wildflowers, and grasses. This takes a few turns along a flat section, follows the edge of a marsh area on the left, and dips back into a forested area alongside Sheldon Road.

It comes to #4 at mile 1.4, where there's a choice to go left or straight. Keep going straight, with Sheldon on the right. The same happens at #5, but stay on the straight and, well, not really narrow, but wide-ish trail. At mile 1.9, the trail swings to the east (left) and comes up to #6, where there's a turn left that you'll return to later in the ride, but for now go straight, paralleling Mead Road to the right.

The two-track gets a bit more rolling and takes more twists and turns through this area. There are some detour options at #7, #8, #9, and #10, but save them for another ride. Stay to the right in all cases and follow the outer boundaries of the trail system. At #11, turn right toward #12 (left takes you back to #8, where you could find yourself in an endless loop, only to be found weeks later, dazed and delirious—though happy, of course, because you're riding your bike).

The view opens onto a field on the right as it skirts the forest edge. The numbering system gets a bit disorienting at #12, as you get three directional options, and they all seem valid. What's worse, there are clear views over a wide area with trails crisscrossing, and rather than making things easier it adds to information overload. Stay to the right and head toward #13 along the field, then along a line of evergreen trees. At #13 (mile 3.5) the trail takes a sharp left, heading north up a rise. In less than 0.1 mile, take another left (Marker #14) and continue uphill along an open section of the trail to #15 at mile 3.8. This is another wide-open crossroads. You'll return here later to begin tackling the most challenging parts of the trail, but for now head across the open area toward #16, where it plunges once again into the leafy forest.

From #16 (mile 3.9), head to #17. Turn right at #17 and ride to #18, then left to #19. Notice that up to this point the route has followed the sequential

Bike Shops

KLM Bike & Fitness: 2680 Rochester Rd., Rochester Hills, MI 48307; (248) 299-0456; klmfitness.com

Main Street Bicycles: 5987 26 Mile Rd., Washington, MI 48094; (586) 677-7755; mainstreetbicycles.com

RBS Rochester Bike Shop: 426 S. Main St., Rochester, MI 48307; (248) 652-6376; rochesterbikeshop.com

Stoney Creek Bike: 58235 Van Dyke Rd., Washington, MI 48094; (586) 781-4451; stoneycreekbike.com

numbering system. That will now end. There will also be moments covering short sections of the trail you've previously trodden. The next segment of the trail will do that, in part, in order to get to a section of the trail listed as a black (difficult) section. At #19, you're sitting at the exit of that trail, but you need to get to the beginning in order to follow it in the designated direction. Do that by heading straight west to #5. This should look familiar. From there turn left (south) and after the curve east you'll arrive at #6. Turn left, headed toward #19. This isn't really a "difficult" section of trail, as it's relatively flat single-track with only a few light obstacles, some tighter twists, and a couple of board-walks. But it is a change from the two-track encountered so far. It's worth taking for the more intimate beauty and change of venue.

From #19, take a right, back to #18. From #18 go left to #20. This gets back on the designated blue trail. This trail section is wide once again, but it does earn its blue label with some rolling hills and one rather spiky climb. The climb occurs between #22 and #23 at mile 6.4, and its biggest challenge besides pitch is the somewhat loose gravel. By the time #23 comes along, it's all just a fun roller-coaster ride along a wide wooded trail. The shrub layer is minimal, so there's little to inhibit views well into the forest. It's another unique natural system along the trail.

Turn right at #29 to begin a segment of the black trail. This is where the black designation is something to pay attention to. The trail narrows once again to single-track, begins to twist and turn as standard procedure, and adds some steeper terrain into the mix. Like all of Stony Creek, it has a smooth flow throughout, but technical skills are in more demand on the remaining black sections.

To say it's a climb to the top of a hill, then a roll back down the other side would be an oversimplification, but not entirely untrue. It does steadily climb to about mile 7.6, but there are also a lot of small convoluted rolls and twists and biting rises to get there. The same for the descent. It dips and swoops like a hawk looking for its next meal. It passes #24, eventually arriving at an opening at blue segment #21 for a quick left to #20, then another left through the forest to #16. Roll to #15 and take a left, heading once more onto the black trail. Single-track returns as you enter the forest on the right swing of the trail headed toward #25. More noticeably, the trail slants up and begins a series of tightly crafted chicanes known as the Snake. It pops into an opening at #25, mile 9.2, on the highest spot of the mountain bike trail with long-range views south.

At the north end of the opening, the trail Ys, with the right headed against trail traffic to #26 and the left continuing on the black trail to #28. Go

Cyclist on a two-track section of the trail

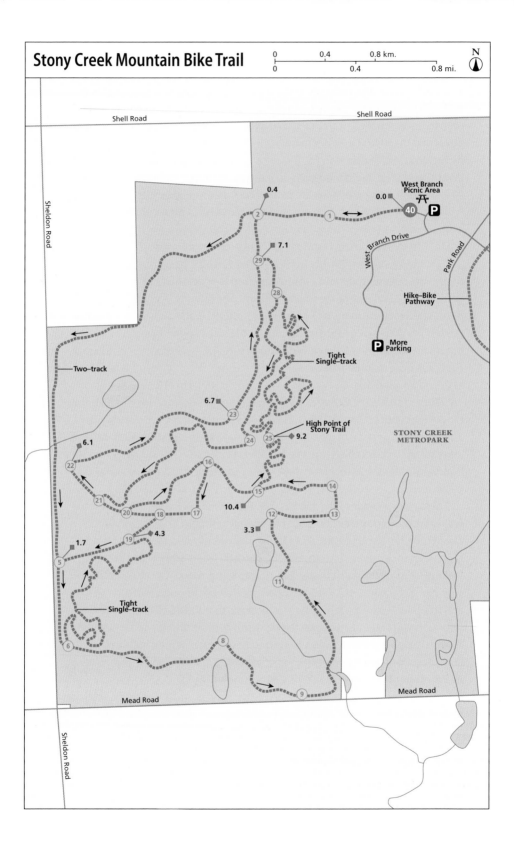

left to #28. It dives into a dense, shrub-lined thicket that opens onto more forested, coiling single-track. Since it's coming from the high point, most of this
is descending, though there is one short, distinct exception beginning at mile
10.2 that rises to a level area before winding farther down the hill. And, again,
none of this is one steady descent, but that is the general theme.

Marker #28 leads on to #29, where you'll turn right (north) and ride to #2.
Turn right. From here back it's a two-way trail, so watch for oncoming cyclists.
Go straight past #1 and keep going to the parking lot trailhead.

MILES AND DIRECTIONS

0.0   Leave the parking lot headed west on a wide two-way trail.

0.4   Continue straight at Trail Marker #2. Stay to the right on the consecutively numbered two-track trail and pass #4, #5, #6, #7, and so on all
the way to #12.

3.3   Turn to the right at Trail Marker #12 and go to #13.

3.5   Turn left at #13.

3.6   Turn left at #14. Stay to the right on the trail heading toward #15.
Continue following the markers consecutively to #19.

4.3   At Trail Marker #19 continue on to Trail Marker #5.

4.5   This may look familiar at #5, as it's ground you've recently covered,
but it's also a way to access the one-way single-track that leads
from #6.

4.7   At Trail Marker #6 turn left onto the single-track and weave through
this wooded and marshy area with boardwalks and a few gentle created obstacles back to #19.

5.7   Turn right at #19 and retrace your tire tracks back to #18.

5.9   Turn left at #18, headed toward #20.

6.1   Turn right at #22.

6.7   Stay to the left at #23 and roll through this beautiful section of woodland.

7.1   Turn right at #29 onto the more challenging single-track section. This
is a short two-way trail.

7.2   Stay to the right at #28. Begin one-way.

7.7 Turn right at #24, headed toward #21.

8.3 Turn left at #21, headed toward #20.

8.4 Turn left at #20, headed toward #16.

8.7 From #16 continue on to #15.

8.9 Turn left at #15, headed back into the challenging trail section that climbs through the forest to #25, the high spot in the trail system.

9.2 At #25 head across to the north side of the open area and go straight into the narrow thicket rather than to the right. This gets you on the winding single-track that will lead back to #28.

10.5 Head past #28 to #29.

10.6 Turn right, toward #2.

10.7 Turn right at #2 and head back on the two-way two-track to the parking area trailhead.

11.2 Arrive back at the trailhead.

RIDE INFORMATION

Local Events/Attractions
The **Metroparks** have events throughout the year. See www.metroparks.com for up-to-date information.
Massive Fallout: A connected four-trail mountain bike trail/bike path group ride put on by the Clinton River Area Mountain Bike Association (CRAMBA) in October of each year; massivefallout.org

Restaurants
Downtown Cafe: 606 N. Main St., Rochester, MI 48307; (248) 652-6680

Restrooms
Start/Finish: At West Branch Picnic area trailhead
Water spigot at trailhead restroom

Southeast Michigan Bicycle Resources

Ann Arbor Bicycle Touring Society
aabts.org

Ann Arbor Velo Club
www.aavc.org

Clinton River Rider Bicycle Club
www.lmb.org/crr

Easy Riders Bicycle Touring Club
www.lmb.org/easy

Flying Rhino Cycling Club
www.flyingrhinocc.com

Huron-Clinton Metroparks
www.metroparks.com

League of Michigan Bicyclists
www.lmb.org

M-Bike
www.m-bike.org

The Michigan Department of
Natural Resources
dnr.org

Michigan Mountain Bike Association
(MMBA)
mmba.org

The Michigan Trails & Greenways
Alliance
www.michigantrails.org

Wolverine Sports Club
www.wolverinesportsclub.com

Index

About the Author

Rob Pulcipher is a freelance writer and photographer who focuses on the outdoors. The author of *Dirt Road Washtenaw,* a cycling guide to the back roads of that county, he lives in Ann Arbor and has ridden his bike throughout Michigan for more than twenty years as a racer and as a recreational enthusiast.

Come Ride With Us!

INTERNATIONAL MOUNTAIN BICYCLING ASSOCIATION

You've just purchased, or are about to purchase, the mountain bike of your dreams. Where will you take your new steed? Who will you ride with? Joining IMBA's network of chapters, clubs and patrols taps you into a friendly network of experienced mountain bikers. They host rides for all skill levels, build trails and get together before and after rides to share stories and plan the next adventure. Find a local group by visiting imba.com/near-you.

FIVE RECENT ACCOMPLISHMENTS

1) *Built incredible trails.* IMBA's trailbuilding pros teamed with volunteers around the nation to build sustainable, fun singletrack like the 32-mile system at Pennsylvania's Raystown Lake.

2) *Won grants to build or improve trails.* Your contributions to IMBA's Trail Building Fund were multiplied with six-figure grants of federal money for trail systems.

3) *Challenged anti-bike policies.* IMBA works closely with all of the federal land managing agencies and advises them on how to create bike opportunities and avoid policies that curtail trail access.

4) *Made your voice heard.* When anti-bike interests moved to try to close sections of the 2,500-mile Continental Divide trail to bikes, IMBA rallied its members and collected more than 7,000 comments supporting keeping the trail open to bikes.

5) *Put kids on bikes.* The seventh edition of National Take a Kid Mountain Biking Day put more than 20,000 children on bikes.

FIVE CURRENT GOALS

1) *Host regional bike summits.* We're boosting local trail development by hosting summits in distinct regions of the country, bringing trail advocates and regional land managers together.

2) *Build the next generation of trail systems* with innovative projects, including IMBA's sustainably built "flow trails" for gravity-assisted fun!

3) *Create "Gateway" trails* to bring new riders into the sport.

4) *Fight blanket bans against bikes* that unwisely suggest we don't belong in backcountry places.

5) *Strengthen its network* of IMBA-affiliated clubs with a powerful chapter program.

FOUR THINGS YOU CAN DO FOR YOUR SPORT

1) *Join IMBA.* Get involved with IMBA and take action close to home through your local IMBA-affiliated club. An organization is only as strong as its grassroots membership. IMBA needs your help in protecting and building great trails right here.

2) *Volunteer.* Join a trail crew day for the immensely satisfying experience of building a trail you'll ride for years to come. Ask us how.

3) *Speak up.* Tell land-use and elected officials how important it is to preserve mountain bike access. Visit IMBA's web site for action issues and talking points.

4) *Respect other trail users.* Bike bans result from conflict, real or perceived. By being good trail citizens, we can help end the argument that we don't belong on trails.

YOU BELONG WITH IMBA **JOIN**

Join IMBA at www.imba.com or call 1-888-442-IMBA